Artificial Intelligence of Things (AIoT)

This book is devoted to the new standards, technologies, and communication systems for Artificial Intelligence of Things (AIoT) networks. Smart and intelligent communication networks have gained significant attention due to the combination of AI and IoT networks to improve human and machine interfaces and enhance data processing and services. AIoT networks involve the collection of data from several devices and sensor nodes in the environment. AI can enhance these networks to make them faster, greener, smarter, and safer. Computer vision, language processing, and speech recognition are some examples of AIoT networks.

Due to a large number of devices in today's world, efficient and intelligent data processing is essential for problem-solving and decision-making. AI multiplies the value of these networks and promotes intelligence and learning capabilities, especially in homes, offices, and cities. However, several challenges have been observed in deploying AIoT networks, such as scalability, complexity, accuracy, and robustness. In addition, these networks are integrated with cloud, 5G networks, and blockchain methods for service provision. Many different solutions have been proposed to address issues related to machine and deep learning methods, ontology-based approaches, genetic algorithms, and fuzzy-based systems.

This book aims to contribute to the state of the art and present current standards, technologies, and approaches for AIoT networks. This book focuses on existing solutions in AIoT network technologies, applications, services, standards, architectures, and security provisions. This book also introduces some new architectures and models for AIoT networks.

Artificial Intelligence of Things (AIoT)

New Standards, Technologies and Communication Systems

Edited by
Kashif Naseer Qureshi and Thomas Newe

CRC Press
Taylor & Francis Group
Boca Raton London New York

CRC Press is an imprint of the
Taylor & Francis Group, an **informa** business

Designed cover image: Shutterstock

First edition published 2024
by CRC Press
2385 NW Executive Center Drive, Suite 320, Boca Raton FL 33431

and by CRC Press
4 Park Square, Milton Park, Abingdon, Oxon, OX14 4RN

CRC Press is an imprint of Taylor & Francis Group, LLC

ISBN: 9781032552996 (hbk)
ISBN: 9781032553078 (pbk)
ISBN: 9781003430018 (ebk)

DOI: 10.1201/9781003430018

Typeset in Minion
by KnowledgeWorks Global Ltd.

Contents

Preface

In today's hyperconnected world, where technology permeates every aspect of our lives, the Artificial Internet of Things (AIoT) has emerged as a transformative force. With billions of devices connected to the internet, ranging from household appliances to industrial machinery, people, processes, data, and things to modernize activities, the AIoT has brought unprecedented convenience and efficiency. However, it has also exposed us to new challenges in terms of scalability, routing, resource allocation, and security. *Artificial Intelligence of Things (AIoT): New Standards, Technologies and Communication Systems* is a timely and essential book that delves into the intricate world of AIoT. As we continue to witness the rapid proliferation of connected devices, it is crucial to understand the existing network demands, especially of the artificial intelligence integration. This book serves as a comprehensive guide for individuals and organizations seeking to navigate the ever-evolving landscape of AIoT processes and services.

The authors of this book, with their deep expertise and extensive experience in the field of AI and IoT, provide valuable insights into the unique requirements, challenges, and risks associated with the AIoT. They meticulously analyze the diverse range of devices, networks, and applications that constitute the AIoT, shedding light on potential AI-based applications, standards, and protocols. By presenting real-world case studies and practical examples, they offer actionable strategies to adopt AI in IoT networks for better services and data communication.

This book suggests two parts of security fundamentals: Part I—Artificial Intelligence Evolution in Internet of Things Networks and Its Fundamental Concepts, and Part II—Data Communication Systems for AIoT Networks. These security fundamentals go beyond theoretical concepts, equipping readers with the necessary knowledge and tools to proactively address different areas of AIoT. The book explores cutting-edge technologies, such as artificial intelligence and blockchain, and their application in enhancing AIoT security. It emphasizes the importance of adopting a holistic approach to cybersecurity, encompassing not only technical measures but also organizational policies, user awareness, and regulatory frameworks. As the digital landscape continues to evolve, AI becomes paramount. The interconnected nature of the AIoT presents both immense opportunities and profound risks.

This book serves as a beacon of knowledge and guidance, empowering readers to understand the AI functionalities in the AIoT ecosystem. I commend the authors for their comprehensive research, diligent analysis, and commitment to advancing AI in the context of the IoT. Their work will undoubtedly make a significant contribution to the field and will serve as a valuable resource for AI and IoT professionals, researchers, and policymakers alike. I encourage readers to delve into the pages of *Artificial Intelligence of Things (AIoT): New Standards, Technologies and Communication Systems* and embark on a journey towards understanding the intricate challenges and developing robust solutions for increasingly interconnected world.

I believe that *Artificial Intelligence of Things (AIoT): New Standards, Technologies and Communication Systems* will be useful to readers who are beginning to approach this complex technical topic, since it puts together many different perspectives, application examples, and specific solutions. At the same time, it will be a useful reference for the more experienced researcher who aims at going deeper into a specific vertical application of AIoT networks, or who looks for possible open questions and/or future research topics to be explored.

Dr. Kashif Naseer Qureshi
Department of Electronic & Computer Engineering,
University of Limerick, Limerick, Ireland

Acknowledgements

This work received support from the Higher Education Authority (HEA) under the Human Capital Initiative-Pillar 3 project, Cyberskills.

CYBER SKILLS

Cyber Skills is an HEA Human Capital Initiative funded under pillar 3 that brings together Ireland's leading experts in cybersecurity education. Munster Technological University, University of Limerick, and Technological University Dublin are collaborating to provide pathways and micro-credentials to address skill shortages in the area of cybersecurity. Our programs are designed to provide industry-based learners with the knowledge and skills designed to enhance their careers with cybersecurity expertise.

Cyber Skills is the only resource in Ireland where you will find courses and modules that have been specifically designed and created by industry and academic experts. Working closely with our industry partners, including Dell, Mastercard, ADI, J&J, etc., we have designed courses informed by the needs of the workplace to enhance the skills of IT cybersecurity professionals in a wide variety of industries.

Cyber Skills benefits from the first of its kind world class cloud-based Cyber Range and mobile Cyber Range unit. These Cyber Ranges provide a secure, sandboxed area which simulates real-world feel scenarios and environments where students can test their new skills in an environment that can replicate their work-based systems. Labs and assignments will be used to reinforce the content from the lectures and a full range of scenarios will provide the opportunity to test the vast array of techniques required to keep ahead in this challenging and ever changing environment.

Since its foundation, Cyber Skills has recruited over 14 academic staff who come from multi-disciplinary backgrounds, with a passion for cybersecurity. Combining years of experience with expert knowledge, our lecturers enable students to achieve their academic and career progression goals.

All programmes delivered by Cyber Skills are aligned to the internationally recognised NIST-NICE Cybersecurity Workforce Framework. This framework allows Cyber Skills to provide clear guidance to learners on the work role tasks, knowledge, and skills being covered in their selected course so that they may select a course that suits the work role they are in or planning to apply for.

About the Editors

Kashif Naseer Qureshi is an Associate Professor of Cybersecurity in the Department of Electronic and Computer Engineering at the University of Limerick, Ireland. He is also actively involved in the Cyber Skills project, an HEA-HCI Pillar 3 initiative, Ireland. He received a Ph.D. degree from the University of Technology Malaysia (UTM) and holds two master's degrees in Computer Science and Information Technology from reputable universities. He is the Co-Principal Investigator in Cyber Reconnaissance and Combat project funded by higher education commission. His research interests focus on the security, trust, and privacy concerns for Internet of Everything (IoE), Internet of Vehicles (IoV), Electronic Vehicles (EV) charging management planning and recommendation systems, and Internet of Things (IoT) and use cases implementation in wireless and wired networks. He is active member of LERO, the Science Foundation Ireland Research Centre for Software in University of Limerick (UL). His name is included in the top 2% scientists for consecutive 3 years from Stanford University, Stanford, California. He has published various high-impact factor papers in international journals and conference proceedings and served on several conferences IPCs and journal editorial boards. He has written number of book chapters and edited five books in Springer, CRC, and Elsevier Publishers related to Cybersecurity, Privacy, and Trust architectures. He has also part of various research projects related to wireless communication, routing, and cybersecurity domains in the United Kingdom, China, Ireland, Malaysia, Canada, Dubai, Vietnam, and Pakistan.

Prof. Thomas Newe is a Professor in Cyber Security in the Department of Electronic & Computer Engineering at The University of Limerick, Ireland and is a Principal Investigator in the SFI Smart Manufacturing Centre, Confirm and a Funded Investigator in the SFI Centres; Lero-Software Research Centre, and MaREI-Marine and Renewable Energy Research Centre. He holds a B.Eng. in Computer Engineering, a Master in Engineering in Security Protocol Design, and a Ph.D. in Formal Logic for Security Protocol Verification. He has been a University of Limerick faculty member since 1994. Tom is a board member of Cyber Ireland, an initiative that brings together Industry, Academia, and Government to represent the needs of the Cyber Security Ecosystem in Ireland, and a founding member of Cyber Skills, a HEA-HCI Pillar 3 initiative that aims to address the global shortage of cybersecurity professionals. His research interest includes many topics under the general areas of cybersecurity for Data, Networks, the Internet of Things, and Smart Collaborative Robotics. He has to date graduated 16 Ph.D. students in these areas.

I

Artificial Intelligence Evolution in Internet of Things Networks and Its Fundamental Concepts

CHAPTER 1

Artificial Internet of Things

A New Paradigm of Connected Networks

Kashif Naseer Qureshi and Thomas Newe

Department of Electronic & Computer Engineering, University of Limerick,
V94 T9PX Limerick, Ireland

1.1 INTERNET OF THINGS

The Internet of Things (IoT) is one of the demanding and emerging technologies, where billions of devices are communicating for different services. These networks are based on integrated and heterogeneous networks. The popularity of IoT has multiplied swiftly due to its usage in all fields of life such as transportation, education, and enterprise development. Devices are connected over the internet and can communicate with each other with or without human support. Recently, the concepts of smart homes, smart industries, and smart cities have changed the lifestyle where everything is connected like home appliances, communication devices, smart meters, smart watches, and smart cars. Different enabling technologies are involved in IoT networks including the following: embedded systems, cloud and edge computing, blockchain, data analytics methods, and AI networks. Around the globe, the adoption of IoT in the form of different projects has achieved milestones in terms of demand, popularity, efficiency, and usage (Khalid et al. 2023). IoT networks transform the world into digital, smart, and modern networks. Different smart devices and intelligent systems are integrated by using cloud and edge networks. These networks also generated the big data which is streamed to the cloud services for further data management and analysis. There are several cloud services adopted and popular for data handling such as Google Cloud Platform, Microsoft Azure, Oracle, and IMB Waston Cloud. Fog computing is introduced as a horizontal system-level architecture for data distribution where data control, storage, and networking functions are closer to the network. Edge computing is another concept that is closer to end users and networks (Naseem et al. 2022). Fog and edge computing are used for better latency, security, and data reliability, and have better response time. Standard protocols are used for communication like Open Platform Communication United Architecture (OPC-UA). IoT solutions require data handling systems for data management like Not Only SQL (NoSQL). Another service Google IoT framework is used for easy and secure data management services.

1.2 ARTIFICIAL INTELLIGENCE

AI has changed the traditional IoT networks, converted the services into more intelligent networks, and received tremendous interest from communities and industries. The amazing and attractive services of AI technology have resulted in the adoption of more advanced communication applications. Machine and deep learning methods have been adopted to meet real-time processing demands. AI also provides human intelligence in machines, allowing them to perform multiple and complex tasks. This field is a multidisciplinary area of computer science to make machines smarter and more capable of learning, reasoning, and perceiving in order to solve problems. AI is categorized into two main types: narrow and general. The narrow AI performs specific tasks within limited domains like virtual personal assistance, image recognition, and recommendation systems. Popular examples of narrow AI are Siri and Alexa. On the other hand, general AI provides strong Artificial General Intelligence (AGI) which is able to perform any task that human beings can do. AGI functions like human intelligence to perform tasks, to understand and learn, and to apply this intelligence in different domains. Machine Learning (ML) methods are involved to train models and perform tasks such as predict and data analysis. Some other AI methods are natural language processing, robotics, expert systems, and computer vision. The AI methods are useful to improve the industry's processes, decision-making, fast automation, and solve complex challenges.

1.3 ARTIFICIAL INTERNET OF THINGS

Artificial Internet of Things (AIoT) is a new concept where machine and deep learning technologies meet the new application requirements in real-time manners. IoT network devices have limited resources in terms of storage, energy, and processing capabilities. These constraints increase the different Quality of Service (QoS) challenges and issues. The combination of AI and IoT enhances the sensing and communication services to achieve high performance. The intelligence is used at macro and micro levels in AIoT networks. This intelligence starts with self-driving to control home appliances. In AIoT networks, several smart devices, sensor nodes, data storage devices, and data processing capabilities are interconnected with cloud and edge networks (Qureshi and Abdullah. 2014). AIoT devices sense the surroundings and store, transmit, and broadcast the data. The traditional IoT networks without AI devices have limited features in terms of data analysis, automation, and adaptation, whereas the AI-based IoT networks offer voice services for users. These devices can answer queries as per user and application requirements such as calling cabs, playing music, controlling smart home appliances, making restaurant reservations, and more functions. Alexa is one of the voice services used for products like Amazon Echo. Siri and Google are other examples of voice assistance with some extra features like a conversation with users. These AI based IoT applications are used for multiple tasks such as wake word detection, text and speech conversion, contextual reasoning, question answering, and dialogue management.

Another usage of AI in IoT is robotics which can interact with human beings. These applications are capable of understanding, expressing, and reciprocating certain human emotions. The recent development in the field of robotics makes these machines more responsive to understanding human emotions, body movements, facial expressions, and

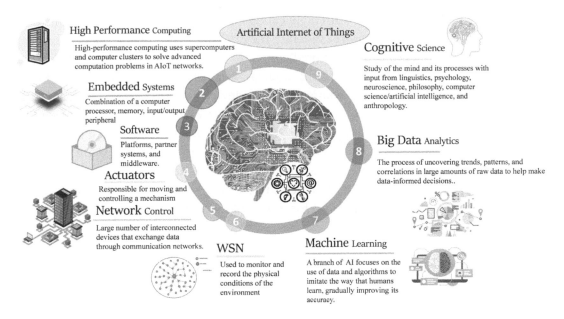

FIGURE 1.1   Emerging fields of AIoT networks.

tone of voice. These AI-based machines recognized four human emotions including sadness, joy, surprise, and anger. Sophia is one of the examples and considered a social humanoid robot. This robot is capable of expressing emotions through its eyes and facial expressions. Sophia is the world's first robot who received citizenship of a country. Another example is the robotic kitchen which is a fully functional robot with arms, a hob, an oven, and a touch-screen. This robot is able to prepare food and has a food recipe repository. AI-enabled smart devices are also used in smart homes for monitoring and identification, by using neural networks, deep learning and computer vision, and transfer learning. Smart ovens, smart electric meters, smart refrigerators, and light systems are used to manage and predict the usage and processes of users. Security systems like Skybell, which can answer the door by using a voice assistant feature system, are another example. An additional AI-enabled example is effective as a cabin sensor for automobile networks. Industries are another beneficial area where AI-based applications provide financial and statistical analysis for better prediction and decision-making. Figure 1.1 shows the emerging fields in AIoT networks.

1.4   APPLICATIONS

There are a number of IoT applications especially designed for industries, smart homes, transportation, education, and healthcare systems that have gained popularity. The smart factories concept is used where the machinery or industrial devices are equipped with smart sensors and devices for sensing and monitoring the operations of the machine. The machines are connected to infrastructure or central control systems and provide real-time access to information and control capabilities. Industrial AIoT applications increase the productivity, real-time operations, efficiency and the quality of products. There is a wide range of industrial AIoT applications such as predictive maintenance, tracking and management, remote monitoring, quality control, energy management, and safety and security applications. These AIoT applications are providing real-time machinery monitoring and management control systems. The data are analyzed and collected from different sensors and used for further prediction and analysis. The tracking of machinery faults and other complexity issues have also been resolved by using the tracking applications like inventory tools, equipment, and device connectivity. Energy control is another tremendous application of AIoT in industries where energy consumption is monitored. This is accomplished by analyzing data patterns and establishing optimized usage, distribution, and smart management practices. Quality is always a main concern for industries, and quality is more manageable by using AIoT applications where the data are collected from various stages and processed accordingly. Supply chain optimization is also achieved using AIoT applications for shipment tracking and monitoring the temperature and humidity.

Smart homes AIoT applications also offer real-time automation and control management systems such as lighting control, security cameras, appliances control, energy management, and security control systems. Users can control all their home appliances remotely through smart mobile devices. The most prominent IoT applications for smart homes are energy control, energy management, smart metering, and security control systems. The IoT-based security system integrates motion sensors, cameras, door and window sensors, and smart lock systems to control access. Energy management IoT applications also help the users to control or optimize energy use by using adjustment temperature settings of central heating or air condoning systems. Smart lighting control and management systems also provide ways to automate the systems based on schedule, preferences, or motion detection data. These strategies reduce energy bills and costs and create ambiance and enhance users' convenience. Another example of an AIoT application is voice assistance, like Amazon Alexa or Apple Siri, to control the home thermostat and temperature.

The use of AI in IoT networks has gained popularity due to numerous benefits and existing applications services and efficiencies. AI improves the IoT network's reliability, intelligence, and efficiency to process and analyze the data locally and make decisions. How various AIoT applications are deployed is discussed as follows:

1. **Data Analytics:** AIoT devices generate a vast amount of data that need analysis and interpretation. AI is integrated into this area where ML can be used to identify patterns, anomalies, and trends. These services provide valuable insight to users to avoid any potential failures.

2. **Decision Making:** The AI methods are integrated with IoT devices which are connected with edge and cloud computing for decision-making processes. The AI methods improve this process in real-time and provide better decision-making.

3. **Prediction Processes:** The AI applications are used to predict the equipment condition and failure status before any emergency situation. ML models are used to identify patterns by analyzing the sensor's data. These applications are reducing downtime and increasing production.

4. **Energy Management:** These applications are used to optimize energy consumption in AIoT networks by dynamically adjusting the power usage based on patterns and energy demand. These applications save and manage energy.

5. **Security Applications:** The AI models also improve IoT networks and provide security by detecting threats and anomalies in real-time. The AI models are used to detect unusual behavior and trigger alerts or take prevention measures to stop data breaches.

6. **Language Processing:** These applications use natural language processing techniques in AIoT devices where users interact by using voice commands or written text. These applications are making the user experience more efficient and intuitive.

7. **Smart Home Management:** AI-based smart home applications are used to check the user's preferences and habits to manage smart home services. The most popular AI-based applications are temperature control, appliance management, and personalized home device management.

8. **Traffic and Parking Management:** These AI-based applications are used to optimize traffic flow, especially in urban areas, by using different resources like GPS, cameras, and sensors. Another AI application is traffic prediction and providing data analysis for decision-making. These applications are used to reduce congestion issues and improve traffic efficiency.

9. **Smart Healthcare:** These AI-based applications are used to monitor the patient's health conditions and vital signs such as temperature, heart rate, and body movement. The collected data are also analyzed and provide timely alerts to healthcare professionals in case of an emergency.

10. **Environmental Monitoring:** The IoT sensors are integrated with AI and used for monitoring environmental factors like water quality, weather conditions, and air quality. These applications are also managing a potential disaster situation by predicting environmental changes and signs.

1.5 THE CONVERGENCE OF AIoT

Advanced technologies have brought significant advancement in all fields of life. These technologies transform processes from the fields of healthcare to those of smart living systems. The new area of AIoT is another step and advancement where the convergence of these technologies opens new innovations, revolutionizes industries, and overall enhances the quality of life. This convergence also opens new research and concepts for the future. The convergence of AI and IoT creates a symbolic ecosystem where smart devices and sensors collect, process, and analyze the data and initiate automated actions. AI algorithms are used to connect and gather data from smart devices and create a link between the physical and virtual worlds. There are various advantages of the AI and IoT convergence, but one of the key advantages is its ability to enhance connectivity and provide deeper insight into the data. The traditional IoT networks are generating massive data which need more advanced systems for data analysis. The AI systems provide real-time data analytics for possible meaningful patterns. This new concept also empowers business and individuals toward better decision-making and increases the system's productivity and efficiency.

This convergence also improves the automation and efficiency of processes and tasks. The AI algorithms can identify patterns and predict future events for quick decisions and reduce the need for human intervention in daily activities. Intelligent automation not only improves the processes but also minimizes human errors and monitoring tasks. The integration of AI and IoT also revolutionizes the way technologies can interact. Data analysis also provides an adaptive experience to enhance the user's engagement and satisfaction. These systems also have a positive impact on transforming industries' automation and manufacturing processes. In the agriculture sector, AIoT systems can optimize irrigation systems for better crop management and improve productivity with less waste. In healthcare systems, smart AIoT applications are used to monitor patients remotely on a real-time basis for their diagnosis and personal treatments. With advanced AI-enabled devices, the manufacturing sector can also streamline its production processes to enhance productivity and supply chain management systems. These systems reduce the cost, minimize downtime, and provide greater sustainability. Table 1.1 describes the new convergence of AIoT networks and other areas.

TABLE 1.1   New Convergence of AIoT Networks with Other Areas

AIoT-based Convergence Solutions	Technologies and Architecture	Used Methods	Description
Architecture Convergence			
ThriftyEdge (Chen et al. 2018)	Architecture for Edge and Fog Computing	Delay-aware task graph partition algorithm for resource occupancy	Proposed a resource-efficient computational offloading mechanism
Application-Aware Real-Time Edge Convolutional Neural Network (AWARE-CNNs) (Sanchez et al. 2020)	Model for Edge Networks	Used deep learning algorithms on IoT devices	Proposed an application-aware real-time edge acceleration of CNNs Accelerators for real-time applications
Edge AI for IoT (Sivabalan and Minue. 2022)	AI-based Model for Edge Networks	Used ML Technologies	Proposed AI-based ML model to transform the raw data into events
Sensing and Monitoring Convergence			
Sensing and Deep Reinforcement Learning (DRL) (Zhang et al. 2020)	Edge-enabled IoT	Deep Deterministic Policy Gradients (DDPG) algorithm and Double-dueling-deterministic Policy Gradients (D3PG)	Propose a quality of experience model for computational offloading.
Multi-hop ad hoc IoT (Kwon, Lee and Park. 2019)	AI-enabled IoT networks	Deep reinforcement learning approach	Propose a multi-hop based on a deep reinforcement learning approach for devices' connectivity
5G Intelligent Internet of Things (5G I-IoT) (Wang et al. 2018)	Cellular and IoT Networks	Big data mining, Deep learning, and Reinforcement learning	Propose a solution for the effective utilization of channels and QoS

1.6 AIoT ARCHITECTURE

AIoT architecture is based on two main modules including Mobile Edge Computing (MEC) and AI. These two main areas are further categorized into several techniques and standards. This section discusses both modules' components, functionalities, applications, and processes. The main objective of AIoT architecture is to process and analyze data by using two cutting-edge technologies. The interconnection of devices unlocks new and enhanced decision-making, real-time, and predictive analytics. The MEC module contains several components, like sensors and devices, to collect and sense the data from the environment and transmit it over the network. The devices are connected to each other and further connected with cloud and edge computing for synchronized and controlled transfer of the data. Edge computing is one of the concepts where the processing is closer to the network. Edge computing also reduces latency and bandwidth consumption and enhances network privacy and security, whereas cloud computing serves as a centralized repository to handle the data and provides the computational power required for complex AI algorithms and ML models. On the other hand, the second module is based on AI and ML techniques processing massive data to derive meaningful data patterns and predictions. The sensed data from the first module is further managed by using AI analysis.

1.6.1 Mobile Edge Computing Module

Different smart technologies are used in this module like sensor nodes, actuators, and devices. These devices are integrated with information systems and further linked with edge and cloud computing. The IoT network devices generate the data from different applications and forward it for further processing. The cloud, edge, and fog networks are used to maintain the data. Edge computing addresses the limitation of cloud computing. Fog computing is another extension of cloud computing and is located between edge and cloud computing modules. This concept provides low latency computation by using the horizontal, system-level architecture to distribute the data storage, control, and networking functions closer to the local networks. The objective of fog is the same as edge and cloud, but only fog offers the distributed architecture with low bandwidth and latency. Whereas, fog computing has suffered from high scalability issues. To address this concept, edge computing is used where the shared processes and computing provide the services at the device level and reduces the data movement toward cloud computing. The edge devices are used as tools for computing power movement and offloading computational capabilities from cloud to edge (Ali et al. 2022). Fog and edge computing are integrated with IoT networks and use different standards and protocols. The well-known protocols used in these modules are Machine-to-Machine (M2M), Open Platform Communication United Architecture (OPC UA), Highway Addressable Remote Transducer Protocol (HART), and WirelessHart and Data-Distribution Service (DSS) (Vaclavova et al. 2022.; Wang, Nixon and Boudreaux. 2019). Big Data Analytics (BDA) is also one of the requirements of this module.

Routing and communication are also performed in this module where the network needs in-time data delivery and an efficient routing mechanism. As with the integration of AI in IoT, there is a need to adopt more advanced architecture. This module also utilizes the Software Defined Network (SDN), Network Function Virtualization (NFV), and Content Delivery Network (CDN). The SDN networks provide flexible and cost-effective solutions for AIoT networks and dynamically handle IoT data. The 5G and 6G technologies are also adopted to deploy complex devices and manage communication channels.

1.6.2 AI Module

This module utilizes AI for better decision-making processes for IoT applications and services. The AI methods have solved multiple issues of traditional networks such as fast decision-making, optimization, and data management (Song et al. 2020). There are some other challenges related to access to IoT devices, signal processing, and resource management whenever the IoT devices access the resources by using a contention-based random-access procedure. Random-access selection leads to access collisions, latency, interference, and outage. AI Deep Reinforcement Learning (DRL) is used to address these issues in traditional IoT networks by making a proper decision on random access processes. This module has an AI-based contusion random access to improves the initial access of the network. Another AI feature for IoT networks is used in this module to adjust the transmission parameters and improve the QoS. AI helps to adjust the frequency bands and set the users' priorities as per their needs and requirements. The Deep Q-Networks (DQN)-based spectrum access strategy is used to set the spectrum sensing and its distribution (Chander et al. 2022). This module is also utilizing the central controller by using the ML technique for effective base station selection. The ML models are also used to train the statistical model for wireless networks. The AI and ML methods are also used for more precise modeling of the interference. Resource allocation is another issue that increases the number of devices. The ML-based clustering method is used to address this issue by forming clusters.

Open radio access controllers are also used in ML methods for network functions. Implementation of Deep Learning (DL) in radio networks provides better resource allocation, spectrum, and mobility management. There are different AI methods like Long Short-Terms Memory (LSTM), Reinforcement Learning (RL), and Deep Neural Networks (DNN) utilized for resource allocation in AIoT networks.

1.7 COMMUNICATION AND NETWORKS

Wireless communication in AIoT uses different multiple access techniques like Frequency Division Multiplexing (FDM), Orthogonal Frequency-Division Multiple Access (OFDMA), and Code-Division Multiple Access (CDMA). These standards are used for short messages and voice calls in the networks. The 5G networks are used in IoT networks for smart services by using the Mobile Broadband (eMBB) and Ultra-Reliable and Low Latency Communication (URLLC) standards for communications. The 6G concept for AIoT uses networks with 1 GHz. up to 1 Tbps bandwidth. The 6G also provides low latency services which are ten times less than 5G. The routing protocols for data communication play a crucial role in AIoT networks. The scalable routing protocols are used in these networks due to a massive number of smart devices and sensor nodes. Many AIoT application requirements are in-time data delivery on a real-time basis. Low latency is required for timely delivery of the data because of time-sensitive AI applications, as resources are limited in smart devices in terms of storage, processing power, and energy, energy-efficient routing protocols are needed to improve the node's battery lifetime and extend the operational time. There are different routing protocols designed to address the energy issues in these networks. Reliability and QoS are needed for AIoT applications, especially for smart healthcare, transportation, and disaster management applications. Some applications prioritize low latency whereas some need to prioritize high data throughput. The routing protocols must be able to provide reliable QoS support as per the application's needs. The AIoT networks are heterogeneous and dynamic and use adaptable routing protocols to handle diverse data types. Security is another main requirement to protect data integrity, user confidentiality, and system availability. Context-aware routing is needed for better decisions based on real-time information as per application requirements and network conditions. Resource awareness is another requirement of any routing protocol to avoid overburdening certain nodes and to optimize resource utilization. AIoT networks can benefit from various existing routing protocols like OLSR (Optimized Link State Routing Protocol), and RPL (Routing Protocol for Low-power and Lossy Networks) (A. Ahmed et al. 2017). The choice of the routing protocol depends on the specific use case, network architecture, and the desired performance metrics.

1.7.1 AI Usage in Communication Systems

Several AI methods have been adopted for communication systems and fulfill the AIoT network requirements. Figure 1.2 shows the layer-wise operations with AI and ML-based algorithms.

Several AI and ML-based solutions have been proposed for AIoT networks to establish reliable and secure data communication services. Heuristic algorithms are used to find the heuristic value of artificial network nodes. This type of method is applicable where there is no solution to the existing problem. Some examples of heuristic algorithms are Generic Algorithm (GA), Ant Colony Optimization (ACO), and Particle Swarm Optimization (PSO) (Qureshi, Ahmad, et al. 2020). Supervised learning is also used for mapping the input and output variables by using training datasets. Examples of supervised learning are Support Vector Machine (SVM) and K-Nearest Neighbour (KNN). On the other hand, the unsupervised learning method is used without training the dataset by computing the input data for output. The well-known unsupervised methods are Principle Component Analysis (PCA) and K-mean clustering. Reinforcement learning is also utilized by using different elements like agent, environment, action, and state. Some well-known examples of reinforcement methods are Q-Learning, and State Action Reward State Action (SARSA). DL methods are used to analyze the data sets for device localization, routing optimization, network access, and channel estimation. DRL and Federated Learning (FL) are also used for different applications in AIoT networks. These methods are used to solve complex problems, such as resource allocation, and ensure security and privacy (Qureshi and Iftikhar. 2020).

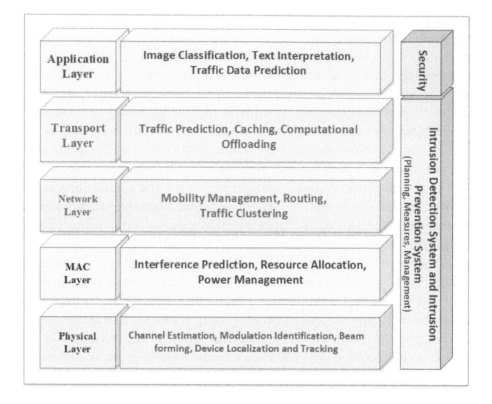

FIGURE 1.2 Layer wise operations with AI and ML-based algorithms.

1.8 EXISTING CHALLENGES AND ISSUES

While offering a number of benefits, AIoT technologies also possess new challenges and concerns. As communication systems, fixed and mobile networks, wired and wireless enable technologies, and the open nature of network architecture are developed, they open various communication, connectivity, resource allocation, and security challenges (Qureshi, Din, et al. 2020). As these networks combine the features of AI and IoT, networks and systems are more complex and interconnected. The existing challenges need to be addressed for better services and network operations. The details of some major challenges are as follows:

1. **Data Routing:** The smart devices are communicating with each other by using wired and wireless networks. The routing is always a major issue especially when the network is congested or fewer resources are available (Qureshi, Abdullah, et al. 2014). Disconnectivity, best pathfinding, delay, and network overhead are always the main concern of IoT networks. As AI processes are integrated with IoT networks and need real-time decisions, so routing needs more smart systems and standards for better data communication processes.

2. **Data Storage and Management:** AIoT networks generate a large amount of data from different smart and fixed devices. Data storage and its management are always a major issue for these networks. These networks require scalable storage management

systems and effective architecture to avoid overwhelming the network and ensure timely processes.

3. **Privacy and Security:** This challenge is one of the top priorities of the system due to the increased number of interconnected smart devices and the exchange of user data. Security is always a major concern of these networks for different reasons, such as new vulnerabilities and malware, and lack of security solutions and awareness. AIoT networks are vulnerable to cyber-attacks, privacy violations, and cyber-attacks. There is a need to adopt more smart encryption methods, strong authentication, and robust access controls to safeguard the network and its data.

4. **Interoperability:** Interoperability and scalability are always challenges due to different manufacturers and their protocols and standards. Compatibility is always an issue especially when different companies have their own standards, protocols, and processes. There is a need to design the devices to create cohesive and functional AIoT networks.

5. **Real-time Data Processing:** Real-time data processing is always a major requirement of these networks. The different areas are integrated with smart devices like autonomous vehicular systems, industrial automation, smart homes, and smart healthcare. These areas need real-time data processing with low latency and high throughput to maintain the requirements of the network for responsive AIoT systems.

6. **Energy Management:** Traditional IoT devices are often constrained by limited energy resources. This issue increases when the AI system is integrated with more capabilities due to additional strain on energy requirements (ALiero et al. 2021). Energy management and solutions are needed to address this issue in terms of models, architecture, and protocols. The energy management solutions require extending operational lifetime and reducing environmental impact.

7. **Resource Allocation:** AI algorithms are used in IoT networks and require more resources such as processing power, storage, energy, and communication requirements. Resource allocation is always a major concern of these networks especially when the resources are limited to handle complex algorithms. Optimizing AI models for better deployment on resource-constrained devices is a significant challenge.

8. **Data Management:** The AIoT applications need high-quality and reliable data for better, in-time, and accurate decisions. The networks must require that data integrity is maintained and that cleaning is performed to address the issues like data bias, data drift, and anomalies to ensure the network performance and trustworthiness of AI models in IoT networks.

9. **Ethical and Legal Challenges:** There are various ethical and legal challenges related to ownership, transparency, and consent in AIoT networks. There is a pressing need to establish new laws and rules to ensure data integrity where the AI decisions are unbiased and align with ethical laws and regulations. Mature ethical policies gain the public and users' trust and avoid potential legal issues.

Addressing the above-discussed challenges and issues in the AIoT network needs strong collaboration among all stakeholders. The technology developers, policymakers, industries, and end users should consider the discussed challenges to propose any new system for these networks. These networks are evolving with new effective solutions and reaching full potential with fewer risks and maximum benefits.

1.9 SECURITY IN AIoT NETWORKS

Security is one of the main concerns due to the rapid growth of malware, spam, and security attacks. AIoT networks are in use across the globe and are interconnected with other cloud and edge-based technologies. To ensure security, users' privacy and trust establishment are crucial at the large-scale network level. Security attacks need detection and prevention solutions to monitor the unauthorized access of networks and systems and to protect them from any alteration or breach. There are many well-known attacks that exist in AIoT networks such as Denial of Service (DoS) attacks, micro probing, and reverse engineering attacks. DoS attacks occur when a service is made unavailable for the user by an attacker by the attacker overloading the capacity of the infrastructure. This attack results in a loss of reputation for the vendor. A DoS attack is conducted by botnets targeting a single target from different IPs. DoS attacks can be carried out using User Datagram Protocol (UDP), Internet Control Message Protocol (ICMP), Simple Network Management Protocol (SNMP), and Transmission Control Protocol (TCP) protocol packets. These packets are flooded into the system such that the system becomes unavailable to genuine requests (Carl et al. 2006). The micro-probing attack is performed by an attacker who has complete physical access to the hardware. The attacker gains access to the semiconductor chip directly so that he can observe and interfere with the hardware's low-level configurations. These attacks may exploit the one-time programmable OTP memories, rewrite passwords in memories using UV light rays, fuse polysilicon read and write using advanced tools, and inject fault in the system controller IC (Shi et al. 2016). Reverse engineering is used to get information about the hardware type, algorithms, and authentication being used. These are invasive attacks which can give an insight into the inner surface of hardware, and the system can be cloned after reverse engineering. A system or a node can be replicated and introduced in the original network to spy or divert the traffic from the destination. There are many other security attacks that exist and disturb AIoT network's operations.

1. **Network Attacks:** A Network is vulnerable to attack because an illegitimate user can pretend to be an authorized user and can compromise traffic. Network attackers can get access to the central device or system and manipulate themselves as original users and can sniff packets and generate fake packets towards the nodes resulting in an increase in illegitimate traffic, performance effects, and stealing key parameters of a system.

2. **Node Capture Attacks:** A node capture attacker steals the security parameters of a device from memory and can then exploit either hardware or software configurations for the purpose of launching further attacks or eavesdropping on the communication

of the network. Node capture can be a result of vulnerabilities in the configuration of the device, unauthorized access to the central controller, or reverse engineering (Shaukat et al. 2014).

3. **Monitoring and Eavesdropping:** Eavesdropping is to intercept traffic or sniff it to steal information that can be useful to gain further unauthorized access and know about the system infrastructure. After getting such critical security parameters, an attacker can do the most impactful attack. Monitoring a system actively on live traffic also helps attackers to find out vulnerabilities in the network.

4. **Traffic Analysis:** Network traffic analysis is performed passively on captured traffic to analyze the network traffic pattern. This analysis helps the attacker to understand the network speed, size, origin, type, and content of files being shared on the network. This is achieved by network state monitoring tools.

5. **Replication Attacks:** Sensor nodes are captured, and reconfigured using secure parameters such as code, id, and keys, and then these nodes are sent to the network. An attacker can now eavesdrop and monitor the network communication or may handle the whole network, insert wrong information, shut down some nodes, etc. This replication is camouflaged, and till the time the system detects some vulnerabilities, massive harm to the network may have occurred (Khurum. 2019).

6. **Side Chanel Attack:** Side channel attacks are based on power, traffic, system time, and fault analysis rather than utilizing vulnerability in the hardware or algorithm level implementation. The attacker wants to get security critical parameters using this method (Zhou and Feng. 2005).

7. **Power Analysis:** This analysis provides a solution to analyze the power consumption by using oscilloscope power traces when cryptographical operations are performed in the device. Correlational power analysis is used to derive the secret key. Power consumption is analyzed, and the algorithm estimated using power consumption peaks against each instruction or subset of instructions. The power consumption of a few instructions is known to estimate unknown parameters.

8. **Traffic Analysis:** Traffic analysis can be considered as a type of side-channel analysis in which metadata of traffic transmitted in the medium is analyzed to get information about the system. It can be used as a fingerprinting technique to gather critical information about infrastructure. This attack is like eavesdropping and traffic analysis.

9. **Timing Analysis:** This is a side-channel attack in which an attacker tries to get the time of execution of cryptographic operations. If a precise measurement of time for each operation is known, an attacker can backtrace to the input and hence cryptographic keys are obtained and the system is compromised.

10. **Fault Analysis:** Flawless algorithm implementation cannot be guaranteed. A single fault can be exploited to generate false projected output, and even a calculated

disturbance in a system can cause a change in a program counter and cause a program to exhibit more and missed instructions.

11. **Software Attack:** Third-party, malicious software and spyware through the internet or email attachment (phishing), or other cleverly disguised software instructions are software attacks that are very harmful to the system.

12. **Trojan Horse Attacks:** A Trojan horse usually comes from some form of social engineering. It creates a backdoor for a command and control server to further exploit vulnerabilities in the system already created by a Trojan. Complete user system access can be gained by hackers using this.

13. **Logic Bombs:** A logic bomb is like a malicious logic programme meant to cause harm at some point in the future but inactive at the present. A time and date are specified when that part of the code activates. These attacks exploit AIoT software architecture and configuration and damage to the whole infrastructure unless the system is recovered.

14. **Worms and Viruses:** Viruses are typically Portable Executable (PE) files or are attached as plugins to either Word files or pdf files. The infected host file should be removed to get rid of the virus attack. A worm, however, is application independent and does not need the support of any other Word or pdf files. Worms spread through internet connectivity. Each worm can grow its infection in the network itself.

15. **Denial of Services Attacks:** A DoS attack is accomplished by flooding traffic, e.g., ICMP or too many TCP connection requests. These attacks are malicious attempts to disrupt the normal functioning of a targeted server, service, or network, making it temporarily or indefinitely unavailable to its intended users.

16. **Crypto-Analysis Attack:** Crypto-analysis or cryptanalysis leads to the identification of the type of crypto algorithm and the decoding of key parameters to break the fully or partially cryptographic algorithm. It is the study of cipher types and cryptosystems. Many algorithms based on ML and pattern matching exist for such attacks (A. W. Ahmed et al. 2017).

17. **Cipher Text only Attack:** During a cipher text-only attack, the attacker just has obtained cipher text from a target. The goal is to recover plain text so that the secret key may be guessed to further decrypt all the cipher messages. A number of possible strings are saved, and the output of the algorithm is generated. The two most important methods which are based on given text are attack on two-time pad and frequency analysis.

18. **Known Plain Text Attack:** In a Known Plain text attack, the attacker has access to the plain text as well as its corresponding cipher text. The goal is to guess the secret key used behind it. It provides more opportunities to guess accurate keys. A simple

substitution can easily be detected using this attack. Enigma cipher and the simple XOR cipher can easily be detected.

19. **Chosen Plain Text Attacks:** During chosen plain text attacks, a cryptanalyst can choose random plain text to pass to the device and receives corresponding cipher text. The goal is to acquire an encryption key or alternatively to create an algorithm even if the key is not acquainted. The attacker is analyzing behavior with respect to input and output.

20. **Man in the Middle Attack:** A MITM attack is difficult to intercept. A controlled device is inserted between the inbound and outbound network flow of the system by which the attacker can gain the transcript of whole communication between the two parties.

These attacks are a deep concern of the AIoT networks. Companies need to adapt advanced systems and technology to protect their privacy and data. AIoT services are needed without delay. Because of unavailability and compromised traffic, these attacks are becoming more advanced and critical for the systems.

1.10 IoT SECURITY CHALLENGES AND SOLUTIONS

Table 1.2 represents security issues, addressed vulnerabilities, identity of the affected layer in networks, the threat or attack's security level, and the threat or attack's proposed solution.

TABLE 1.2   Security Issues and Proposed Solutions for AIoT Networks

S.No.	Security Threats and Attacks	Consequences	Affected Layers	AIoT Levels	Proposed Solutions
1.	Unavailability and redundancy	Service interruption	Network layer	Mid-Level	Timestamp and nonce attributes allow for protecting layers from replay attacks and verification of fragmentation by hashing chains.
2.	Insecurity of internal network	Spoofing of source IP	Network layer	Mid-Level	Authenticate using Elliptic curve SS
3.	Buffer overflow	Unavailability of buffer	Network layer	Mid-level	Sending complete fragmented packets using split buffer
4.	Internet service provider interruption	Man-in-the-middle attacks	Network layer	Mid-level	Packet filtering on a behavior basis
5.	Network security for authenticating user	Violation in data confidentiality	Transport and Network layer	Mid-level	Using cryptographic encryption algorithms and hash functions like RSA, SHA.

TABLE 1.2 *(Continued)*   Security Issues and Proposed Solutions for AIoT Networks

S.No.	Security Threats and Attacks	Consequences	Affected Layers	AIoT Levels	Proposed Solutions
6.	Security threats on the transport layer	Violation in confidentiality	Network and Transport layer	Mid-level	Using AES/Sha-based cipher, IPSEC compression, DTLS header compression, Identification, and authorization using AES/CCM-based security
7.	Session creation and renewal	DOS attack	Network layer	Mid-level	Authorization using a private key and encryption based on a symmetric key.
8.	Constrained internet application protocol	DoS	Application and Network layer	High and Mid-level	Tunnel filtering method
9.	Vulnerable graphical user interfaces	Violation of privacy, DoS, interruption in the network	Application layer	High level	Allow only strong passwords, and identify backdoors, and vulnerabilities using SQL injection and cross-site scripting.
10.	Vulnerable software	Violation of privacy, DoS, interruption in the network	Network, Transport, and Application layer	All security levels	Software should be updated every time, use encryption techniques with validation and verification
11.	Middleware security	Violation of privacy, DoS, interruption in the network	Network, Transport, and Application layer	All security levels	Implementation of security policies, crypto key management techniques, use of authentication approaches

1.11 CONCLUSION

AIoT is one of the new concepts for smart networks. These networks provide monitoring, sensing, and data communication services by using AI methods for better prediction, data analysis, and decision-making. AIoT applications use intelligent and enabling technologies, smart architectures, complex network topologies, and intelligent information systems. This chapter discussed AIoT network architecture in detail including data communication, AI, and edge and cloud modules. It also covered layer-wise AI usage in IoT networks where several ML and DL methods are presented in detail. This chapter also covered the applications, AI usage in IoT networks, existing issues, and challenges. Security and existing attacks and their behavior are also discussed to understand the network requirements. This chapter will help new researchers in this area to understand all the operations, AI usage, and other concerns.

REFERENCES

Ahmed, Abdul Wahab, et al. "A Comprehensive Analysis on the Security Threats and Their Countermeasures of IoT." *International Journal of Advanced Computer Science and Applications* 8.7 (2017): 489–501.

Ahmed, Aneeqa, et al. "Link-Based Penalized Trust Management Scheme for Preemptive Measures to Secure the Edge-Based Internet of Things Networks." *Wireless Networks* (2022).

Ali, Zulfiqar, et al. "Edge Based Priority-Aware Dynamic Resource Allocation for Internet of Things Networks." *Entropy* 24.11 (2022): 1607.

ALiero, Muhammad Saidu, et al. "Smart Home Energy Management Systems in Internet of Things Networks for Green Cities Demands and Services." *Environmental Technology & Innovation* 22 (2021): 101443.

Carl, Glenn, et al. "Denial-of-Service Attack-Detection Techniques." *IEEE Internet computing* 10.1 (2006): 82–89.

Chander, Bhanu, et al. "Artificial Intelligence-Based Internet of Things for Industry 5.0." *Artificial Intelligence-Based Internet of Things Systems* (2022): 3–45.

Chen, Xu, et al. "Thriftyedge: Resource-Efficient Edge Computing for Intelligent IoT Applications." *IEEE Network* 32.1 (2018): 61–65.

Khalid, Bushra, et al. "An Improved Biometric Based User Authentication and Key Agreement Scheme for Intelligent Sensor Based Wireless Communication." *Microprocessors and Microsystems* 96 (2023): 104722.

Khurum, Abbas. "Tutorials for Internet of Things (IoT)." (2019).

Kwon, Minhae, Juhyeon Lee, and Hyunggon Park. "Intelligent Iot Connectivity: Deep Reinforcement Learning Approach." *IEEE Sensors Journal* 20.5 (2019): 2782–91.

LIM, Se-jung. "E-Healthcare System in Smart Cities Using AI-Enabled Internet of Things: Applications and Challenges." *International Journal of Intelligent Systems and Applications in Engineering* 11.7s (2023): 655–60.

Naseem, Shahid, et al. "Artificial General Intelligence-Based Rational Behavior Detection Using Cognitive Correlates for Tracking Online Harms." *Personal and Ubiquitous Computing* 27 (2022): 119–137.

Qureshi, Kashif Naseer, and Abdul Hanan Abdullah. "Adaptation of Wireless Sensor Network in Industries and Their Architecture, Standards and Applications." *World Applied Sciences Journal* 30.10 (2014): 1218–23.

Qureshi, Kashif Naseer, et al. "A Dynamic Congestion Control Scheme for Safety Applications in Vehicular Ad Hoc Networks." *Computers Electrical Engineering* 72 (2018): 774–88.

Qureshi, Kashif Naseer, et al. "Nature-Inspired Algorithm-Based Secure Data Dissemination Framework for Smart City Networks." *Neural Computing and Applications* 33 (2020): 10637–56.

Qureshi, Kashif Naseer, et al. "Link Quality and Energy Utilization Based Preferable Next Hop Selection Routing for Wireless Body Area Networks." *Computer Communications* 149 (2020): 382–92.

Qureshi, Kashif Naseer, and Abeer Iftikhar. "6 Contemplating Security." *Security and Organization within IoT and Smart Cities*. CRC Press, 2020. 93.

Sanchez, Justin, et al. "AWARE-CNN: Automated Workflow for Application-Aware Real-Time Edge Acceleration of CNNs." *IEEE Internet of Things Journal* 7.10 (2020): 9318–29.

Sen, Jaydip. "Security in Wireless Sensor Networks." *Wireless Sensor Networks: Current Status and Future Trends* 407 (2012).

Shaukat, Haafizah Rameeza, et al. "Node Replication Attacks in Mobile Wireless Sensor Network: A Survey." *International Journal of Distributed Sensor Networks* 10.12 (2014): 402541.

Shi, Qihang, et al. "A Layout-Driven Framework to Assess Vulnerability of ICs to Microprobing Attacks." *2016 IEEE International Symposium on Hardware Oriented Security and Trust (HOST)*. 2016. IEEE.

Sivabalan, S, and R Minu. "Edge AI for Industrial IoT Applications." *Applied Edge AI: Concepts, Platforms, and Industry Use Cases*. CRC Press, 2022. 147–70.

Song, Hao, et al. "Artificial Intelligence Enabled Internet of Things: Network Architecture and Spectrum Access." *IEEE Computational Intelligence Magazine* 15.1 (2020): 44–51.

Vaclavova, Andrea, et al. "Proposal for an IIot Device Solution According to Industry 4.0 Concept." *Sensors* 22.1 (2022): 325.

Wang, Dan, et al. "From IoT to 5g I-IoT: The Next Generation Iot-Based Intelligent Algorithms and 5g Technologies." *IEEE Communications Magazine* 56.10 (2018): 114–20.

Wang, Gang, Mark Nixon, and Mike Boudreaux. "Toward Cloud-Assisted Industrial IoT Platform for Large-Scale Continuous Condition Monitoring." *Proceedings of the IEEE* 107.6 (2019): 1193–205.

Zhang, Jing, et al. "Dynamic Computation Offloading with Energy Harvesting Devices: A Hybrid-Decision-Based Deep Reinforcement Learning Approach." *IEEE Internet of Things Journal* 7.10 (2020): 9303–17.

Zhou, YongBin, and DengGuo Feng. "Side-Channel Attacks: Ten Years after Its Publication and the Impacts on Cryptographic Module Security Testing." *IACR Cryptology ePrint Archive* 2005 (2005): 388.

CHAPTER 2

Advanced AIoT Applications and Services

Raja Waseem Anwar, Alaa Ismael

German University of Technology - Muscat & Arab Open University - Muscat

Kashif Naseer Qureshi

Department of Electronic & Computer Engineering, University of Limerick, V94 T9PX
Limerick, Ireland

2.1 INTRODUCTION

In the evolution of contemporary civilization, Artificial Intelligence (AI) is a key technology that has the potential to enhance human potential and bring about significant benefits. In the meantime, the IoT has the potential to build a massive network of connected intelligent devices. It can handle a variety of relationships between people and things and has a sizable capacity. Additionally, it is capable of facilitating the quick transmission of a variety of information to greatly improve people's quality of life and productivity. If these two technologies can be effectively paired, it will have a favourable impact on the design and advancement of industrial equipment. Autonomous vehicles, smart homes, and computer network businesses all can benefit from the use of the IoT and AI (Mukhopadhyay et al. 2021). AI is a method that enables machines to function and behave like people. In 1956, Dartmouth University introduced the concept of "artificial intelligence" for the first time. The idea of AI has since been gradually expanded and gained attention due to fast, intelligent, and cost-effective processes. Although the development of AI is taking longer than predicted, and it has not had a lengthy history, its development has never come to a halt. Many new AI systems are being developed now, having been first developed 40 years ago, and they are having an impact on the advancement of other technologies (Yao. 2019).

The devices are connected via a vast network called the IoT. These devices collect and disseminate the information as per their usage and deployment. With the advancement in communication systems, IoT-based applications and technologies that are built on AI are assisted by a variety of different sorts of sensors. In recent decades, with continuous evolution in smart and digital technologies, AIoT has attracted the attention of many academics and emerged among the most widely used technologies due to their offered benefits, such as maximizing data collection, processing, and decision-making. AIoT has a wide

DOI: 10.1201/9781003430018-3

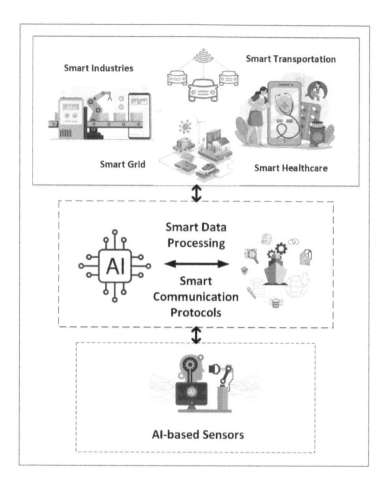

FIGURE 2.1   AI-based sensors for IoT applications.

range of offered benefits such as enhancing operational efficiencies through precise predictions based on collected and historical data, increased scalability among different IoT domains and deployed services, improved productivity with enhanced risk management, and reduced downtime (Ślusarczyk. 2018). The fundamental convergence of AI and IoT applications is depicted in Figure 2.1.

Almost all systems today employ sensors. The existing networks are found in smart homes, places of employment, retail establishments, and healthcare facilities, and smartphones are using smart sensor nodes for sensing and monitoring the surrounding environment. The IoT ecosystem cannot exist without sensors. In many applications and disciplines, such as device and data management, computation, security, trust, and privacy, the expansion of IoT networks creates important concerns. The growth of the digital economy is directly linked to this expansion. Smart cities, smart businesses, remote monitoring, smart meters, and automated processes are all made possible by the IoT (Phan et al. 2023). Applications and services offered by the IoT today and in the future have the potential to dramatically ease, accelerate, and enrich users' lives due to the integration of AI (Kuzlu, Fair and Guler. 2021).

Utilizing AI algorithms to analyze the enormous volumes of data that IoT sensors produce in a variety of applications is an emerging trend in the integration of AI with IoT. Additionally, by providing innovative opportunities and features while dramatically minimizing human contact, this integration speeds up the processes. AI and IoT have been combined to make it possible to give machines intelligence to perform activities that previously required the human mind. Additionally, AI-based systems are developing quickly in terms of their versatility, adaptability, processing speed, and ability to make decisions. AI, employed in computers, will eventually be able to reason similarly to humans. This trend, which will speed up the digital transformation of industries, will benefit several IoT-based applications.

2.2 ARTIFICIAL INTELLIGENCE AND ITS IMPORTANCE

Studying AI aims to make computers more capable and to behave more like humans. The digital transformation of smart industries has adopted this new technology and changed the traditional data communication process. Furthermore, AI entails computational devices capable of replacing human expertise in performing specific tasks. Through collaborations across many other disciplines, AI has become more interdisciplinary and is used in many disciplines, such as philosophy, computer science, mathematics, statistics, biology, physics, sociology, and psychology (Qureshi et al. 2013). The adoption of AI-based solutions in the IoT is rapidly transforming the entire process because the devices produce an enormous amount of data that can be leveraged by using data-driven technology. Through improved efficiency and helpful decision-making, AI and the technology that makes up IoT subset have improved accessibility, integrity, availability, scalability, confidentiality, and interoperability for connecting devices (Anwar and Ali. 2022). Consisting only of a piece of hardware with a sensor node that sends data and equipped with location services like GPS, these systems utilize fewer resources and are cost-effective due to smart and tiny size sensor nodes (Lu and Da Xu. 2018).

Over the past few years, the IoT has made considerable advancements. According to the International Data Corporation (IDC), there will be 41.6 billion IoT devices, or "things," by 2025, and 79.4 ZB of data will be generated as a result (Li, Xu and Zhao. 2015). Because IoT connects multiple items to networks for intelligent services and permits interaction between the real world and computer communication networks, future IoT systems must take privacy and security precautions (Hajjaji et al. 2021). IoT is unquestionably raising the bar for innovation and productivity in both the industrial sector and daily life. It shows a sizable network where individuals, gadgets, and objects are all linked for data exchange and interaction.

AIoT networks have a significant impact in different fields of life, such as better governance, economics, transportation, and healthcare systems. Through work automation, increased productivity, anxiety reduction, smart homes and cities, among other contexts, AIoT networks have the potential to make life better. IoT-enabled devices are used to monitor, recognize, and comprehend a scenario of environmental circumstance without the assistance of a human. It is now possible to design and manage cutting-edge apps and improvements by using AI to evaluate the massive amount of IoT data that is now available. The emergence of AI coincides with a technological earthquake that enhances human welfare and well-being. It has been shown that AI is highly capable in a variety of domains, including face recognition, credit scoring, decision-making, and autonomous driving (Naseem et al. 2022).

Since its inception, the IoT has benefited from the convergence of three visions: things-, internet-, and semantic-orientation. IoT is a "global network of interconnected objects," to use semantic terminology. The fundamental objective of AIoT is to make it easier for autonomous networked actors to share real-time information.

2.2.1 Convergence of IoT and Artificial Intelligence

The study of AI focuses on how to make computers smart so they can carry out tasks that earlier needed human intelligence. AI systems have grown rapidly in terms of their capacity, functionality, flexibility, and computational efficiency. IoT is a network of physical items, or "things," that are equipped with software, sensors, and other features to allow for online communication with other things. AI and IoT will become more and more integrated (Alshehri and Muhammad. 2020). The intimate integration of AI technology and the IoT creates new possibilities for the IoT in various domains. Figure 2.2 depicts the layered technologies in AIoT networks.

AIoT is made up of many different kinds of hardware, software, and networking protocols, and they all have security flaws. As a result, the attack surface for the entire network has increased. The IoT is also a decentralized network of intelligent items that can sense, process, and talk to each other. The main idea behind AIoT is to use cutting-edge technology and make it a natural part of everyday life. Yet, it is anticipated that the development of smart gadgets will lead to the definition of new lifestyle standards, norms, and services (Anwar, Zainal, Outay, et al. 2020). Every AIoT component works with clearly defined objectives and is largely self-sufficient. However, it is challenging to design generic architecture for smart cities due to the wide variety of devices,

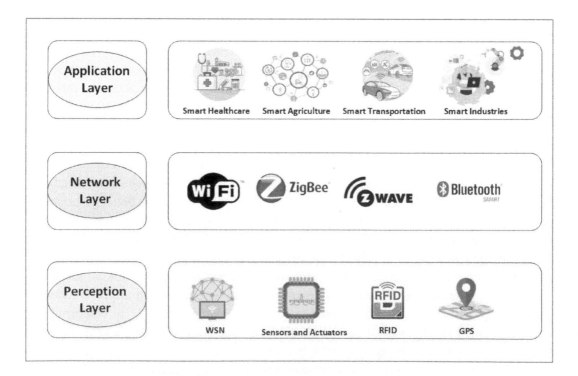

FIGURE 2.2 AIoT layer architecture.

underlying technology, and need to integrate components. The fundamental framework for communication in a smart city has three layers: the Network layer, the Application layer, and the Hardware or Perception layer. Together, these levels enable communication between diverse entities and other network elements (Anwar, Zainal, Abdullah, et al. 2019).

a. **The convergence of AI at the Application Layer:** At this layer, consumers can directly access numerous applications, but there are new challenges due to the exponential growth of applications as well as the varied and personalized service requirements. For example, even when consumers are looking for the same information, their needs may vary. However, AI contributes to helping understand personalized services and enhances user satisfaction. Also, user profiles help significantly in providing adaptive services. The Application layer of AI provides users with adaptive services. AI may assist with in-depth user profile analysis and learn hidden information with data mining techniques when users suggest a specific requirement for a particular application (Jabraeil Jamali et al. 2020).

b. **The Convergence of AI at the Network Layer:** The second layer and core element of IoT architecture is the Network layer, which connects the Application and the Perception layers. Data aggregation from different sensors is the main duty of the Network layer. The Network layer's communication efficiency can be increased by choosing the best routing path, which is crucial. Most prefer to select a routing path for lightweight networks, like Wireless Sensor Networks (WSN), based on predetermined rules or information. Through knowledge-enabled and data-driven techniques, AI significantly contributes to optimal routing path selection, network scheduling optimization, Quality of Service (QoS) improvement, effective connection establishment, and effective communication (Ghosh, Chakraborty, and Law. 2018).

c. **The Convergence of AI at the Perception Layer:** The Perception layer is the foundational element of the architecture, sometimes referred to as recognition. It takes in the surrounding environment, collects real-time information, then delivers it to the Network layer for processing. Data is the fundamental building block of IoT and AI, which open up an enormous number of possibilities for mining value-added services. When AI converges at the Perception layer, it enables technological advances in handling exploding data. AI is appearing at an opportune time (Chang et al. 2021).

AIoT applications produce a lot of information. As a result, it is crucial to develop and implement reliable AI techniques for dimensionality reduction, noise reduction, and potentially redundancy removal in data pre-processing and preparation. In order to facilitate the creation of AIoT applications, we believe that the network compositional layers will continue to evolve AI approaches and methodologies. The field of AI encompasses a number of technological developments, such as machine learning, deep learning, and natural language processing. The architecture of interconnected IoT systems is improved by combining AI-based techniques at various IoT compositional layers to handle a variety of data for self-management activities. Innovations (AI, bots, and Augmented Reality/Virtual Reality (AR/VR)) use combined IoT knowledge to make intelligent judgments, enhancing human capabilities and improving machine/thing capabilities to better manage and govern IoT and other areas such as fog and edge computing (Lai et al. 2021).

2.2.2 Artificial Intelligence in IoT Applications

In a variety of IoT scenarios, AI techniques are enabling hundreds of different applications. Smart cities, smart buildings, smart homes, smart transportation, smart healthcare, environmental monitoring, agriculture, and smart grids are some of the AI applications in the consumer and industrial IoT. More specifically, by assisting with application design and development as well as infrastructure and application maintenance, AI has demonstrated its effectiveness in numerous areas. Artificial neural networks (such as deep learning techniques), fuzzy logic, and evolutionary computation are currently the most widely used AI technologies in IoT applications. These technologies are used for a variety of tasks, including regression, classification, multidimensional signal processing, sensor calibration, measurement, data fusion, prediction, decision support, security, and data transmission (Deng et al. 2020). In addition, every IoT application uses a unique set of communication protocols and has the option to include security and privacy protection measures.

Also, production from the AIoT is significant. AIoT devices regularly produce more data than any human being can handle or use productively, including data on health, the environment, warehouses, and logistics. Additionally, these IoT components benefit greatly from AI approaches. Due to restrictions in communication technologies, a sizable number of IoT applications are created on portable, lightweight, and energy-efficient devices. AI-based IoT has many applications across numerous industries and offers many benefits like increased productivity, cost savings, and positive user experiences. AI programs can gradually learn the most significant patterns and trends. They are capable of detecting certain occurrences that require human intervention (Herath, Karunasena and Herath. 2021).

- **Smart Cities:** A smart city is a big concept that includes both the city's physical infrastructure and concerns affecting its residents and society. A community that plans adequate investments in public transportation and services could offer better life quality and resource management that enable thoughtful and sustainable socioeconomic growth (Kassens-Noor and Hintze. 2020). There are several uses for AI, including security, the stock market, search and rescue, and transportation. The creation of smart cities involves a number of intricate factors, including economic restructuring, environmental protection, governance, and transportation concerns (Kar et al. 2019). Smart buildings can be constructed sustainably by leveraging electronic devices, software-driven systems, or other cutting-edge technologies in the form of AI that can adapt to the surroundings of the building in order to optimize or increase the system's performance.

- **Smart Healthcare:** The term "smart healthcare" refers to platforms for health systems that connect people, resources, and organizations while making it simple to enter health records using devices like wearable appliances, the IoT, and the mobile Internet. An important component of connected life is smart healthcare. One of our fundamental needs is healthcare, and it's anticipated that in the near future, smart healthcare will generate several billion dollars. The IoT, the Internet of Medical Things (IoMT), medical sensors, AI, edge computing, cloud computing, and next-generation wireless communication technology are a few of the components of smart health-care (Bellini, Nesi and Pantaleo. 2022; Ahmed et al. 2022). AI-integrated healthcare systems now significantly benefit from the IoT. The detection method for diabetes and heart-related disorders uses a convergence of IoT and AI technologies. However, there are many obstacles standing in the way of next-generation healthcare, including reliability, network latency, and bandwidth.

- **Smart Agriculture:** IoT networks have the potential to transform agriculture by providing crop, weather, and soil conditions in real time. This will allow for precision agriculture and the efficient use of resources like water and fertilizer. Automation in agriculture is a hot topic and a significant source of concern worldwide. The need for food and employment grows along with the global population. The conventional farming techniques are insufficient to achieve these objectives. With the use of AI, new automated procedures have been created that have changed agriculture (Ciruela-Lorenzo et al. 2020). Social, economic, and environmental sustainability are all being improved by smart agriculture in the agricultural sector. Thanks to Wireless Sensor Networks' (WSN) explosive expansion, the IoT has been shown to be a useful tool for automating agriculture and making judgments. IoT devices that can trigger responses to changes in plants and environmental circumstances are created by using AI techniques on IoT devices to regulate smart irrigation, harvesting, and greenhouse factors.

- **Smart Manufacturing:** Sensors, which are embedded in all the parts connected to the manufacturing process, are a crucial aspect of AIoT. These sensors serve as the "senses" for gathering information about a product's availability, production, storage, distribution, and consumption in order to promote industrial supply chain optimization, proactive maintenance, and product quality control. IoT with AI provides automation, preventive maintenance, and real-time monitoring of production processes in the industrial sector, which makes Industry 4.0 deployment easier. This results in greater efficacy, less downtime, and better product quality (Ghahramani et al. 2020).

- **Smart Transportation:** AIoT networks can benefit the transportation sector through intelligent traffic management, Vehicle-to-Vehicle (V2V) and Vehicle-to-Infrastructure (V2I) communication, and the development of autonomous vehicles. The majority of the world's biggest cities encounter logistical, traffic, and transportation issues. Using AI in the creation and management of a sustainable transportation system might be highly beneficial. The intelligent transportation system is a collection of control systems, sensors, actuators, and Information and Communication Technologies (ICTs) that generates massive amounts of data and will significantly affect future transportation in the modern smart city (Qureshi and Abdullah. 2013).

The handling of real time traffic flow data in urban environments, which is a crucial component of the development of smart transportation systems, effectively requires the employment of ML, AI, and Deep Reinforcement Learning (DRL) approaches. Intelligent public transportation, traffic management, manufacturing, safety management, and logistics are all impacted by AI.

- **Smart Retail:** AIoT networks can improve customer experiences in the retail industry by enabling tailored marketing, in-the-moment inventory management, and intelligent payment systems. An increasing number of businesses and customers are now emphasizing the effectiveness and experience of shopping. The growth of IoT and AI, as well as the uptake of smartphones and mobile payments, are driving the increase in unstaffed retail purchases (De Vass, Shee and Miah. 2021). Utilizing AI and machine learning gained from production data can result in intelligent automation.

- **Environmental Monitoring:** Environmental monitoring is the idea of designing a space with integrated sensors, displays, and computer equipment to aid users in comprehending and managing their surroundings. For example, artificial neural networks are used to interpret data from AIoT sensors to analyze the data collected from networks (Shaikh, Naidu and Kokate. 2021). Neural networks and deep learning are the AI methods used most often in this situation.

- **Smart Mobility:** An intelligent transportation and mobility network is known as a smart mobility network. Parking, intelligent routing, autonomous and sustainable transportation, supply chain resilience, and traffic management are some of the essential elements of smart mobility (Herath, Karunasena and Herath. 2021).

- **Smart Education:** Due to the significant role that AI applications have played in a range of educational disciplines, the education sector has gotten a lot of attention lately. Utilizing IT and its AI-based applications is one of the major advancements in smart education (Qureshi et al. 2023).

- **Smart Governance:** IoT networks have the potential to change a variety of industries and improve quality of life by fostering a more connected, efficient, and intelligent society. Additionally, smart governance refers to the application of technology and innovation to improve planning and decision-making in governing bodies. Smart governance is made possible by the IoT. Bringing together data from several government departments can give authorities access to a wealth of information from a variety of sensor data (from weather-related data to environment-related data) (Zhou and Kankanhalli. 2021). The integration of IoT and AI helps in urban planning, disaster management, decision making, and e-governance.

2.3 SECURITY REQUIREMENTS FOR IoT APPLICATIONS

The most important issue for new and advanced AIoT applications is cybersecurity. Any security breach can have disastrous consequences, including loss of money, information, bodily injury (if the wrong data is entered into the system), disrupting other activities, and impairing decision making. Without sacrificing security or intelligence, AIoT's secure infrastructure can be expanded. Due to the configuration of these environments, particularly the weak connections and open data interchange, they are exposed to a variety of threats and serious security concerns (Singh et al. 2022).

Protecting physical assets, data, and networks from threats, attacks, and vulnerabilities, both known and undiscovered, is the primary objective of IoT security. Additionally, a huge amount of information is produced by a diverse variety of devices, and this information is used for decision making. Furthermore, the acquired data is regarded as the most valuable asset and requires adequate security to safeguard data Confidentiality, Integrity, and Availability (CIA). While integrity ensures that tasks are carried out by the person who is authorized to do them, it also involves belief in the veracity of the resources within a system. Table 2.1 lists the numerous security requirements that the various AIoT components must take into account during the design and authentication phases (Zikria et al. 2021).

The AIoT environment must protect its data's integrity and take the required security measures to prevent attackers from harming or tapping into communications. The secrecy of data and system communications, as well as total security, must be maintained in order to help make data and transactions feel more readily available, legitimate, and validated. Additionally, it can be challenging or impossible for AIoT devices to carry out computation-intensive and latency-sensitive security activities, especially for massive data streams, due to their limited memory, computational power, radio bandwidth, and battery resources (Li et al. 2018).

TABLE 2.1   Security Requirements for IoT

Security Requirements	Description
Confidentiality	The data is safe and only accessible to authorized users because unlawful access is prevented.
Integrity	End-to-end encryption and digital signatures can be used to ensure data integrity in an IoT setting.
Availability	The term "availability" refers to the process of ensuring timely and dependable access to and use of data, tools, and services.
Authentication	A network of interconnected things, including devices, people, services, providers, and processing units, is known as the IoT. Each IoT device needs to be able to recognize and authenticate other IoT devices.
Authorization	Only those with authorization may access the provided tools and services.
Non-repudiation	An IoT network requirement for cyber-security is non-repudiation, which provides evidence of what entities have done.
Data Freshness	Allowing for the assurance that all data produced by devices are up-to-date, time-tamped, and unaffected by an opponent who might have manipulated the data or retransmitted older communications.
Anonymity	Anonymity refers to ensuring the privacy and security of the data against possible adversaries.
Scalability	The system's ability to keep its current devices and services while adding new ones.
Attack Resistance	Ability to defend against a variety of potential attackers.

2.4 SECURITY ATTACKS IN IoT APPLICATIONS

Because many IoT devices lack proper security, hackers have developed a variety of methods to attack them from different angles. The IoT device itself, as well as its hardware and software, the network to which it is attached, and the application with which it communicates, all serve as potential attack surfaces (Domingo. 2021). Before attempting an attack on a particular device, IoT attackers usually investigate it to identify any vulnerabilities. The most common way to do this is to buy an identical IoT device. The adversary then builds a test attack using reverse engineering to analyze the device's outputs and available attack possibilities. This can be done, for instance, by disassembling the device and examining the internal hardware to understand the software (such as the flash memory), or by fiddling with the microcontroller to find sensitive data or trigger undesirable behavior. To prevent reverse engineering, it is essential that IoT devices implement hardware-based security. Many cybersecurity experts are looking to AI to protect systems against cyberattacks. Here are a few hazardous attacks that could harm IoT devices if they were installed by someone with malicious intent (Radanliev et al. 2020).

a. **Physical Attack:** Physical attacks, which are typical of the low-tech variety, make use of the target device's hardware in some way to the attacker's advantage. There are numerous sorts of physical attacks. These include attacks like network outages, in which the device's connection to the network is cut off to interfere with its operations, cause physical damage, or inject malicious code that prohibits correct performance (Abdul-Ghani, Konstantas and Mahyoub. 2018).

b. **Man-in-the-Middle (MITM) Attack:** MITM attacks are among the most common ones against IoTs. In terms of computers in general, an MITM attack allows the attacker to act as a proxy by intercepting communication between two nodes. In this attack, transmitted communications can be intercepted, their contents can be changed or erased, and harmful content can even be added. This is done so that the recipient is unaware of these facts and will therefore treat any messages it receives as though they were sent with authorization (Cekerevac et al. 2017).

c. **False Data Injection Attacks:** False Data Injection (FDI) attacks may be used by an attacker after a MITM attack to get access to any or all of the devices on an IoT network. An FDI attack involves the attacker subtly altering IoT sensor readings to fabricate data in order to avoid detection (Zhang et al. 2021).

d. **Sybil Attack:** In this attack, once an adversary seizes control of an IoT node, the perpetrator may attempt to assume a new identity near another node. A single rogue node impersonates a huge number of other nodes in this kind of attack (Arshad et al. 2021).

e. **Botnets:** Another frequent attack on IoT devices is the deployment of a large number of devices to build botnets and perform Distributed Denial of Service (DDoS) attacks. A DDoS uses attacks from numerous entities to achieve this objective. A Denial of Service (DoS) attack is a deliberate effort to hinder lawful usage of a service.

DDoS attacks seek to overwhelm the target service's infrastructure and obstruct regular data flow. The four steps of a DDoS attack are typically recruiting, exploitation and infection, communication, and attack. In the recruitment stage, the attacker looks for vulnerable machines to use in the DDoS attack against the target; in the exploitation and infection stage, the attacker takes advantage of the weak points and injects malicious code; the attacker evaluates the infected machines, determines which are online, and chooses when to schedule attacks or upgrade the devices during the communication stage; and throughout the attack, the attacker sends commands to the affected machines (Om Kumar and Sathia Bhama. 2019).

Despite the fact that AIoT offers a lot of conveniences, it is vulnerable to security and privacy problems such as malicious attacks and privacy leakage. IoT devices tend to be vulnerable to malicious techniques, such as bogus data injection attacks and DDoS attacks, but can still be successful in IoT contexts since they have limited processing and storage resources. However, to protect IoT applications from these malicious attacks, it is necessary to explore other security solutions, such as using the blockchain along with AI.

2.5 CONCLUSION

With the ongoing growth of data, connections, and services, IoT has entered a period of significant challenges. It is vital to address these problems and achieve high efficiency with the current infrastructure, given the conflict between scarce resources and extremely demanding criteria. Applications with an IoT focus are assisting in gathering huge amounts of sensor fusion data from many sources. However, the fusion of AI and IoT can reshape how data can be managed, allowing for intelligent responses from corporations, economies, and enterprises. Increasingly more IoT devices are producing data, which makes it increasingly challenging to collect, process, and analyze data in real time. Individuals' fundamental needs benefit from the convergence of IoT and AI streams to govern smart sensing systems. The collaborative integration of AI with IoT has significantly advanced the development of AIoT systems that assess and respond to environmental stimuli more intelligently without human intervention.

REFERENCES

Abdul-Ghani, Hezam Akram, Dimitri Konstantas, and Mohammed Mahyoub. "A Comprehensive IoT Attacks Survey Based on a Building-Blocked Reference Model." *International Journal of Advanced Computer Science and Applications* 9.3 (2018): 355–73.
Ahmed, Aneeqa, et al. "Link-Based Penalized Trust Management Scheme for Preemptive Measures to Secure the Edge-Based Internet of Things Networks." *Wireless Networks* (2022).
Alshehri, Fatima, and Ghulam Muhammad. "A Comprehensive Survey of the Internet of Things (IoT) and AI-Based Smart Healthcare." *IEEE Access* 9 (2020): 3660–78.
Anwar, Raja Waseem, and Saqib Ali. "Smart Cities Security Threat Landscape: A Review." *Computing and Informatics* 41.2 (2022): 405–23.
Anwar, Raja Waseem, et al. "Security Threats and Challenges to IoT and Its Applications: A Review." *2020 Fifth International Conference on Fog and Mobile Edge Computing (FMEC)*. 2020. IEEE.

Anwar, Raja Waseem, et al. "BTEM: Belief Based Trust Evaluation Mechanism for Wireless Sensor Networks." *Future Generation Computer Systems* 96 (2019): 605–16.

Arshad, Akashah, et al. "A Survey of Sybil Attack Countermeasures in IoT-Based Wireless Sensor Networks." *PeerJ Computer Science* 7 (2021): e673.

Bellini, Pierfrancesco, Paolo Nesi, and Gianni Pantaleo. "IoT-Enabled Smart Cities: A Review of Concepts, Frameworks and Key Technologies." *Applied Sciences* 12.3 (2022): 1607.

Cekerevac, Zoran, et al. "Internet of Things and the Man-in-the-Middle Attacks–Security and Economic Risks." *MEST Journal* 5.2 (2017): 15–25.

Chang, Zhuoqing, et al. "A Survey of Recent Advances in Edge-Computing-Powered Artificial Intelligence of Things." *IEEE Internet of Things Journal* 8.18 (2021): 13849–75.

Ciruela-Lorenzo, Antonio Manuel, et al. "Digitalization of Agri-Cooperatives in the Smart Agriculture Context. Proposal of a Digital Diagnosis Tool." *Sustainability* 12.4 (2020): 1325.

De Vass, Tharaka, Himanshu Shee, and Shah J Miah. "IoT in Supply Chain Management: A Narrative on Retail Sector Sustainability." *International Journal of Logistics Research and Applications* 24.6 (2021): 605–24.

Deng, Shuiguang, et al. "Edge Intelligence: The Confluence of Edge Computing and Artificial Intelligence." *IEEE Internet of Things Journal* 7.8 (2020): 7457–69.

Domingo, Mari Carmen. "Deep Learning and Internet of Things for Beach Monitoring: An Experimental Study of Beach Attendance Prediction at Castelldefels Beach." *Applied Sciences* 11.22 (2021): 10735.

Ghahramani, Mohammadhossein, et al. "AI-Based Modeling and Data-Driven Evaluation for Smart Manufacturing Processes." *IEEE/CAA Journal of Automatica Sinica* 7.4 (2020): 1026–37.

Ghosh, Ashish, Debasrita Chakraborty, and Anwesha Law. "Artificial Intelligence in Internet of Things." *CAAI Transactions on Intelligence Technology* 3.4 (2018): 208–18.

Hajjaji, Yosra, et al. "Big Data and IoT-Based Applications in Smart Environments: A Systematic Review." *Computer Science Review* 39 (2021): 100318.

Herath, HMKKMB, GMKB Karunasena, and HMWT Herath. "Development of an IoT Based Systems to Mitigate the Impact of Covid-19 Pandemic in Smart Cities." *Machine Intelligence and Data Analytics for Sustainable Future Smart Cities*. Springer, 2021. 287–309.

Jamali, Jabraeil, Mohammad Ali, et al. "IoT Architecture." *Towards the Internet of Things: Architectures, Security, and Applications* (2020): 9–31.

Kar, Arpan Kumar, et al. "Moving Beyond Smart Cities: Digital Nations for Social Innovation & Sustainability." *Information Systems Frontiers* 21 (2019): 495–501.

Kassens-Noor, Eva, and Arend Hintze. "Cities of the Future? The Potential Impact of Artificial Intelligence." *AI* 1.2 (2020): 12.

Kuzlu, Murat, Corinne Fair, and Ozgur Guler. "Role of Artificial Intelligence in the Internet of Things (IoT) Cybersecurity." *Discover Internet of Things* 1 (2021): 1–14.

Lai, Ying-Hsun, et al. "Study on Enhancing AIoT Computational Thinking Skills by Plot Image-Based VR." *Interactive Learning Environments* 29.3 (2021): 482–95.

Li, Jiaqi, et al. "AI-Based Two-Stage Intrusion Detection for Software Defined IoT Networks." *IEEE Internet of Things Journal* 6.2 (2018): 2093–102.

Li, Shancang, Li Da Xu, and Shanshan Zhao. "The Internet of Things: A Survey." *Information Systems Frontiers* 17 (2015): 243–59.

Lu, Yang, and Li Da Xu. "Internet of Things (IoT) Cybersecurity Research: A Review of Current Research Topics." *IEEE Internet of Things Journal* 6.2 (2018): 2103–15.

Mukhopadhyay, Subhas Chandra, et al. "Artificial Intelligence-Based Sensors for Next Generation IoT Applications: A Review." *IEEE Sensors Journal* 21.22 (2021): 24920–32.

Naseem, Shahid, et al. "Artificial General Intelligence-Based Rational Behavior Detection Using Cognitive Correlates for Tracking Online Harms." *Personal and Ubiquitous Computing* (2022).

Om Kumar, CU, and Ponsy RK Sathia Bhama. "Detecting and Confronting Flash Attacks from IoT Botnets." *The Journal of Supercomputing* 75 (2019): 8312–38.

Phan, Vu Hien, et al. "An IoT System and Modis Images Enable Smart Environmental Management for Mekong Delta." *Future Internet* 15.7 (2023): 245.

Qureshi, Kashif Naseer, and Abdul Hanan Abdullah. "A Survey on Intelligent Transportation Systems." *Middle-East Journal of Scientific Research* 15.5 (2013): 629–42.

Qureshi, Kashif Naseer, et al. "Internet of Things enables smart solid waste bin management system for a sustainable environment." *Environmental Science and Pollution Research* 30.60 (2023): 125188–125196.

Radanliev, Petar, et al. "Future Developments in Standardisation of Cyber Risk in the Internet of Things (IoT)." *SN Applied Sciences* 2 (2020): 1–16.

Shaikh, Rumana Abdul Jalil, Harikumar Naidu, and Piyush A Kokate. "Next-Generation WSN for Environmental Monitoring Employing Big Data Analytics, Machine Learning and Artificial Intelligence." *Evolutionary Computing and Mobile Sustainable Networks: Proceedings of ICECMSN 2020.* 2021. Springer.

Singh, Ashish, et al. "AI-Based Mobile Edge Computing for IoT: Applications, Challenges, and Future Scope." *Arabian Journal for Science and Engineering* 49 (2022): 1–31.

Ślusarczyk, Beata. "Industry 4.0–Are We Ready?" *Polish Journal of Management Studies* 17.1 (2018): 232–48.

Yao, Wenbo. "The Application of Artificial Intelligence in the Internet of Things." *2019 International Conference on Information Technology and Computer Application (ITCA).* 2019. IEEE.

Zhang, Zhenyong, et al. "On Feasibility of Coordinated Time-Delay and False Data Injection Attacks on Cyber–Physical Systems." *IEEE Internet of Things Journal* 9.11 (2021): 8720–36.

Zhou, Ya, and Atreyi Kankanhalli. "AI Regulation for Smart Cities: Challenges and Principles." *Smart Cities and Smart Governance: Towards the 22nd Century Sustainable City* (2021): 101–18.

Zikria, Yousaf Bin, et al. "Next-Generation Internet of Things (IoT): Opportunities, Challenges, and Solutions." *Sensors* 21.4 (2021): 1174.

CHAPTER 3

Tri-Tier Architectures for AIoT Networks

Muhammad Ahmed

Department of Computer Science, Bahria University Islamabad Pakistan

Kashif Naseer Qureshi

Department of Electronic & Computer Engineering, University of Limerick, V94 T9PX Limerick, Ireland

3.1 INTRODUCTION

Over the years, research and advancement in the field of the internet has now proven the success of it in every single field of science and the day-to-day life of every person. This has provided the advancement and betterment to the society. The Artificial Internet of Things (AIoT) is an emerging technology in the areas of the internet, networking, and communication. This new technology is bringing to light the experience of the intelligent presence of internet-based physical devices which can not only communicate with humans but also with each other (machine-to-machine). The existence of such a developed and internetworking environment has massive scope, and it will provide great opportunities in terms of growth in every business, market, and industry. All that advancement in technology will improve quality of life. Since it is an emerging area of research, it is too early to define the impact of AIoT applications in different domains and fields. There are some formal architectures available for the AIoT environment; working on them and using their existing protocol suits could provide us with grounds for the development of AIoT and ensure the co-existence and cooperation of different technologies. With the great interest in AIoT and the large amount of research on it, there are many proposed architecture designs.

One of the main reasons for the growth toward 5G technology is the rapidly increased number of interconnected computing devices. These devices include embedded devices which could be assigned and attached to other objects. Billions of devices are expected every year on cellular networks; about 28 billion devices were added just in 2017 (Liyanage, Braeken, et al. 2020). IoT is described as the worldwide network of billions of physical devices that are linked together.

In addition, with highly computational and resourceful devices like computers and smartphones, the IoT environment enables heterogeneous devices and objects to

DOI: 10.1201/9781003430018-4

communicate over the Internet. Through this networking model, IoT makes the entire internet a working area for the devices. This inter-communicative heterogeneous environment makes the devices smart, that is, able to access, gather, and process data, and then take action on that data accordingly. This interconnected and intercommunicating IoT environment is going to increase the data and computational resources all over the internet. To accommodate such technology, the internet demands an infrastructure and technologies which can co-exist with the existing infrastructure and computational technologies. One such alteration is Multi-Access Edge Computing (MEC) formerly known as Mobile Edge Computing (Liyanage, Ahmad, et al. 2018). Analogically, IoT devices are the nervous system of the new information area while the computational brain power of IoT devices resides in the decision-making technologies like Artificial Intelligence (AI), Machine Learning (ML), edge computing, cloud computing, etc.

At the start, computer networking aimed to access and share expensive resources efficiently and economically. However, with the emergence of Transmission Control Protocol/Internet Protocol (TCP/IP) protocol suites, it grew enormously, resulting in a huge worldwide network known as the Internet. All this time, the internet has been evolving, and advancements are occurring in it. These years of advancements and developments in the internet have paved the path for new technologies like IoT (Perera et al. 2013). IoT's path is similar to that of the Internet; it is the result of a merger of several perspectives, including those that are Things-oriented, Internet-oriented, and Semantic-oriented (Atzori, Iera and Morabito. 2017). AIoT, as described, allows people, things, and AI methods to connect anytime, anywhere, with anything, and with anybody, potentially through any connection, network, or service.

3.2 ARTIFICIAL INTELLIGENCE

AI is the term used to describe a machine's capacity to emulate or enhance human intelligence, such as reasoning and learning through experience. Although AI has long been employed in computer programs, now it is applied and integrated into about every computer-related service and product (Abhishek. 2022). AI is a subfield of computer science that studies how to utilize computers to replicate and enhance human brain function. Its definition is "A computer system and human knowledge and behavior with capabilities such as learning, inference, judgment, resolving the issue, memory, knowledge and understanding of the human natural language" (Li. 2009). AI can be divided into two parts: theoretical research and engineering studies. Theoretical research deals with the understanding of the human brain and the development of these patterns and intelligent theories for machines. Engineering studies deal with the design and development of theoretical research.

The field of AI covers numerous fields of study and has recently gained popularity in the public, business, and academic sectors (Boyd and Wilson. 2017). In particular, the self-learning algorithm serves as the foundation of the present AI evolution and can have significant implications across many fields (Holdren and Smith. 2016). The importance of artificial intelligence is being highlighted by the rapid changes brought about by the digitization of information in the workplace, especially in the business sector (Castro and New. 2016). AI has the potential to increase the economic growth of developed countries by 2 percent within 15 years (Purdy and Daugherty. 2016). AI can provide benefits and bring change in both the public and private sectors. By maximizing its support of industry, AI could provide the intelligent automation of systems and virtual workforces which could be a cost-efficient approach for industries (Bataller and Harris. 2016). Another way to define AI is as a capital-labor hybrid to replicate labor activities at a much greater scale and speed, and even to perform some tasks beyond the capabilities of humans (GSS Asia, 2017). For these reasons, nearly every major IT firm is investing more in the research and development of AI and related technologies (Horvitz. 2016).

3.2.1 Applications of Artificial Intelligence

The rapid development of AI across all technological domains has opened up numerous avenues for boosting productivity across all sectors of the economy. Artificial intelligence provides highly advanced, self-aware computational programs that pretend to work like a human brain. Applications of AI are present in about every field of technology. Following are some applications in different fields.

There are several cases where understanding the connections between transportation system characteristics is challenging, AI can solve those complex problems which existing traditional techniques cannot solve. Usage of AI techniques in the transportation sector provides many advantages. Research shows the benefit of AI in transportation by transforming the roadside traffic sensors into smart grid agents which can automatically detect any accident on the road and can also forecast future traffic conditions (Klügl, Bazzan and Ossowski. 2010). AI is also bringing rapid improvement in the field of Intelligent Transportation Systems (ITS). These systems use a wide range of technologies and forms of communication to accomplish their goals of easing traffic and enhancing drivers' experiences on the road. They gather crucial information that can be used by ML systems. (Liu et al. 2018) developed a system that uses reinforcement learning techniques to enhance traffic control policies in real-time.

To help traffic managers reduce congestion, numerous attempts have been undertaken to pinpoint exactly when and where an incident occurred, as well as what caused it. These attempts could be manual (reported by humans) or could be automated by neural networks. Manual reports can have delays, but the automated reports gathered by AI systems can be more rapidly responsive. Furthermore, the implanted sensors on the roads allow the AI system to measure the characteristic flow before and after the incident. A system was designed and tested which uses a classification neural network approach to detect any incident on the freeway (Dia and Rose. 1997). Through AI deep learning techniques, we can detect real-time incidents from social media (Gu, Qian and Chen. 2016). Twitter has proven to be an effective, low-cost approach for monitoring motorways and major routes for incidents.

The use of AI in airline operations has been acknowledged. ML, software/hardware, and applications (such as smart maintenance and flight route optimization) could all benefit from the use of AI. Authors Oza, Castle, and Stutz. 2009 developed a system which is called Aviation Safety Reporting System (ASRS). The system was created to collect data from extremely dense aviation reports and adapt the Support Vector Machine (SVM) and Mariana algorithms. The results show the effectiveness of the SVM) technique to perform the consistent document classifications. Authors, Budalakoti, Srivastava and Otey, demonstrated that the unsupervised ML approach is reliable for application in increasing landing safety.

3.3 AI USAGE IN AIoT NETWORKS

AI is an extensive field that includes a variety of ideas. Most of the recent research focuses on AI technologies. Both the private and public sectors, including industries looking upon the use of AI technologies (Prediger. 2017) for healthcare, manufacturing, business, and even the auto sector, have all benefited from the application of AI. With the benefits of AI there are also some issues involved such as cybersecurity and cyberattacks (Dilek, Çakır and Aydın. 2015). AI has also contributed new technologies and ideas to the field of computing and information technology. These approaches, techniques, and models use AI techniques which make them the sub-branches of AI. Some of these models are Natural Language Processing, Deep Learning, Robotics, and Computer Vision (Ashley; Jackson. 2017). The purpose of AI is to develop computer systems with human-like intelligence. AI has provided significant advancement in industries where robots are working in the fields of manufacturing and assembling. All these robots use AI techniques to do the given task like a human does.

ML is a form of AI that analyzes a system's data and its patterns to draw conclusions (Alpaydin. 2020). Another branch of AI is robotics, which involves the engineering of autonomous machines to carry out formerly human-only jobs (Patil. 2016; Dirican. 2016). The advancement in robotics with the help of AI is leading engineers to create self-driven intelligent vehicles (Makridakis. 2017).

3.3.1 Machine and Deep Learning

An emerging field of AI is ML. The machine learning paradigm uses different AI models and approaches to allow system automation (Marsland; Alpaydin. 2011). The techniques of ML focus on computer data programs that access and understand data. ML enables the system to learn new things on its own (Acemoglu and Restrepo. 2018). ML uses AI approaches to learn from experiences (Qureshi, Ahmad, et al. 2020). Deep Learning (DL) is an AI technique that mimics the working of the human brain, its pattern creation, and how it processes the data. DL techniques use this information to make strategic decisions like humans. Because DL can learn unsupervised data from unstructured data, it is also known as a Deep Neural Network. Deep knowledge facilitates the gathering of massive amounts of unstructured data, which is very hard for humans to understand and analyze (Mathew, Amudha and Sivakumari. 2021).

3.3.2 Biometrics

With the advancement of technology, the systems have become so much more complicated that the security of the data systems has become a priority for many enterprises. The use of biometric identification has been a game changer in terms of data system security. Biometric technology makes use of several physical characteristics which are unique in every person and uses them as security features for that specific person.. AI can use these unique human properties, such as fingerprints, iris, and facial structures, for the security recognition of that specific person (Akhtar et al. 2018; Rodgers. 2018). The data collected from these unique human properties are then sent to different specific nodes, which the AI system can easily comprehend, to perform required actions on it.

3.3.3 Artificial Intelligence in Vehicles

An important development of AI is in the field of transportation and making an Intelligent Transportation System (ITS) (Qureshi and Abdullah. 2013). The ITS makes a transportation system intelligent through the communication between transportation units for further decision making. In Vehicular Ad Hoc Networks (VANETs), vehicles use wireless communication to get run time information of the environment to make transportation better and safer (Taherkhani and Pierre. 2015). Research aiming at network traffic prediction using the relationship between road and network traffic parameters shows that the machine learning technique random forest (RM) is the best option to solve the traffic flow prediction problems in VANETs (Sepasgozar and Pierre. 2022). (A new approach was developed to improve the network traffic prediction in Aldhyani et al. 2020) Using sequence mining, the proposed approach predicts the traffic of the network intelligently. Adaptive Neuro-Fuzzy Inference System (ANFIS) and Long Short-Term Memory (LSTM) were used as a time series model. A new technique for the prediction of network traffic in Long-Term Evolution (LTE) is proposed by Stepanov et al. 2020. To predict the traffic in a network the model uses three machine learning algorithms SVM, Bagging, and Radio Frequency (RF) on cellular traffic datasets.

IoT is a very vast and emerging field with the capability of interconnecting and processing the data of billions of devices like sensors and actuators. Every IoT device can perform basic functions on data, such as gathering, storing, transmitting, and processing, in order to take required actions. The processing capability of an IoT-enabled device decides the smartness of that device. A non-smart device has limited capabilities in processing data in comparison with smart devices which have a much greater level of processing and can take actions accordingly. A better IoT system, on the other hand, will contain artificial intelligence and may serve the true purpose of automation and adaptation.

3.3.4 AI-Enabled Voice Assistants

Voice Assistants are cloud-based services. Users can use them as personal assistants. They carry out a variety of functions by engaging with applications developed by third parties and other smart devices available in the surroundings. Using the user's vocal instructions, they may do a variety of functions, including responding to questions, turning on/off lighting, contacting cabs, playing music, etc.

Some famous voice assistants are the following:

- Amazon created the famous voice assistant ALEXA, it can be utilized in products such as Amazon Echo, Amazon Tap, and others. Alexa has a kit called Alexa Skills Kit (ASK) that can be used to improve specific skills by personalizing it according to the user's needs and requirements.

- Siri, which is the production of Apple Inc., also serves the same purpose and is used in the Apple Home pod.

- Google Assistant on Google Home has extra features that allow it to recognize six different people and obtain their information to speak with them.

3.3.5 Robots

Recent developments in robotics have led to the creation of more human-like machines that can interact with people while understanding, recreating, and expressing human emotions. Robots are a fine example of IoT as different sensors, actuators, and AI approaches help them to grow and evolve with time which means that they can continuously learn new things.

- SoftBank Robotics developed a humanoid robot which is named Pepper. That robot can communicate with humans and act as a human companion. It can understand human emotions through facial expressions, bodily movements, tone of voice, and phrases, among other things. Furthermore, Pepper can detect four different emotions: happiness, sorrow, rage, and surprise. It also reacts according to the detected emotion with touch, and expressions. It also has the functions of IoT and can connect to other devices. It can also be used commercially as a customer care representative.

- Sophia from Hanson Robotics is a socially active robot. It can effectively communicate with humans as it has a wide range of facial expressions, the ability to make contact according to the situation, and can conduct an interesting conversation. It's the first robot that owns citizenship. It has given many interviews on different platforms and performed on stage by singing songs.

- The robotic kitchen from Moley Robotics is a kitchen integrated with various robots. It has a wide range of recipe libraries. It has a touch screen to select your desired recipe to prepare. After selection, it can use its robotic arms, hob, and oven to prepare food like an expert cook.

3.3.6 Smart Devices

Other than robots and Voice Assistants, smart devices/objects are also being used to make human tasks simpler and easier. Such devices are AI-enabled and can perform voice recognition, facial recognition, object identification, speech identification, and expression detection by using neural networks, Computer Vision, etc.

- Smart Oven by June acts as a perfect cook. According to the user requirements, it can cook food precisely by watching it in the oven using an HD camera and built-in thermometer. The oven can be operated through Alexa too.

- Honeywell created a doorbell that is HD Wi-Fi enabled named SkyBell. The doorbell can operate the door opening or closing function by using a smartphone or Voice Assistant. It can send a live transmission to the user's phone by using its live camera. Users can even communicate with the person at the door from a remote location.

- Smart Lights by Deako can connect with Alexa and Google Assistant. Users can control the light's colour and intensity with just a voice command.

- Affective Created Automotive AI uses AI to enable the use of taxis called robo-taxis. It is an in-cabin sensor AI model which is utilized in high-performance automobiles. This AI system can detect road signs and decrease or increase its speed accordingly which reduces the risk of accidents. It has built-in microphones and a camera that can detect the facial expressions and cognitive state of the occupants and can therefore react accordingly.

3.4 ARCHITECTURE OF AIoT

AIoT has provided an environment where billions and trillions of devices can interconnect through the internet. With the increase of AIoT, these numbers are expected to grow exponentially. By the end of 2025, the number of devices is expected to grow to 75.44 billion, with an anticipated increase of 10 devices per person (Alavi et al. 2018). As these devices are exceptionally large in number and heterogeneous in nature, IoT requires a flexible layered architecture for seamless connectivity between them. AIoT functions at the Application layer, Network layer, and Perception layer (Atzori et al. 2017; Lin et al. 2017; Wu et al. 2010) Figure 3.1 shows the flow of information between these three layers in the architecture of the AIoT.

- **Perception Layer:** Since the Perception layer is concerned with smart devices, such as tags or sensors, whose purpose is to collect data about physical objects, it is also known as the Device layer. The main roles of this layer are to collect data, update the state of the smart device, and send that data to the next layer.

- **Network Layer:** The Network layer is the layer that uses different connecting devices (switches, routers, etc.) for data communication between different heterogeneous networks. It provides the best routing paths for seamless data transmission. Depending upon the environment, it uses different communication technologies which could be Wi-Fi, LTE, fibre optics, and Bluetooth.

- **Application Layer:** The Application layer processes and analyzes the gathered data from the Perception layer, and then by using that data, performs the required services and necessary actions. It provides services in different domains including intelligent transportation, smart homes, smart cities, and e-health systems.

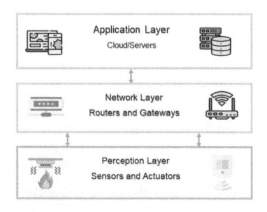

FIGURE 3.1   Tri-Tier AIoT architecture.

3.4.1 Cloud Computing

Cloud computing is a network access approach that allows for ubiquitous, on-demand, and affordable access to a shared pool of programmable computing resources like storage, processing, services, and on-demand applications. These cloud resources can be easily deployed and monitored with minimal management (Mell and Grance. 2011). Cloud computing can be referred to as network-enabled services which offer adaptable Quality of Services (QoS) on demand via the Internet (Hu et al. 2011). Cloud computing services are on-demand resources for sharing on the internet. The entity or organization that shares these resources with the clients is called a Cloud Service Provider (CSP). The client accessing the cloud can use those shared resources on demand (Hu et al. 2011). Cloud computing focuses on the client-server model, and on that basis, it provides three main service models, namely Software-as-a-service, Platform-as-a-service, and Infrastructure-as-a-service. The client requests the service using software or hardware of the Abstraction layer from the CSP) which then provides the requested service from the above three models (Ali, Khan and Vasilakos. 2015). Figure 3.2 shows the cloud architecture for AIoT networks.

AIoT is the next booming technology of the internet which is going to revolutionize the internet. AIoT allows the world's billions of internet-connected devices to connect, exchange data, and ultimately enhance the quality of human lives. Cloud computing provides on-demand computational power and scalable network access. With the collaboration of IoT and cloud computing, a new area of the internet is going to explode all over the world. It is critical to investigate the common characteristics of computing technologies. The same is the case with AIoT and cloud computing, as both of these technologies have common features. Their integration can improve and enhance both technologies (Buyya et al. 2009). Cloud computing provides the platform to share computational resources all

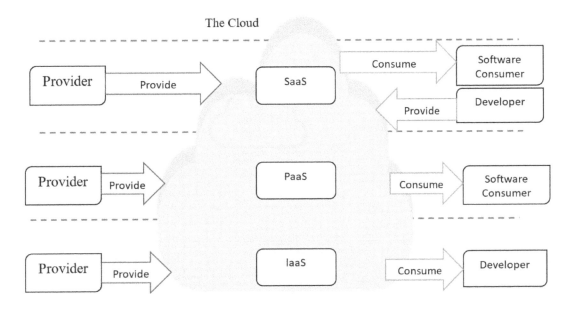

FIGURE 3.2 Cloud architecture for AIoT networks.

over the internet. Through providing on-demand resources, cloud computing has solved many ongoing problems on the internet. But with the combination of both AIoT and cloud computing, the future environment of the internet is going to change (Babu, Lakshmi and Rao. 2015).

Application and data exchange are two key components of the cloud-based AIoT concept. AIoT enables the transmission of worldwide applications, while automation facilitates the distribution and collection of data at minimal cost. The cloud is an efficient and inexpensive method of linking, administering, and monitoring the data through built-in apps and custom portals (Rao et al. 2012).

The cloud-based IoT platforms are available for different networks, like in the eHealth sector (Dang et al. 2019). The purpose of new research and the integration of cloud with smart networks is to explore the different internet technologies to enhance the eHealth sector and other services.

3.4.2 Edge Computing

Edge computing is a data networking paradigm that emphasizes processing data as close to the network as feasible. This helps to minimize latency and data transfer needs (Cao et al. 2020). According to Shi et al. 2016, "Edge computing is a distributed computing paradigm that brings computation and data storage closer to the location where it is needed, to improve response times and save bandwidth." Figure 3.3 shows the architecture of edge computing for AIoT networks.

Edge computing transmits the data that is processed and handled by millions of AIoT devices (Zhao et al. 2020). With time, as the internet evolves, emerging technologies require real-time computational power and resources. Cloud computing and real-time cloud services tend to provide promising solutions (Papcun et al. 2020). Edge computing provides an approach to evaluate the data of IoT devices on the edge before reaching to the main cloud or fog. That approach provides more rapid and scalable IoT processing.

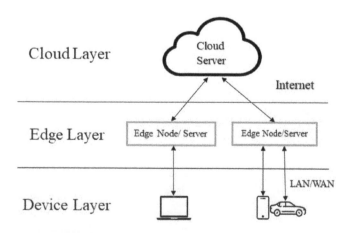

FIGURE 3.3 Edge computing for AIoT networks.

3.5 AI BASED SOFTWARE DEFINE NETWORK

The Software Define Network (SDN) is a model where all the decision-making of the overall network behaviour is done by a central software program. SDN divides the network into two-parts: data planes and control planes. All network devices that become packet-forwarding devices are included in the data plane. Decision-making control logic is carried out in the controller, which becomes the control plane. The SDN uses a software program to manage the network, hence it is very easy to introduce new technologies in the SDN network without disrupting existing programs. It is also easy to use a software program to manage the network rather than using a fixed set of commands in network devices (Qureshi, Alhudhaif, et al. 2020). Another advantage of the SDN is that it provides a central approach to control and configure the network rather than configuring it on every device of the network individually. The controller is used for that purpose since it has global knowledge of the network and can make network-wide forwarding decisions for the network traffic (Kim and Feamster. 2013; McKeown. 2013). Figure 3.4 shows the architecture of SDN for AIoT networks.

Open-Flow (OF) is a very suitable and effective approach for SDN-related networks (Lee et al. 2014; McKeown et al. 2009). In OF, the provider can test the new protocols in the deployed network without disturbing and affecting the production application. There are three main parts of the OF which are as follows:

- **Flow Tables:** These are installed in the switches.

- **OF Controller:** The Controller is the remote host machine.

- **OpenFlow Protocol:** This allows the controller to securely communicate with switches.

As the interest in AIoT grows, the demand for wide-area deployments of subnetworks also grows. These subnetworks can make it possible to have multiple heterogeneous wireless technologies coexist in the same place in a single environment.

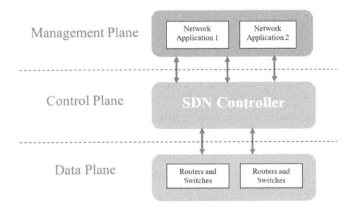

FIGURE 3.4   SDN architecture for AIoT networks.

For seamless communication and management between such different technologies in IoT, SDN provides its layered architectural platform to manage such distributed heterogeneous networks easily. The authors developed an SDN-based approach to provide differentiated quality levels in heterogeneous IoT environments to complete different tasks (Qin et al. 2014). To promote interoperability in heterogeneous smart home devices, an SDN-based intelligent support system for IoT was developed (Qureshi, Alhudhaif, et al. 2022)

To solve various problems, several ML and AI techniques have been used; these problems include routing (Nazar et al. 2022), traffic classification (Soysal and Schmidt. 2010), flow clustering (McGregor et al. 2004), intrusion detection (Xu and Wang. 2005), load balancing (Kim and Kim. 2013), fault detection (Moustapha and Selmic. 2008), QoS and Quality of Experience (QoE) optimization (Mushtaq, Augustin and Mellouk. 2012), and admission control and resource allocation (Testolin et al. 2014). Recent studies have revealed a significant tendency in the scientific community to use AI methods in SDNs.

The supervised techniques mostly used for AI-based SDN networks are supervised DL, SVM, Neural Networks (NNs), ensemble methods, and Decision Tree (DTs). Authors, Chen and Yu, developed a Collaborative Intrusion Prevention Architecture (CIPA). CIPA architecture uses the NN technique and provides a distributed intrusion prevention system. The CIPA system has simple and parallel computational abilities whereby it has low computational overhead. Authors, Bendriss et al. 2017 Bendriss, Yahia. and Zeghlache. 2017, developed a novel method for implementing Service Level Agreement (SLA) in SDN and Virtualized Network Functions (NFV). Their research focused on predicting service level objective violations for streaming services via NFV and SDN. The findings demonstrated that Long Short-Term Memory (LSTM) is more reliable and effective than Feedforward Neural Networks (FFNNs). Authors, Phan, Bao and Park. 2016, by combining SOM with SVM developed a new method that gives 97.6% effectiveness of Distributed Denial of Service (DDoS) detection in SDN. Authors in Rego et al. produced a multimedia transmission system which detects the problem and corrects the errors from the transmission in the SDN-based IoT environment. The system consists of two parts; the first one uses the SVM technique to detect the network traffic type. The second one tells the SDN controller which action is required to perform on the data to ensure the QoS.

3.6 CONCLUSION

Typical IoT architectures provide data communication and sensing services to the users. The integration of AI and their ML and DL methods have changed the traditional IoT networks into smarter, more cost-effective, and intelligent AIoT networks. There are some special requirements of AIoT networks, such as proper architectures based on SDN networks, cloud, edge-based networks, and mobility-based architectures. This chapter discussed traditional IoT networks and the emergence of AI in IoT networks. This chapter also proposed a tri-tier architecture for AIoT networks for more scalable, flexible, energy-efficient, and interoperable-based architectures where the systems can serve better. AI-empowered IoT architecture is based on emerged cloud, fog, and edge systems tailored with ML and DL methods and capabilities. The functions and technologies are discussed to understand the functionalities of the proposed architecture. The proposed architectures support and provide all the required services of AIoT networks.

REFERENCES

Abhishek, Kumar. "Introduction to Artificial Intelligence." 10 May 2022. Web2023.

Acemoglu, Daron, and Pascual Restrepo. "Artificial Intelligence, Automation, and Work." *The Economics of Artificial Intelligence: An Agenda.* University of Chicago Press, 2018. 197–236.

Akhtar, Zahid, et al. "Biometrics: In Search of Identity and Security (Q & A)." *IEEE MultiMedia* 25.3 (2018): 22–35.

Alavi, Amir H, et al. "Internet of Things-Enabled Smart Cities: State-of-the-Art and Future Trends." *Measurement* 129 (2018): 589–606.

Aldhyani, Theyazn HH, et al. "Intelligent Hybrid Model to Enhance Time Series Models for Predicting Network Traffic." *IEEE Access* 8 (2020): 130431–51.

Ali, Mazhar, Samee U Khan, and Athanasios V Vasilakos. "Security in Cloud Computing: Opportunities and Challenges." *Information Sciences* 305 (2015): 357–83.

Alpaydin, Ethem. *Introduction to Machine Learning.* MIT Press, 2020.

Ashley, Kevin D. *Artificial Intelligence and Legal Analytics: New Tools for Law Practice in the Digital Age.* Cambridge University Press, 2017.

Atzori, Luigi, Antonio Iera, and Giacomo Morabito. "Understanding the Internet of Things: Definition, Potentials, and Societal Role of a Fast Evolving Paradigm." *Ad Hoc Networks* 56 (2017): 122–40.

Atzori, Luigi, et al. "The Social Internet of Things (SIoT)–When Social Networks Meet the Internet of Things: Concept, Architecture and Network Characterization." *Computer Networks* 56.16 (2012): 3594–608.

Babu, Shaik Masthan, A Jaya Lakshmi, and B Thirumala Rao. "A Study on Cloud Based Internet of Things: CloudIoT." *2015 Global Conference on Communication Technologies (GCCT).* 2015. IEEE.

Bataller, Cyrille, and Jeanne Harris. "Turning Artificial Intelligence into Business Value." *Today.* Rttrieved from: https://pdfs.semanticscholar.org/a710/a8d529bce6bdf75ba589f42721777 bf54d3b.pdf (2016).

Bendriss, Jaafar, et al. "AI for SLA Management in Programmable Networks." *DRCN 2017-Design of Reliable Communication Networks; 13th International Conference.* 2017. VDE.

Bendriss, Jaafar, Imen Grida Ben Yahia, and Djamal Zeghlache. "Forecasting and Anticipating SLO Breaches in Programmable Networks." *2017 20th Conference on Innovations in Clouds, Internet and Networks (ICIN).* 2017. IEEE.

Boyd, Matthew, and Nick Wilson. "Rapid Developments in Artificial Intelligence: How Might the New Zealand Government Respond?" *Policy Quarterly* 13.4 (2017).

Budalakoti, Suratna, Ashok N Srivastava, and Matthew Eric Otey. "Anomaly Detection and Diagnosis Algorithms for Discrete Symbol Sequences with Applications to Airline Safety." *IEEE Transactions on Systems, Man, and Cybernetics, Part C (Applications and Reviews)* 39.1 (2008): 101–13.

Buyya, Rajkumar, et al. "Cloud Computing and Emerging It Platforms: Vision, Hype, and Reality for Delivering Computing as the 5th Utility." *Future Generation Computer Systems* 25.6 (2009): 599–616.

Cao, Keyan, et al. "An Overview on Edge Computing Research." *IEEE Access* 8 (2020): 85714–28.

Castro, Daniel, and Joshua New. "The Promise of Artificial Intelligence." *Center for Data Innovation* 115.10 (2016): 32–35.

Chen, Xiao-Fan, and Shun-Zheng Yu. "CIPA: A Collaborative Intrusion Prevention Architecture for Programmable Network and SDN." *Computers & Security* 58 (2016): 1–19.

Dang, L Minh, et al. "A Survey on Internet of Things and Cloud Computing for Healthcare." *Electronics* 8.7 (2019): 768.

Dia, Hussein, and Geoff Rose. "Development and Evaluation of Neural Network Freeway Incident Detection Models Using Field Data." *Transportation Research Part C: Emerging Technologies* 5.5 (1997): 313–31.

Dilek, Selma, Hüseyin Çakır, and Mustafa Aydın. "Applications of Artificial Intelligence Techniques to Combating Cyber Crimes: A Review." *arXiv preprint arXiv:1502.03552* (2015).

Dirican, Cüneyt. "The Impacts of Robotics, Artificial Intelligence on Business and Economics." *Procedia-Social and Behavioral Sciences* 195 (2015): 564–73.

GSS Asia, "Artificial Intelligence to transform businesses, societies" 2017. https://www.gessasia.com/news-center/news/artificial-intelligence-transform-businesses-societies

Gu, Yiming, Zhen Sean Qian, and Feng Chen. "From Twitter to Detector: Real-Time Traffic Incident Detection Using Social Media Data." *Transportation Research Part C: Emerging Technologies* 67 (2016): 321–42.

Holdren, John P, and Megan Smith. "Preparing for the Future of Artificial Intelligence." *White House: Washington, DC, USA* (2016).

Horvitz, Eric. "One Hundred Year Study on Artificial Intelligence." Stanford University, 2016.

Hu, Fei, et al. "A Review on Cloud Computing: Design Challenges in Architecture and Security." *Journal of Computing and Information Technology* 19.1 (2011): 25–55.

Jackson, Philip C. *Introduction to Artificial Intelligence*. Courier Dover Publications, 2019.

Kim, Hye-Young, and Jong-Min Kim. "A Load Balancing Scheme Based on Deep-Learning in IoT." *Cluster Computing* 20 (2017): 873–78.

Kim, Hyojoon, and Nick Feamster. "Improving Network Management with Software Defined Networking." *IEEE Communications Magazine* 51.2 (2013): 114–19.

Klügl, Franziska, Ana LC Bazzan, and Sascha Ossowski. "Agents in Traffic and Transportation." *Transportation Research. Part C, Emerging Technologies* 22.1 (2010): 69.

Lee, Byungjoon, et al. "IRIS: The Openflow-Based Recursive SDN Controller." *16th International Conference on Advanced Communication Technology*. 2014. IEEE.

Li, Huoyou "Application of Artificial Intelligence in Computer Aided Instruction." *2009 International Conference on Test and Measurement*. 2009. IEEE.

Lin, Jie, et al. "A Survey on Internet of Things: Architecture, Enabling Technologies, Security and Privacy, and Applications." *IEEE Internet of Things Journal* 4.5 (2017): 1125–42.

Liu, Xiao-Yang, et al. "Deep Reinforcement Learning for Intelligent Transportation Systems." *arXiv preprint arXiv:1812.00979* (2018).

Liyanage, Madhusanka, et al. *A Comprehensive Guide to 5g Security*. Wiley Online Library, 2018.

Liyanage, Madhusanka, et al. *IoT Security: Advances in Authentication*. John Wiley & Sons, 2020.

Makridakis, Spyros. "The Forthcoming Artificial Intelligence (AI) Revolution: Its Impact on Society and Firms." *Futures* 90 (2017): 46–60.

Marsland, Stephen. *Machine Learning: An Algorithmic Perspective*. Chapman and Hall/CRC, 2011.

Mathew, Amitha, P Amudha, and S Sivakumari. *Deep Learning Techniques: An Overview. Advanced Machine Learning Technologies and Applications: Proceedings of AMLTA 2020* (2021): 599–608.

McGregor, Anthony, et al. Flow Clustering Using Machine Learning Techniques. *Passive and Active Network Measurement: 5th International Workshop*. April 19–20, 2004. Springer.

McKeown, Nick. "Software-Defined Networking." *INFOCOM Keynote Talk* 17.2 (2009): 30–32.

McKeown, Nick, et al. "Openflow: Enabling Innovation in Campus Networks." *ACM SIGCOMM Computer Communication Review* 38.2 (2008): 69–74.

Mell, Peter, and Tim Grance. "The Nist Definition of Cloud Computing." (2011).

Moustapha, Azzam I, and Rastko R Selmic. "Wireless Sensor Network Modeling Using Modified Recurrent Neural Networks: Application to Fault Detection." *IEEE Transactions on Instrumentation and Measurement* 57.5 (2008): 981–88.

Sajid Mushtaq, M, Brice Augustin, and Abdelhamid Mellouk. "Empirical Study Based on Machine Learning Approach to Assess the QoS/QoE Correlation." *2012 17th European Conference on Networks and Optical Communications*. 2012. IEEE.

Nazar, Muhammad Junaid, et al. "Software-Defined Networking (SDN) Security Concerns." *Information Security Handbook*. CRC Press. 19–38. 2022.

Oza, Nikunj, J Patrick Castle, and John Stutz. "Classification of Aeronautics System Health and Safety Documents." *IEEE Transactions on Systems, Man, and Cybernetics, Part C (Applications and Reviews)* 39.6 (2009): 670–80.

Papcun, Peter, et al. "Edge-Enabled IoT Gateway Criteria Selection and Evaluation." *Concurrency and Computation: Practice and Experience* 32.13 (2020): e5219.

Patil, Pranav. "Artificial Intelligence in Cybersecurity." *International Journal of Research in Computer Applications and Robotics* 4.5 (2016): 1–5.

Perera, Charith, et al. "Context Aware Computing for the Internet of Things: A Survey." *IEEE Communications Surveys & Tutorials* 16.1 (2013): 414–54.

Phan, Trung V, Nguyen Khac Bao, and Minho Park. "A Novel Hybrid Flow-Based Handler with DDoS Attacks in Software-Defined Networking." *2016 Intl IEEE Conferences on Ubiquitous Intelligence & Computing, Advanced and Trusted Computing, Scalable Computing and Communications, Cloud and Big Data Computing, Internet of People, and Smart World Congress (UIC/ATC/ScalCom/CBDCom/IoP/SmartWorld)*. 2016. IEEE.

Prediger, Lukas. "On the Importance of Monitoring and Directing Progress in AI." *AI Matters* 3.3 (2017): 30–38.

Purdy, Mark, and Paul Daugherty. "Why Artificial Intelligence Is the Future of Growth." *Remarks at AI now: the social and economic implications of artificial intelligence technologies in the near term* (2016): 1–72.

Qin, Zhijing, et al. "A Software Defined Networking Architecture for the Internet-of-Things." *2014 IEEE Network Operations and Management Symposium (NOMS)*. 2014. IEEE.

Qureshi, Kashif Naseer, and Abdul Hanan Abdullah. "A Survey on Intelligent Transportation Systems." *Middle-East Journal of Scientific Research* 15.5 (2013): 629–42.

Qureshi, Kashif Naseer, et al. "Nature-Inspired Algorithm-Based Secure Data Dissemination Framework for Smart City Networks." *Neural Computing and Applications* 33 (2020): 10637–56.

Qureshi, Kashif Naseer, et al. "A Software-Defined Network-Based Intelligent Decision Support System for the Internet of Things Networks." *Wireless Personal Communications* 126.4 (2022): 2825–39.

___. "A Software-Defined Network-Based Intelligent Decision Support System for the Internet of Things Networks." *Wireless Personal Communications* 126 (2022): 2825–39

Rao BBP, et al. "Cloud Computing for Internet of Things & Sensing Based Applications." *2012 Sixth International Conference on Sensing Technology (ICST)*. 2012. IEEE.

Rego, Albert, et al. "An Intelligent System for Video Surveillance in IoT Environments." *IEEE Access* 6 (2018): 31580–98.

Rodgers, Waymond. *Artificial Intelligence in a Throughput Model: Some Major Algorithms*. CRC Press, 2020.

Sepasgozar, Sanaz Shaker, and Samuel Pierre. "Network Traffic Prediction Model Considering Road Traffic Parameters Using Artificial Intelligence Methods in Vanet." *IEEE Access* 10 (2022): 8227–42.

Shi, Weisong, et al. "Edge Computing: Vision and Challenges." *IEEE Internet of Things Journal* 3.5 (2016): 637–46.

Soysal, Murat, and Ece Guran Schmidt. "Machine Learning Algorithms for Accurate Flow-Based Network Traffic Classification: Evaluation and Comparison." *Performance Evaluation* 67.6 (2010): 451–67.

Stepanov, Nikolai, et al. "Applying Machine Learning to LTE Traffic Prediction: Comparison of Bagging, Random Forest, and SVM." *2020 12th International Congress on Ultra Modern Telecommunications and Control Systems and Workshops (ICUMT).* 2020. IEEE.

Taherkhani, Nasrin, and Samuel Pierre. "Improving Dynamic and Distributed Congestion Control in Vehicular Ad Hoc Networks." *Ad Hoc Networks* 33 (2015): 112–25.

Testolin, A., et al. "A Machine Learning Approach to QoE-Based Video Admission Control and Resource Allocation in Wireless Systems." *2014 13th Annual Mediterranean Ad Hoc Networking Workshop (MED-HOC-NET).* 2014. IEEE.

Wu, Miao, et al. "Research on the Architecture of Internet of Things." *2010 3rd International Conference on Advanced Computer Theory and Engineering (ICACTE).* 2010. IEEE.

Xu, Xin, and Xuening Wang. "An Adaptive Network Intrusion Detection Method Based on PCA and Support Vector Machines." *International Conference on Advanced Data Mining and Applications.* 2005. Springer.

Zhao, Zhiheng, et al. "IoT Edge Computing-Enabled Collaborative Tracking System for Manufacturing Resources in Industrial Park." *Advanced Engineering Informatics* 43 (2020): 101044.

CHAPTER 4

Standards and Policies Adoption for AIoT Networks

Adil Hussain

School of Electronics and Control Engineering, Chang'an University, Xi'an, China

Kashif Naseer Qureshi

Department of Electronic & Computer Engineering, University of Limerick,
V94 T9PX Limerick, Ireland

4.1 OVERVIEW

This chapter presents a comprehensive overview of the standards and protocols used in Artificial Internet of Things (AIoT) networks, focusing on the advantages they offer and the bodies responsible for standards creation. International organizations developing standards and protocols for AIoT networks are explained briefly. The session layer, Datalink layer, and Network layer are discussed in detail in terms of routing protocols and standards. The ongoing attempts to establish management and security benchmarks for each of these layers as well as the opportunities for future research and the difficulties faced by AIoT are also discussed in this chapter.

4.2 INTRODUCTION

The Internet of Things (IoT) has been the subject of extensive study in many different fields, such as transportation, urban planning, healthcare, residential automation, and industrial automation. Users, devices, and information resources all participate in an IoT ecosystem by connecting with services. Therefore, interoperability is necessary to ensure smooth communication and compatibility among these components. Security must also be taken into account while discussing interoperability to safeguard information and maintain confidentiality. U.S. industrial firms see interoperability as the primary barrier to implementing IoT technologies (Hahn. 2017). The development of IoT architecture faces big problems with interoperability and security. To successfully integrate IoT in real-world applications, there is a need to address interoperability and security concerns. In addition, a partnership of European business and academic concerns has recently been formed to tackle interoperability and security issues in developing IoT frameworks.

DOI: 10.1201/9781003430018-5

Furthermore, it is anticipated that these partnerships will assume supplementary functions aimed at enhancing the overall quality of life, facilitating business operations, and optimizing the functionality of smart homes (ALiero et al. 2021). One instance of a presently accessible IoT ecosystem is represented by smart homes, which employ sensors designed to remotely regulate temperature, heating, and air conditioning within residential dwellings. Potential future expansions of this system encompass a range of functionalities, including the ability to brew coffee, regulate television usage, monitor health metrics, and operate motor vehicles. The utilization of these applications present additional complexities and necessitate the establishment of standardized protocols to effectively address the wide range of application demands (Hassan. 2018).

AIoT is the idea of combining Artificial Intelligence (AI) technology with IoT communications to improve network processes, human-machine interactions, data organization, and analytics (Chang et al. 2021). IoT devices serve as the brain of the system, while AI controls its every digital action. When AI is combined with IoT, connected devices may perform complex analyses, reach independent conclusions, and conduct independent actions with little to no human intervention. Efficiency and effectiveness are mostly driven by "smart" gadgets. The optimization of systems, the generation of important insights into performance, and the facilitation of informed decision-making are all made possible by the data analytics supplied by AIoT. In addition, AI improves IoT by employing Machine Learning (ML) methods and bolstering decision-making (Phan et al. 2023). Connectivity, communication, and data exchange are all areas in which IoT helps AI. AIoT, the combination of smart devices, has a transformational effect that helps both technologies. The proliferation of IoT technologies across multiple sectors has increased the amount of unstructured data produced by humans and machines alike. The abundance of data generated by the IoT can be put to good use with the help of data analytics solutions, which can be provided by AIoT.

A more intelligent IoT system would incorporate AI and may achieve the desired outcomes of automation and adaptability. Standards are viewed by many in the business community as the greatest obstacle to widespread adoption. This is a natural consequence of the introduction of any novel technical format or concept. The battle between Betamax and VHS and the one between HD DVD and Blu-ray are two examples of standards wars that resulted in an undisputed market leader. The growth of the Transmission Control Protocol/Internet Protocol (TCP/IP) model, which enabled the original internet, will serve as a template for discussions surrounding IoT standards. The format is less important than overall utility and functionality (Haqiq et al. 2022).

4.3 OVERVIEW OF STANDARDS AND ORGANIZATIONS

One definition of a standard is *a document developed and adopted by consensus of appropriate organizations.* Its goal is to standardize a process or create a set of principles for a particular field so that everyone can perform at their best. In the field of Information and Communication Technology (ICT), the term *standard* typically refers to a set of agreed-upon protocols that facilitate the transmission of information and communication services and their use by multiple, distributed computer systems over a shared network. Consequently, standards play a crucial role in facilitating the development and deployment of IT (Hasan and Qureshi. 2018). In essence, a standard can be defined as a predetermined specification, and the standardization process pertains to the methods or actions used to establish and determine these standards. Furthermore, organizations responsible for setting standards can classify them as either de jure or de facto.

ICT international standards include rules and guidelines that make it easier for information technologies to progress and be used. Thus, adhering to these standards can facilitate the successful implementation of ICT systems. So, it's important to think about the standards not only when doing the work, but also when doing the study. Several well-known standards, such as network protocols and data formats, have been used to build systems in the IoT area. A number of well-known international standardization bodies, such as the International Organization for Standardization (ISO), the International Electrotechnical Commission (IEC), the International Telecommunication Union (ITU), and the Internet Engineering Task Force (IETF), are also helping to make standards for the IoT networks. These standards, which have been extensively disseminated through a number of publications, cover a vast array of topics, including architecture, framework, network protocols, and definitions. In addition, adopting standardized protocols can effectively improve both interoperability and security. These protocols offer a dependable structure to guarantee compatibility and safeguarding measures (E. Lee et al. 2021).

4.3.1 Standards and Organizations

This section overviews the standards groups involved in developing IoT standards. Furthermore, it elucidates the characteristics of their endeavors towards standardization. Standards encompass diverse information, from granular details to abstract concepts, contingent upon their intended objectives. Specific standards offer comprehensive specifications to ensure precise interoperability among various systems or representations without any loss of information. Example network protocol measures that provide thorough specifications for facilitating efficient communication between a sender and a receiver include IEEE 802.11, CoAP, and WebSocket. Similar to how documents within web pages can be described using structured formats like HTML, CSS, and XML, which are all part of Web standards, if network standards are applied correctly, interoperability and security can be ensured.

However, particular standards provide abstract information, such as a software's framework, reference model, and architectural design. The fundamental goal of these guidelines is to provide high-level ideas that may be applied across a wide range of software, system, and environment development projects. Additionally, the standards are created by experts in their respective disciplines. Therefore, conceptual norms offer practical constraints for developing software and infrastructure. As a result, abstract standards can improve productivity, reduce development and management times, and reduce risks. Furthermore, applying contemporary technologies that adhere to these established standards is straightforward. The benefits of implementing standards are outlined as follows:

- Standards facilitate the seamless exchange of operations and information, ensuring compatibility and preventing any loss of information through adherence to standardized formats.

- Standards can assure security.

- Providing reasonable criteria is essential for developing and managing systems, frameworks, software, and environments.

- Implementing standards can significantly enhance the efficiency of development processes by reducing time and mitigating risks.

The application of contemporary technologies can be predicated upon adherence to these established standards.

4.3.1.1 International Organization for Standardization

In the realm of information technology, the ISO (International Organization for Standardization)/IEC (International Electro-Technical Commission) JTC (Joint Technical Committee) is a joint body charged with developing global benchmarks. In 1987, the ISO and the IEC formed a JTC 1 to work out any discrepancies or overlaps among their respective standards. In 2016, during the first JTC meeting, Subcommittee 41 (SC 41) was established to deal solely with IoT-related issues. SC 41 is mostly interested in industrial IoT, real-time IoT, edge computing, sensor networks, reliability, requirements, and wearables. There are currently twenty-one written standards and nineteen work programs that are being used. Not only does SC 41 contribute to establishing standards for the IoT, but several other subcommittees (SCs) and working groups (WGs) play a significant role in this regard as well. SC 31 emphasizes the implementation of automatic identification and data capture techniques.

Additionally, SC 31 is involved in an IoT project that aims to establish a system for unique identification, as outlined in standard 29161:2016 (ISO/IEC). Information security, cyber-protection, and personal data privacy standards are currently being developed by Standard Committee 27 (SC 27). One such standard is 27030 (ISO—ISO/IEC), which defines best practices for protecting users' data and identities when using IoT. The ITU has released a standard known as SG6, which pertains to telecommunications and the exchange of information among systems. This standard, referred explicitly to as TR 29181-9:2017 (ISO), falls under the domain of IT and addresses the concept of the network of everything. Its goal is to define the networking of everything as a problem and to specify what must be done to solve it in the context of future networks. The IoT is just one part of a larger whole, and network standards define all of its characteristics. Standardized architecture evaluation frameworks have been built in the fields of software and systems engineering, specifically SC 7. This framework, known as ISO/IEC/IEEE 42030:2019 (ISO/IEC/IEEE), encompasses the evaluation of architectures, including those about the IoT.

4.3.1.2 Electrical and Electronics Engineers Standards Association

The Institute of Electrical and Electronics Engineers (IEEE) is dedicated to advancing electronic and electrical engineering. Within this institute, a Standards Association (SA) known as IEEE-SA has been established to focus specifically on developing and implementing standardized practices, The IEEE-SA is an authoritative standardization organization that is responsible for the development of international standards in diverse domains of electronic and electrical engineering, encompassing areas such as ICT, including software and system engineering, wired and wireless communications, healthcare, smart grids, and computer technology, among others.

The IEEE-SA has formed IEEE P2413, a working group dedicated to creating IoT standards. Standards for an architectural framework that can be used for IoT systems are the primary emphasis of IEEE P2413. The architectural framework separates out unique IoT abstractions and then finds commonalities among them (Logvinov et al. 2016). In addition, the IEEE-SA has compiled 80 IoT guidelines (E. Lee et al. 2016). In addition to networks, data types, electric power management, interfaces, Wireless Access in Vehicle Settings (WAVE), terminology definition, and health informatics, these guidelines cover a vast array of topics. The IEEE-SA offers a variety of network-related standards designed for IoT and RFID (IEEE 21451-7), WiMAX (IEEE 802.16), and Wi-Fi (IEEE 802.11) technologies. In addition, the IEEE P1901 committee is developing standards to improve the functionality and efficacy of broadband over power line networks in IoT applications. Also, IEEE-SA has compiled a comprehensive list of the 46 IoT standards currently in development (Kiyani et al. 2022). Emerging standards include interoperability, network infrastructure, interface protocols, security, WAVE, and smart grid systems.

4.3.1.3 International Telecommunication Union

Since its founding in 1865, the ITU has functioned as a United Nations (UN) specialized organization concerned with telecommunications and related technologies. There are three divisions within the ITU: research and development (ITU-D), radio communication (ITU-R), and standardization (ITU-T). The ITU-T brings together specialists to develop international standards. The standards that establish normative guidelines in this context are called ITU-T recommendations. It is important to note that these recommendations are not mandatory until they are officially incorporated into the legal frameworks of individual nations. ITU-T publishes both normative standards and non normative content in the form of technical papers and reports on a broad spectrum of topics. In addition, this division of the ITU is responsible for publishing the ITU-T Handbooks on a variety of topics pertaining to information and communication technologies. The operation, network planning, quality of service, implementation guide, outside plant, electromagnetic effect protection, measurement methods, security, mobile systems, formal languages, and formal language usage could be among the topics covered.

The ITU-T consists of eleven study groups dedicated to standardizing various aspects of ICT. These study groups encompass a range of topics and areas of focus. For instance, SG2 examines operational aspects, while SG3 is concerned with economic and policy matters. SG5 is concerned with the environment and the circular economy, while SG9 is dedicated to high-speed Internet and television. While SG12 focuses on performance, service quality, and user experience, SG11 is in charge of establishing protocols and test requirements. Transport, access, and home networks are the focus of SG15, while the future of networking and cloud computing is investigated by SG13. The IoT, smart cities, and communities are the focus of SG20: multimedia is the primary concern of SG16 and SG17. The standardization of IoT technologies falls under the purview of SG20. This includes fostering machine-to-machine (M2M) communication and setting up pervasive sensor networks, as well as developing more extensive frameworks for IoT and techniques to ensure compatibility among IoT applications.

Additionally, it is noteworthy that the ITU-T encompasses a diverse range of study groups specifically focused on the standardization efforts pertaining to the IoT. The signaling requirements, protocols, and test specifications fall under the purview of SG 11.

The primary objective of SG11 is to standardize the process of developing test specifications to address global interoperability testing challenges. This includes many things, such as technical means, services, Quality of Service (QoS), and testing factors. Moreover, the IoT ecosystem is emphasized in SG11. Standards for next-generation networks are being developed by SG 13 of the ITU, with a focus on meeting the connectivity needs of the IoT.

Moreover, SG11 standards are primarily concerned with ensuring sufficient support for the IoT over future networks via cloud computing. Multiple ITU Study Groups, including those concerned with the IoT, collaborate under Study Group 16 to develop standards for multimedia coding, systems, and applications. Furthermore, Study Group 17 (SG17) pertains to the examination of security matters, with a particular emphasis on safeguarding applications and services within the realm of the IoT, from a security perspective.

4.3.1.4 Internet Engineering Task Force

There is a worldwide group called the Internet Engineering Task Force (IETF) whose mission is to improve the Internet. It actively promotes the adoption of voluntary standards for things like automated network management, the IoT, upcoming transport technologies, and privacy and security on the Internet. IETF encompasses more than 100 active working groups. Among these working groups, a subset is dedicated to developing protocols tailored to the IoT. In October 2014, the IETF formed an advisory group called the IoT Directorate (IOTDIR). This division is heavily involved in IoT standardization work. The IETF divides its standards into two distinct groups, *proposed standards* and *Internet standards.* These standards are seen as being well understood and described as having a stable specification because it addresses recognized design choices. As a result of widespread scrutiny and widespread attention, it has been declared valuable. However, it is essential to note that different experiences could potentially lead to a modification or even withdrawal of the specification, as mentioned earlier, before its progression.

The definition of the Internet standard refers to a specification or protocol that has been widely adopted and recognized as a standard for the Internet. It stands out because of its advanced technology and the widespread opinion that the protocol or service in question offers the Internet community many benefits. The IETF also provides research and standardization-relevant information in the form of nonstandard publications. Informational specifications, experimental specifications, and historical specifications are the three main categories of nonstandard specifications. An *informational specification* is defined as a document published for the benefit of the Internet community at large. It should be noted that this specification does not necessarily reflect a consensus or recommendation from the Internet community. The *experimental specification* is defined as a component of a research or development endeavor. The term *historic specification* refers to a specification rendered obsolete due to the introduction of a more recent specification or for other reasons. A specification is given a number in the Internet Standard (STD) series by the IETF before it is officially recognized as an Internet standard. Meanwhile, RFC numbers are given to any and all additional specifications, whether they be proposed standards or not.

The IETF includes the Internet Research Task Force (IRTF), which, along with the Association for Computing Machinery (ACM), organizes yearly workshops on applied networking research. There are now 14 active sub-study groups within the IRTF, each dedicated to investigating a certain aspect of the Internet. These communities discuss a wide range of issues, from protocols to applications, to architecture, to technology. Different groups are looking into different aspects of the Internet, such as the crypto forum, network computing, decentralized Internet infrastructure, universal Internet access, human rights protocol considerations, Internet congestion control, information-centric networking, measurement and analysis for protocols, network management, coding for efficient network communications, path-aware networking, privacy enhancements and assessments, and quantum Inter, to name a few. The Thing-to-Thing Research Group's (T2TRG) primary focus is on examining open questions in the field of IoT. The group is especially interested in architectures and Application Programming Interfaces (APIs) that improve IP-to-API communication.

4.3.1.5 One Machine-to-Machine

Since 2012, the multinational group known as oneM2M has been working toward a unified global standard for machine-to-machine (M2M) and IoT communications. Eight groups working on ICT standards have joined forces. The oneM2M program is distinguished by its extensive network, which includes roughly 200 partners and members. The Technical Plenary (TP) within the oneM2M framework assumes the responsibility of developing and overseeing the creation of technical specifications and reports that cater to the market requirements of oneM2M. This is achieved by establishing three distinct working groups, each focused on specific topics. The first WG is responsible for creating the RDM (Requirements and Domain Models), while the second WG is in charge of the SDS (System Design and Security). Working Group 3's overarching mission is to investigate and assess the Testing and Developers Ecosystem (TDE).

oneM2M is responsible for the creation, endorsement, and maintenance of technical specifications, which are also known as standards and technical reports. The Machine-to-Machine (M2M) and IoT industries have distinct requirements, so these standards and studies address interoperability and security to meet those requirements. There have been five separate occasions on which oneM2M has released technical papers and specifications. The initial and subsequent versions were amended in the succeeding iterations, with the subsequent iteration being officially authorized by the oneM2M Technical Plenary in December 2018. The current versions (drafts 4 and 5) are only useful for research because they need to be revised before they can be published.

4.3.1.6 Open Connectivity Foundation

The Open Connectivity Foundation (OCF) is a group of businesses working together to create universally acknowledged standards for IoT ecosystem interoperability. The OCF's standardization initiatives have the support of a number of major players in the telecommunications and device industries. The primary areas of focus for the organization are twofold. Firstly, it aims to assist manufacturers with materials such as specifications, codes, and certified programs that enable interoperability among IoT devices and legacy systems. Secondly, it seeks to improve the user experience with machines that comply with the OCF standards.

The OCF has formulated specifications, also known as standards, to facilitate the process of certification and interoperability. There are five basic categories of specifications, including those for frameworks, security, bridges, resources, and onboarding. Several ISO/IEC JCT 1 standards, including the ISO/IEC 30118 family of papers, were developed using OCF requirements. With the support of the OCF, an open-source project known as IoTivity (Mandza and Raji. 2021) was developed. The initiative's overarching objective is to hasten the adoption of interoperability standards and certification programs for the IoT.

4.4 IoT ECOSYSTEM

The structure of the IoT ecosystem, illustrated in Figure 4.1, consists of the Market, Acquisition, Interconnection, Integration, Analytics, Application, and Services layers. Smart grids, smart homes, and smart healthcare are just a few examples of the application domain's Market layer. Applications rely heavily on the second layer, Acquisitions, which is made up of sensors and smart devices. The classification and spatial arrangement of sensors exhibit variability contingent upon the particular applications. Temperature sensors, humidity sensors, electricity meters, and webcams are just a few examples of the many uses for sensors. The third layer, known as the Interconnection layer, is responsible for relaying sensor data to a central server or the cloud. In this context, the data is integrated with additional datasets, including geographical, population, and economic data.

Moreover, the aggregated data undergoes thorough examination using ML and data mining methodologies. There is a need for the development of sophisticated collaboration and communication software at the application level to facilitate the operation of extensive distributed applications, such as Software Defined Networking (SDN) and Services Oriented Architecture (SOA). Ultimately, the upper layer consists of all the services of

Services	Energy, Entertainment, Health, Education, Transportation...
Apps and SW	SDN, SOA, Collaboration, Apps, Clouds
Analytics	Machine Learning, Predictive Analysis, Data Mining, ...
Integration	Sensor Data, Economy, Population, GIS, ...
Interconnection	DECT/ULE, WiFi, Bluetooth, ZigBee, NFC, ...
Acquisition	Sensors, Cameras, GPS, Meters, Smart Phones, ...
Market	Smart Homes, Smart Grids, Smart Cities, Smart Health, ...

FIGURE 4.1 IoT ecosystem.

ecosystems. Among these are energy management, health management, schooling, and transportation, among others. Security and management are important parts of all seven layers, which are stacked in a hierarchy, and are shown together.

4.5 LAYER WISE COMMUNICATION STANDARDS

Standards are proposed for all five layers by various prominent organizations such as the IEEE and IETF. IEEE is focused on data links; IETF on networks; and session, security, and management are handled by other organizations. The Datalink layer establishes a connection between two IoT system elements: two sensors or one sensor and a gadget called a "gateway" that connects a group of sensors to the Internet. Before sending data to the Internet, multiple monitors need to talk to each other and put together a lot of data. Protocols have been made to help with sensor handling, and these protocols are important parts of the Network layer. The communication among different parts of the IoT communication subsystem is facilitated by Session layer protocols. Also, the network and session layers show various protocols for the security and management of IoT. The protocols and standards for IoT are illustrated in Figure 4.2.

4.5.1 Datalink Layer Standards

In this section, the Datalink layer protocol standards, including physical (PHY) and Media Access Control (MAC) layer protocols, are discussed.

4.5.1.1 IEEE 802.15.4e

The IEEE 802.15.4 standard is widely employed in the MAC layer for datalink communication. The standard specifies the framework's configuration, encompassing the construction of headers, the assignment of destination address and source address, and

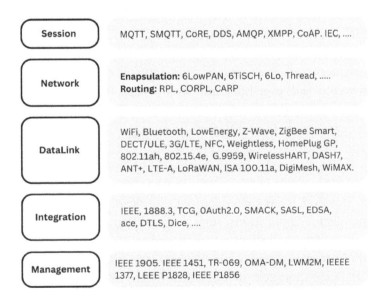

FIGURE 4.2 IoT standards and protocols.

the establishment of communication protocols among nodes. The conventional frame formats employed in networking are ill-suited for IoT devices with limited power resources. The year 2008 witnessed the development of IEEE 802.15.4e, an extension of the existing IEEE 802.15.4 standard, with the primary objective of facilitating low-power communication. The utilization of time synchronization and channel hopping facilitates the establishment of reliable and cost-effective communication in IoT datalinks. The specific features of the MAC protocol include a Slot Frame Structure, Scheduling, Synchronization, Channel Hopping, and Network Formation (Mirzoev. 2014).

4.5.1.2 IEEE 802.11ah

IEEE 802.11ah is the version of the IEEE 802.11 standard with the lowest overhead and that meets IoT requirements. The IEEE 802.11 standards, commonly called Wi-Fi, are widely utilized wireless standards within conventional networking. Digital devices, such as digital T.V.s, laptops tablets, and mobiles, have experienced widespread adoption. But the current Wi-Fi standards aren't good enough for IoT apps because they have too much frame overhead and use a lot of power. So, the IEEE 802.11 working group created the 802.11ah task group with the goal of coming up with a standard that lets sensors and other small devices communicate in a way that is both effective and uses little energy (Park. 2015). IEEE 802.11ah's MAC layer has a Synchronization Framework, an Efficient Bidirectional Packed Exchange Method, a Short MAC Frame Structure, and Null Data Packets.

4.5.1.3 Wireless HART

Wireless HART is a MAC layer standard that utilizes the IEEE 802.15.4 PHY as its underlying technology, with its MAC layer implementing Time Division Multiple Access (TDMA). It encrypts messages with sophisticated encryption techniques and verifies their integrity. This makes it safer and more trustworthy than alternatives. The system is made up of different parts, such as the network manager, the security manager, the gateway that connects the wired and wireless networks, and the wireless devices that serve as field devices, routers, adapters, and access points. This standard offers a wide range of security methods, such as end-to-end, peer-hop, and peer-to-peer. Peer-hop methods protect the connection until the next hop (Kim et al. 2012; Nobre. 2015, Silva and Guedes. 2020), while end-to-end mechanisms secure the connection.

4.5.1.4 Z-Wave

The Z-Wave protocol is a standard for low-power MAC that was originally developed for home automation. However, it has since acquired significant popularity and is now widely employed in numerous IoT applications, such as smart homes and small commercial settings. It's ideal for short communications and works up to 30 meters away in a point-to-point fashion. It employs Carrier Sense Multiple Access with Collision Avoidance (CSMA/CA) for media access and uses short acknowledgement (ACK) messages for dependable transmission. It's organized in a master/slave fashion, where one node issues commands to others and coordinates the network's schedule (Z-Wave).

4.5.1.5 Bluetooth Low Energy

Bluetooth Low Energy, also known as Bluetooth Smart, is a popular short-range communication standard for the Datalink layer in IoT. Its primary application is in car networking. It has a very low latency, 15 times lower than the first generation of Bluetooth. Energy consumption is reduced by as much as ten times compared to standard Bluetooth. An access control mechanism that is contention-free, characterized by low latency and rapid transmission, is employed. The system employs a master/slave configuration and offers two distinct types of frames, namely advertising frames and data frames. The utilization of the advertising framework by slaves involves disseminating it through dedicated channels specifically designated for this objective. To locate and link slave nodes, master nodes use advertisement sensing channels. When the two devices are finally linked, the master will share his wake time and daily routine with the slave. To conserve energy, nodes typically only become active during communication (Gomez, Oller, and Paradells. 2012).

4.5.1.6 ZigBee Smart Energy

ZigBee is one of the IoT protocols that is used the most. It is made for things like smart homes, remotes, and health care systems that need to talk to each other from a middle distance. This network has a few different types of topologies, such as the Star, peer-to-peer, and cluster-tree topologies. In a star topology, the center node is the coordinator. In a tree or cluster topology, on the other hand, the coordinator is at the root. Conversely, in a peer-to-peer topology, the coordinator has the flexibility to be positioned at any place within the network. The ZigBee standard defines two stack profiles: ZigBee and ZigBee Pro. These stack profiles are suitable for low-memory and low-processing-power implementations and offer full-mesh networking. Additional features offered by ZigBee Pro include symmetric-key exchange for increased security, stochastic address assignment for greater scalability, and efficient many-to-one routing for better performance (Zigbee. 2016).

4.5.1.7 DASH7

The DASH7 wireless communication protocol is a new standard for active RFID devices that uses the internationally accessible Industrial Scientific Medical (ISM) band. DASH7 is designed for high-speed, long-range outdoor service that can be expanded. It's an inexpensive option that allows for both IPv6 addresses and encryption. It's well-suited to the IoT since it has a master/slave architecture and can handle bursts of light, asynchronous, transitory traffic. Filtering, Address, and Frame Format are all MAC layer features.

4.5.1.8 HomePlug

The HomePlug Green PHY (HomePlugGP) is a MAC protocol developed by the HomePlug Powerline Alliance, with a primary focus on its application in home automation systems. The HomePlug bundle, which encompasses both HomePlug-AV and HomePlug-AV2, is designed to cater to the PHY and MAC layers. HomePlug-AV serves as the fundamental framework for power line communication. It uses Orthogonal Frequency Division

Multiplexing or OFDM, and it can be modulated in four different ways. It also uses MAC layer techniques called Time-Division Multiple Access (TDMA) and CSMA/CA. Furthermore, HomePlug-AV possesses the capability to adapt its transmission rate in response to the prevailing ambient noise level. IoT applications, including smart homes and smart grids, are the focus of HomePlugGP's development. Its primary goal is to make HomePlug-AV more affordable without sacrificing its interoperability, dependability, or coverage. Therefore, it employs OFDM, with a single modulation just like HomePlug, but it employs secure OFDM encoding to allow for low transmission rates and exceptional dependability. While CSMA is used exclusively by HomePlug-AV at the MAC layer, HomePlugGP makes use of both CSMA and TDMA. Furthermore, HomePlugGP provides a mode that saves energy by simultaneously employing sleeping nodes and awakening them as needed (H. Alliance. 2007).

4.5.1.9 G.9959

This ITU MAC layer standard is for trustworthy, low-bandwidth, half-duplex communication at minimal cost. Because of its great reliability and low power consumption, it is ideal for time-sensitive applications. To conserve power, nodes on the MAC layer can go to sleep when they are out of communication and wake up when they are back in range, and collision avoidance mechanisms, back-off time in the event of a collision, automatic retransmission to guarantee reliability, and a dedicated wakeup pattern are all part of the MAC layer. Unique channel access, frame validation, (ACK, and retransmission (RT) are all features of the G9959 MAC layer (Brandt and Buron. 2015).

4.5.1.10 LTE-A

LTE-A, or long-term evolution advanced, is a set of cellular networking standards created to accommodate IoT and M2M communications. It is the most economical and scalable protocol compared to other cellular protocols. Since its inception in 2009, LTE-A has had many versions that add support for new technologies. The frequency is typically divided into numerous subcarriers, and the medium access technology is Orthogonal Frequency Division Multiple Access (OFDMA). Mobile nodes, the Radio Access Network (RAN), and the Core Network (CN) make up LTE-A's architecture. The CN. monitors and manages mobile devices by recording their IP addresses. Management and data planes, as well as wireless connectivity and radio-access management, are all responsibilities of the RAN. The S1 connection is used for communication between the RAN and the CN Additionally, LTE Rel-13 and LTE Rel-14, the newest iterations of LTE-A, have been designed with special features to accommodate 5G (J. Lee et al. 2016). There are three major new additions in Rel-13: new machine-type communication services, enhanced frequency and carrier aggregation, and enhanced Full-Dimensional Multiple Input Multiple Output (FD-MIMO). To maximize spectrum efficiency, FD-MIMO employs a large number of base station antenna ports. More frequency resources are being consumed by the use of unlicensed spectrum in addition to the licensed spectrum bands. This way, more rounds can be used, and old devices can still work with the new ones. In LTE-A, carrier aggregation was also improved by increasing the peak rate and using frequency resources best. Reduced prices, expanded coverage support, indoor positioning, and the ability to broadcast and multicast in a single cell are just some of the benefits of LTE Rel-13's new services for M2M transmissions. More antenna ports, improved transmission reliability, and decreased feedback are just some of the ways in which LTE Rel-14 is expected to advance FD-MIMO. Reduced latency, vehicle-to-anything, and downlink multi-user transmission were all deemed feasibility studies in Rel-14 (Hoymann et al. 2016), but are now scheduled to be standardized in the upcoming version.

4.5.1.11 LoRaWAN
LoRaWAN is a novel wireless long-distance wide-area network technology that meets the needs of IoT apps by providing low cost, mobility, security, and two-way communication. It is an optimized system for wireless network devices that use little power. It supports technologies such as redundant operation, location-free operation, low cost, low power, and energy harvesting to satisfy the future needs of the IoT while allowing for mobility and user-friendliness (Vangelista and Centenaro. 2019).

4.5.1.12 Weightless
Weightless is a newly developed wireless technology for the IoT MAC layer. It is provided by the Special Interest Group (SIG), a global non-profit organization. Weightless-N was the initial standard to satisfy IoT requirements. To reduce interference, TDMA and frequency hopping are employed. It employs extremely narrow Industrial, Scientific and Medical (ISM) frequency channels below 1 GHz. Weightless-W, on the other hand, shares the same characteristics but employs television band frequencies (Poole. 2014).

4.5.1.13 DECT/ULE
Digital Enhanced Cordless Telecommunications (DECT) is a European cordless phone worldwide standard. DECT/ULE (Ultra-Low Energy), a form of extension, was recently added as a new feature. IoT applications can utilize the low-power, low-cost air interface technology described by LTE-A architecture. This standard has a specialized channel and can handle interference and congestion much better. The original DECT protocol did not allow FDMA, TDMA, or time division multiplexing, but DECT/ULE does (Bush. 2015).

4.5.1.14 EnOcean
EnOcean is a wireless energy-saving technology that is mostly used for automation, but it can also be utilized for other IoT applications. To put it simply, converters can be used to transform kinetic energy or energy from other natural sources into usable forms. This protocol is often deployed in HVAC IoT apps due to its compact packet size (E. Alliance. 2015). Instead of traditional data lines, standards such as Near Field Communication (NFC), and the International Society of Automation (ISA) 100.11a can be utilized. However, the declining usefulness of these standards in comparison to the developing ones outlined in this section means that they are not widely used in the IoT. NFC is mostly used for short-range, ad hoc communication. It uses radio frequency identification to activate the receiver and kick off peer-to-peer connectivity at low frequencies (Kshetrimayum. 2009). In contrast, ANT

is a wireless multicast system that uses a master-slave architecture. It operates at 2.4 GHz and is functionally comparable to Bluetooth low energy (Evanczuk. 2013) which finds its primary application in wireless sensor networks. The ISA standard for wireless networking in industrial automation control is ISA100.11a (Serizawa et al. 2016).

This section briefly discussed the main differences between the different datalink protocols and how they can be used in IoT medium access. In general, Bluetooth and ZigBee are the IoT technologies that are used the most. However, IEEE 802.11ah is the wireless standard that is most compatible with IEEE 802.11, the standard wireless network architecture. HomePlug is used to connect to the Local Area Network (LAN) by various service providers and IoT markets because it is a more secure and stable option. The new technology of LoRaWAN might prove useful in the great outdoors.

4.6 NETWORK LAYER STANDARDS

This section provides a quick overview of some IoT routing standards and protocols. The Network layer of the networking hierarchy consists of two sublayers: the Routing layer, which transmits packets from source to destination, and the Encapsulation layer, which binds packets together.

4.6.1 RPL

The IETF created the Routing Protocol for Low-Power and Lossy Networks (RPL) expressly for use in IoT routing. It's compatible with all the MAC layer protocols we've spoken about, plus a few extras that weren't made with IoT in mind. It is built on Destination-Oriented Directed Acyclic Graphs (DODAGs), which are directed acyclic graphs with just one path from each leaf node to the root and are used to direct traffic. At the outset, every node broadcasts a DODAG Information Object (DIO), claiming to be the network's starting point. Over time, the network will spread DIO, and the whole DODAG will be constructed. A node communicating with another node sends a Destination Advertisement Object (DAO) to parents, and then it is forwarded to the roots. Sending a DODAG Information Solicitation (DIS) is the first step for new nodes joining the network, and receiving a DAO Acknowledgement (DAO-ACK) from the root is confirmation that they have been accepted. An RPL network node can be either stateless (the default) or stateful. A stateless node simply remembers its parent nodes. Only Root knows everything there is to know about the DODAG. Therefore, the Root is the hub of all communication. A stateful node remembers its parent and child relationships to bypass the root node in a Directed Acyclic Graph (DAG) (Winter et al. 2012).

4.6.2 CORPL

CORPL, or Cognitive RPL, is an extended RPL protocol that uses the same DODAG technology. First, it implements opportunistic forwarding, which allows a packet to specify several forwarders while still being sent only to the best next hop. Then, instead of just keeping track of its parent, each node also keeps track of any of its neighbors' changes via DIO messages. Each node dynamically adjusts its neighbors to the collection of forwarders based on the most recent data (Aijaz and Aghvami. 2015).

4.6.3 CARP and E-CARP

The Channel-Aware Routing Protocol (CARP) designed for underwater communication is a distributed network-based routing protocol. Because of its efficiency as a lightweight packet forwarding in IoT networks, when deciding which path to forward data along, it takes into account past measures of consideration protocols that should account for network start-up and data transmission. When a network is set up, the sink sends a HELLO packet to every other node. The data travels from the sensor to sink via intermediate nodes in data forwarding. The subset of the data forwarding process, CARP, doesn't support data recycling. For this reason, CARP data forwarding may not be helpful for applications that need sensor data only when substantial unhelpful changes. E-CARP is an improvement on CARP because it stores previously received sensory data at the sink node. E-CARP uses a ping packet to request updates from the sensor nodes, which are then sent back. Therefore, E-CARP significantly lessens the burden of communication (Basagni et al. 2015).

This section covered three routing protocols applicable to IoT routing sublayers. The most popular and standard distance vector protocol is called RPL. CORPL uses opportunistic forwarding to forward packets at each hop and is used for cognitive networks because it is a nonstandard RPL extension. However, E-CARP stands alone as the only distributed link quality assessment meant specifically for Internet assessment-based networks. E-CARP is mainly employed for submerged communication. The lack of standards prevents its deployment in some IoT contexts.

4.7 NETWORK LAYER ENCAPSULATION PROTOCOLS

The need to adapt IPv6 long addresses for IoT devices within compact and lightweight IoT datalink frames is a matter of concern for standardization efforts. The IETF is working on a set of frame formatting standards at the moment. The goal of these norms is to package IPv6 datagrams into smaller data connection frames appropriate for use in IoT scenarios.

4.7.1 6LoWPAN

IPv6 over Low-Power Wireless Personal Area Network (6LoWPAN) is an early and widely adopted IETF specification in this field. IPv6 headers with large sizes are compressed into a maximum size of 128-byte size of IEEE802.15.4 MAC packets (Culler and Chakrabarti. 2009). Specifications for 6LoWPAN enable a wide range of properties related to address length, networking topology, bandwidth, power consumption, cost-effectiveness, scalability, portability, dependability, and sleep duration. The standards use header compression to decrease the transmission overhead, fragmentation to adhere to IEEE802.15.4's limit frame length of 128 bytes, and multi-hop delivery to get the message to its destination as a quick multi-hop. There are four types of headers used in 6LoWPAN frames: No 6LoWPAN Header (00), Dispatch Header (01), Mesh Header (10), and Fragmentation Header (11). In the No 6loWPAN header case, frames that don't meet the standards of 6loWPAN are dropped. Multicasting and IPv6 header compression both make use of the dispatch header. The Fragmentation Header is used to split down the large IPv6 header into smaller 128-byte chunks, while the Mesh Header is used for broadcasting.

4.7.2 6TiSCH

A new IETF standard, IPv6 Time Slotted Channel Hopping (6TiSCH), was created by the 6TiSCH working group. It describes the TSCH mode for transmitting lengthy IPv6 headers over IEEE 802.15.4e data lines. A channel distribution usage matrix stores the frequencies and time slots in this configuration. Each node in the network has access to a subset of this matrix that includes localized time and frequency information. Nodes within the same interference area work together through coordination and negotiation of transmission times. When numerous surrounding nodes use the same application, scheduling becomes an optimization challenge in which time slots must be assigned. The standard does not specify how scheduling can be accomplished, allowing IoT applications to be as flexible as possible. Instead, it considers scheduling to be an issue unique to each application. Depending on the requirements of the application or the configuration of the MAC layer, scheduling can be centralized or distributed (Dujovne et al. 2014).

4.7.3 6Lo

IPv6 over networks of resource-constrained nodes (6Lo), a newly-assigned IETF group, is working to propose a set of standards for IPv6 frame transmission over various data connections. Even though encapsulation standards like 6LoWPAN and 6TiSCH were created, it is now apparent that additional standards are required to accommodate all types of data communication. For this reason, IEFT established 6Lo. Most of the 6Lo specs are still being worked on and are not yet completed. IPv6 over DECT/ULE, IPv6 over NFC, IPv6 over IEEE 802.11ah, IPv6 over IEEE 485 Master-Slave/Token Passing (MS/TP) networks, and IPv6 over Wireless Networks for Iindustrial Automation Process Automation (WIA-PA) (Hong et al. 2017) are all examples of datalinks for which drafts are currently being developed for the purpose of IPv6 datagrams transmission.

4.7.4 IPv6 over G.9959

When using G.9959 data connections, IPv6 packets must adhere to the frame format established in IETF RFC 7428. Each G.9959 node will be given a unique home network identifier of 32-bit and a controller using a host identifier of 8-bit. So that it can fit in a G.9959 frame, an IPv6 link-local address must be built from an 8-bit host identification from the link layer. In addition, IPv6 packets compress like the headers of 6LoWPAN to fit within frames of G.9959. Regarding security, it's worth noting that RFC 7428 permits encryption purposes using a shared network key. However, end-to-end encryption and authentication are required for security-critical applications, often handled by higher-layer security methods and other protocols (Qureshi, Jeon and Piccialli. 2020).

4.7.5 IPv6 over Bluetooth Low Energy

RFC 7668 (Nieminen et al. 2015) defines the IPv6 over the Bluetooth low energy format. On Bluetooth, fragmentation occurs at the L2CAP sublayer, which stands for Adaptation Protocol and Logical Link Control. Therefore, 6LoWPAN's fragmentation function is being bypassed. Furthermore, multi-hop network generation currently not used effectively by Bluetooth low energy. Instead, the weaker nodes on the edges are routed through a core node. As a result, 6LoWPAN's multi-hop functionality is underutilized.

4.7.6 Summary

This section described the encapsulation of lengthy IPv6 datagrams into small MAC frames. It began with discussing IPv6 over 802.15.4 and 802.15.4e using 6LoWPAN and 6TiSCH. Due to 802.15.4e's prominence as the de facto standard encapsulation framework for IoT; such protocols are crucial. Then, 6Lo specifications are quickly and generally reviewed to demonstrate their presence in IETF standards. These documents deal with 6LoWPAN specifications for transferring IPv6 datagrams through various channel access techniques. Two of the 6Lo specifications that eventually became IETF Requests for Comments are then examined further. The presentation of these standards is significant because it draws attention to the difficulty of achieving interoperability among the many layers of a networking stack, a problem made more complicated by the wide variety of datalink protocols.

4.8 SESSION LAYER PROTOCOLS

Various Session layer protocols for the IoT used for messaging are discussed, including some defined by multiple bodies. The IoT relies on TCP and User Datagram Protocol (UDP), two widely used protocols of the Transport layer. However, different IoT applications call for different sets of message distribution options. Ideally, these features should be implemented via industry-accepted, consistent standards. In this section, we will go over what is commonly called "Session layer" protocols.

4.8.1 MQTT

The Message Transfer Protocol for Telemetry (MQTT) is a standard developed in 2013 by the Organization for the Advancement of Structured Information Standards (OASIS). IBM first debuted it in 1999 (Standard "Mqtt Version 3.1. 1"; Karagiannis et al. 2015). It links together the Application layer, the User layer, the Network layer, and the Communication layer. As can be seen in Figure 4.3, the architecture is a publish/subscribe one, with the three primary parts being Publisher, Subscriber, and Broker. A Publisher in the IoT is a lightweight sensor that links up with the Broker, transmits data, and then falls back to sleep. The applications that are interested in a specific topic or sensory data collection can only subscribe for Broker updates. The Brokers organize sensory input into distinct subjects and distribute them to specific groups of subscribers.

4.8.2 SMQTT

Secure MQTT (SMQTT) is a new and secure version of MQTT (Singh et al. 2015), which allows lightweight attribute-based encryption. This encryption method is widely deployed in IoT software. The encrypted message is broadcast to many additional nodes at once using the multicast feature. The technique can be divided into four phases: preparation, encryption, dissemination, and decryption. During the preparation step, the Broker signed up by the subscribers and publishers will receive a secret master key generated using the key

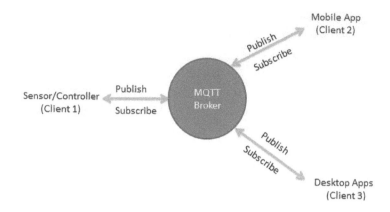

FIGURE 4.3   MQTT architecture.

generation algorithm selected by the developer. Afterward, the Broker encrypts the data before sending the data to subscribers. Decryption is the final step in the process at the end users' end, provided they share the same master secret key. There is no consensus on how to standardize key generation and encryption techniques.

4.8.3 AMQP

The Advanced Message Queuing Protocol (AMQP) is an OASIS standard developed for the banking sector. It employs a Publish/subscribe Architecture based on TCP. As shown in Figure 4.4, the primary distinction between these standards is the Broker's separation into exchanges and queues. The Exchange Component receives the Publisher messages, which then routes them to appropriate queues based on the Publishers' assigned roles. Sensory data is made available to subscribers anytime by connecting them to queues for various subjects (Standard "Oasis Advanced Message Queuing Protocol (Amqp) Version 1.0").

4.8.4 CoAP

Constrained Application Protocol (CoAP) is another Session layer protocol developed in the IETF-constrained RESTful environment (CORE working group, and it aims to provide

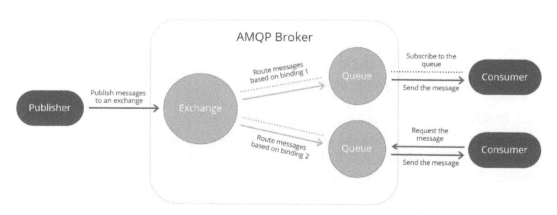

FIGURE 4.4   AMQP architecture.

a low overhead RESTful HTTP interface. The most popular interface for modern web applications is Representational State Transfer (REST). The high cost and power requirements of REST, however, make it inappropriate for IoT platforms. CoAP was created to address issues with REST and open the door for RESTful service usage in IoT applications. Instead of using TCP, it is based on UDP and employs a lightweight technique to ensure dependability. CoAP's structure consists of Message and Request/response layers. The Request/response sublayer is in charge of the actual information exchange, while the Messaging sublayer is responsible for message redundancy and delivery. Confirmable messages, non-confirmable messages, piggyback messages, and standalone messages are the four types of messages that CoAP can handle. Various confirmable and non-confirmable (representing dependable and unreliable transmissions, respectively) request/response communications make use of various modes. In piggyback, the server responds to a message from a client immediately after receiving it within the acknowledgment message. With CoAP messages, the server may take some time to send the acknowledgment. Thus, it is utilized in a separate mode when the answer includes a message that is not part of the acknowledgment. CoAP, as are PUT, PUSH, GET and Delete requests, is used in HTTP to create, insert, retrieve, and delete, respectively (Karagiannis et al. 2015).

4.8.5 XMPP

The Extensible Messaging and Presence Protocol (XMPP) was initially developed to communicate among various chat and message exchange programs. Standardized by IETF over a decade ago, it is based on the XML markup language. Its efficiency and widespread acceptance make it ideal for online deployment. Due to the standardization of XML, it has recently seen an increase in its use for IoT and SDN applications. The decision as to which architecture to adopt in an XMPP implementation is made by the application's developer. Its low-latency support for short messages is optimized for real-time use cases. It is impractical for M2M communications since it does not ensure a certain level of service quality. Additionally, the power consumption crucial for IoT applications is increased by the extra overhead created by XML messages' many headers and tag types. While XMPP's design currently doesn't lend itself well to IoT uses, there is some interest in expanding its functionality to accommodate such uses (Saint-Andre. 2011).

4.8.6 DDS

A messaging standard Data Distribution Service (DDS) was developed by Object Management Group (OMG). It is mainly employed in M2M communications and has a publish/subscribe design (O. Group). This protocol's greatest strengths are its suitability for Broker-less architectures like the IoT and M2M communication and its excellent Quality of Service (QoS) levels. With its 23 QoS tiers, it can meet many standards for quality, such as those related to safety, timeliness, priority, longevity, dependability, etc. It specifies a Publish-subscribe sublayer focused on the data and a Reconstruction sublayer local to the data. The first is required and is in charge of relaying messages to subscribers, while the second is discretionary and facilitates DDS's easy incorporation into the Application layer. The sensory data distribution falls under the Publisher layer's purview.

The Data Writer communicates with the Publishers to reach a consensus on what information and updates should be given to subscribers. Sensory information generated by IoT devices is sent to subscribers. In this context, "topics" refer to the many categories of data that are being distributed to subscribers via "Data Readers," while "data types" refer to the specific categories of data that are being distributed. In other words, in Broker-based architectures, the Broker's role is assumed by the Data Writer and Data Reader.

This section briefly discussed many IoT Session layer standards and protocols. These standards are chosen depending on the applications being used. IoT uses MQTT the most because of the low overhead and power consumption; the choice to be made among these standards is dependent on the organization and the application. XMPP may be the best Session layer protocol for an application designed using XML that can tolerate header overhead. MQTT is suitable for overhead and power-sensitive applications that require Broker implementation. CoAP is the best, if not the only, solution for HTTP-based applications that need REST capability.

4.9 IoT MANAGEMENT STANDARDS

Several management protocols are utilized in the IoT to allow for the management and communication of fundamentally different devices. This section discusses two protocols for dealing with heterogeneity in datalinks and some specific protocols for managing remote devices, emphasizing their applicability in M2M and IoT scenarios. Due to the variety of IoT devices and the requirements at various networking tiers, management protocols play a crucial role in the success of the IoT. IoT applications depend on quickly and efficiently exchanging data among protocols operating at the same or different tiers. Communication among protocols in different layers of the IoT remains difficult despite existing standards for doing so at the same layer.

4.9.1 IEEE 1905.1

Interoperability among the multiple MAC layer protocols used in IoT is essential because of the wide variety of these protocols. The IEEE standard would manage this type of interoperability by adding an abstraction layer on top of the many MAC protocols now in use (I. W. Group). By disguising their differences, the various protocols can communicate with one another without requiring any changes to their design thanks to this abstraction. Control Message Data Units (CMDUs) are communications that can be sent and received between any two devices that adhere to the same communication standards. All devices that conform to IEEE 1905.1 can communicate using a standard "Abstraction Layer Management Entity (ALME)" protocol, the features of which are the following: finding nearby neighbors, exchanging topologies, notifying each other of topology changes, exchanging measured traffic data, exchanging flow forwarding rules, and associating security policies.

4.9.2 Smart Transducer Interface

MAC layer protocols in IoT are diverse and numerous; therefore, interoperability among these standards is essential. This IEEE standard (Malar and Kamaraj. 2014) is meant to manage such interoperability by providing an Abstraction layer on top of all these diverse heterogeneous MAC protocols. Because of this abstraction, disparate protocols can talk to one another while preserving their original designs. CMDUs can be transmitted among devices that adhere to the same protocol. All devices that meet the requirements of IEEE 1905.1 have a common understanding of the ALME protocol. This protocol allows for a variety of services to be provided, such as the discovery of neighbors, sharing of topologies, notification of topology changes, sharing of measured traffic statistics, forwarding of flows, and protection against unauthorized access.

4.9.3 TR-069

Customer-Premises Equipment (CPE) WAN Management Protocol (CWMP), published by the Broadband Forum, is an industry-standard for HTTP-based remote management of M2M devices. The server communicates with the clients or target devices via HTTP messages in this specification. Despite its importance for M2M devices, the standard has had limited adoption in IoT thus far because it relied on HTTP messages (Stusek et al. 2016).

4.9.4 OMA-DM

The Open Mobile Alliance (OMA) created the OMA device management protocol. It is deployed remotely to M2M devices for provisioning, upgrading, and fault management. It's based on XML messages sent over HTTP and may be used with XMPP or any other XML-based transport protocol. Despite this, resource-constrained IoT devices still have difficulty deciphering the protocol's messages (O. M. Alliance *Device Management Architecture*).

4.9.5 LWM2M

The OMA protocol Lightweight M2M (LWM2M) was developed with the management of IoT devices in mind. JASON (JavaScript Object Notation) messages are used for data exchange among clients and servers in certain protocols. It relies heavily on the CoAP session protocol but can also be used with others. The functionalities of devices can be managed across the network using this protocol, and data can be transferred from the server to the devices using this protocol (O. M. Alliance "Lightweight Machine to Machine Architecture").

Several management protocols allowing for the compatibility and diversity of IoT protocols have been highlighted. Transducer and sensor management are handled by IEEE-1451, whereas the variety of IoT MAC layer protocols are handled by IEEE-1905.1. Regarding remote management protocols, LWM2M is preferred and more extensively used for the IoT than TR-069 and OMA-DM. The coordination of IoT protocol stacks at various communication levels remains an open problem.

4.10 IoT PROTOCOLS SECURITY

Securing IoT systems presents a new set of difficulties at each of the networking layers we've discussed so far. Due to their complexity and resource needs, typical security measures like encryption and public critical infrastructure don't seem viable options for IoT devices. This has prompted the development of streamlined security protocols.

4.10.1 Security within IoT Protocol Layers

IoT security is threatened at all levels, including the Datalink, network, Session, and Application layers. This means that security has to be built into the standards we'll talk about in this chapter. 802.15.4e, WirelessHART, 6LoWPAN, and RPL are just a few of the protocols whose Communication layers have built-in security features. Multiple options for security are available in MAC 802.15.4e, and they are activated by setting the "security enabled bit" in the frame control field of the header. Privacy, authentication, integrity, access control, and precisely synchronized temporal communications are all essential for system security. In order to provide its users with the utmost security, the WirelessHART standard uses both established and state-of-the-art cryptographic methods. Indicators for unsuccessful data access, report production on message integrity and authentication, and AES-128 encryption are only a few examples. This means WirelessHART may give varying degrees of protection using the most up-to-date techniques, as needed by the many applications it serves.

Several IETF documents address the security concerns and needs of 6LoWPAN and offer recommendations for mitigating those concerns. EUI-64 interface addresses, for instance, are expected to be unique, although RFC 4944 mentions the potential of duplicates (Montenegro et al. 2007). Security concerns brought forth by RFC 4944 (Hui and Thubert. 2011) are addressed in RFC 6282. Security techniques for resource-limited wireless sensor systems are discussed in RFC 6568 (Kim, Kaspar and Vasseur. 2012). The "Security" header of RPL documents indicates the available security settings. This field specifies the encryption algorithm and strength necessary for the encryption of a message. RPL helps with legitimate data, safeguarding against replay attacks, semantic security, privacy, and managing keys. Unsecured, preloaded, and authenticated RPL security levels exist. Selective forwarding, sinkholes, Sybils, hello floods, wormholes, and DoS attacks are all potential dangers for RPLs. Confidentiality, availability, integrity attacks, and possible defenses against them, are all covered in RFC 7416 (Tschofenig and Fossati. 2016).

4.10.2 TLS/DTLS

Transport Layer Security (TLS) and Datagram Transport Layer Security (DTLS) are two common security protocols. Their primary usage is in Transport layer protocols like CoAP, where they guarantee security and privacy. Security services are provided through TLS over TCP transmission and DTLS over UDP/datagram transfer, respectively. The encapsulation and authentication in TLS and DTLS are handled by two separate protocol layers: Record and Handshaking. These standards' privacy and security methods are discussed in depth in RFC 7925 (Tschofenig and Fossati. 2016). Traditional security techniques such as credentials, signatures, and error handling can be adapted to work with the limited resources of IoT devices utilizing these standards.

4.10.3 Ubiquitous Green Community Control Network Security

The Ubiquitous Green Community Control Network protocol is protected according to standards outlined by IEEE Standard 1888.3. The mechanisms provided by these networks are high quality, energy-efficient, and secure, making them ideal for the IoT. The information must be protected, private, confidential, authenticated, and controlled for access. To ensure safety in such a system, the standard specifies the appropriate architectures and components that must be used. Handshaking, authentication, and access control techniques are only a few of the security mechanisms specifically outlined in the standard.

4.10.4 TCG

Using a variety of use cases and security approaches, the Trusted Computing Group (TCG) has developed guidelines for securing IoT-based heterogeneous applications. Among these measures are those that provide availability, confidentiality, and integrity, as well as those that prevent middleware infections by leveraging Transport Layer Security (TLS). TCGcompatible devices employ these methods, which include Root of Trust for Update (RTU) and Trusted Platform Module (TPM). It is up to the developer to find a happy medium between system security and the complexity and resource requirements of the system; however, standards can help steer developers of IoT applications toward more secure solutions.

4.10.5 OAuth 2.0

In IETF RFC 6749, an authorization system known as OAuth is outlined. It allows reliable third-party servers to manage who can access what. Thanks to this specification, clients can make access requests to owners via an authorization server. Such a server verifies the client's identity and permission levels before granting access. This framework uses HTTP-based messages, which are rarely used for the IoT due to their high overhead (Hardt. 2012). New security concepts and countermeasures are described in RFC 6819 (Lodderstedt, McGloin and Hunt. 2013), which expands OAuth. When OAuth 2.0 is released, there are still dangers and open security vulnerabilities in the protocol that need to be fixed in subsequent iterations. Some instances of these threats include credential leakage, injections, and worries about authorization servers hosted by other parties.

4.10.6 SASL

The IETF has developed the Simple Authentication and Security Layer (SASL) security architecture to facilitate server-based authentication for IoT applications. It employs straightforward messages to authenticate clients using application-level security measures, thus decoupling the application from the authentication procedure. MQTT and AMQP (Melnikov and Zeilenga. 2006) are Session layer protocols that support TLS and SSL.

4.10.7 ACE

IoT platforms can use Authentication and authorization in constrained environments (ACE) security because it is tailored to low-resource devices. In terms of ideas, it's similar to OAuth. However, it is more suited to the IoT because it is based on CoAP communications. The standards have been approved in IETF RFC 7744 (Ludwig et al. 2016), and a new draft is now being worked on (Gerdes et al. 2018).

4.10.8 Blockchain for IoT Security

The use of Blockchain in developing smart contracts and safeguarding IoT platforms is a freshly emerging field of study in IoT security. Distributed ledger technology, like Blockchain, offers built-in security without relying on a single central authority (Tasatanattakool and Techapanupreeda. 2018). It has been studied in various fields, including IoT, but is most known for its application in Bitcoin and other virtual cryptocurrency platforms. IBM and other IoT companies are considering Blockchain solutions for IoT security. Privacy protection in IoT platforms is another area where Blockchain can be helpful (Kianmajd, Rowe and Levitt. 2016).

Due to the importance of addressing vulnerabilities in IoT systems, several proposals, standards, drafts, and studies have emerged to do so. While there are security features built into IoT protocols, these cannot guarantee the system's integrity by themselves. Several protocols, such as ACE and TLS/DTLS, have been proposed by the IETF to increase security and safety in IoT environments. There are other notable continuing drafts that deal with the difficulties and dangers of IoT security. It's worth noting that the IETF has formed a specialized group called DTLS in Limited Contexts (DICE) to address security concerns specific to the IoT. Recent research on improving IoT systems has also been widely discussed.

4.11 CHALLENGES TO ADOPT STANDARDS AND PROTOCOLS

A lot of research has been conducted and standards have been established for the IoT, but creating a useful IoT application is still tricky. Some challenges (Kumar, Vealey and Srivastava. 2016) include mobility, reliability, scalability, management, availability, interoperability, dependability, cost and complexity, and energy harvesting.

4.11.1 Mobility

IoT devices are expected to dynamically switch IP addresses and network affiliations to adapt to their surroundings. Therefore, routing protocols like RPL incur significant overhead whenever a leaf joins the network since they must reconstruct the DODAG. Because of potential disruptions in service and gateway changes, switching service providers is yet another possible complication of mobility.

4.11.2 Reliability

Maintaining a fully functional system that delivers as promised in an emergency response setting is paramount. As a result, the system must be very dependable and quick to collect data, communicate it, and make decisions in IoT applications. The consequences of poor decision-making can be severe.

4.11.3 Scalability

The scalability of an IoT application becomes an issue if millions or even trillions of linked devices are added. Keeping track of where devices are placed and what they can do may be daunting. Also, IoT applications' accommodation for adding new services and devices to the network without interruption is necessary.

4.11.4 Management

The management of IoT devices remotely can be performed using various protocols, but it is still a significant difficulty to manage all IoT applications. A provider's networked devices' failures, configuration, accounting, performance, and security (FCAPS) must be handled.

4.11.5 Availability

IoT platforms must provide services to users and subscribers through software and hardware availability all the time. When software is available, users continue to receive services despite interruptions. The existing devices are readily accessible and support multiple protocols, which is what we mean by "hardware availability." It is also essential that these protocols are small enough to be integrated into the limited IoT devices.

4.11.6 Interoperability

Heterogeneous devices and protocols must be able to communicate with one another to achieve interoperability. The wide variety of IoT platform types makes this a difficult task. Developers and manufacturers should work together to provide interoperability so that users may receive services regardless of the platform or hardware they're using.

4.11.7 Cost and Complexity

Despite the low cost of sensors and smart transducers, it's still expensive to construct an IoT application. Due to the high complexity involved in integrating many protocols and standards, IoT applications are currently unavailable to the general public. One of the biggest obstacles is simplifying the process while cutting costs.

4.11.8 Power Harvesting

IoT devices are still facing power harvesting problems because for small devices with limited resources, there aren't many harvesting solutions. Power management is a concern since IoT devices often need to operate for years without recharging and may be permanently attached to a person's body or environment. Therefore, it appears that a crucial answer for such devices is for energy gathering through motion or another source and transferring it into stored energy. However, the size and power requirements of such converters and collection devices prevent their application to miniature devices.

This section addressed numerous current IoT challenges like reliability, scalability, availability, interoperability, dependability, etc., and mercy efforts that have been made to address businesses' difficulties with mobility, scalability, and management. Furthermore, security remains an unanswered research question.

4.12 CONCLUSION

The Internet of Things (IoT) is being utilized for the development of cities, homes, and more. The combination of Artificial Intelligence (AI) and IoT is becoming very famous. The capability of the sensors of the IoT environment to make decisions is becoming greater.

The adoption of the technology by businesses or consumers is still a valid concern. More and more standards and protocols are being developed to ensure the security, availability, and interoperability of IoT networks. The standards and protocols are designed based on the IoT ecosystem involving Network layer, Session layer, Datalink layer, Management, and Security integration. Many organizations are focusing on the standards and protocols designed for the wide adoption of AIoT. The standards and protocols are designed based on the requirements of the network to make it reliable, secure, and better for the consumers.

REFERENCES

Aijaz, Adnan, and A. Hamid Aghvami. "Cognitive Machine-to-Machine Communications for Internet-of-Things: A Protocol Stack Perspective." *IEEE Internet of Things Journal* 2.2 (2015): 103–12.

ALiero, Muhammad Saidu, et al. "Smart Home Energy Management Systems in Internet of Things Networks for Green Cities Demands and Services." *Environmental Technology & Innovation* 22 (2021): 101443.

Alliance, Enocean. "Enocean–the World of Energy Harvesting Wireless Technology." *EnOcean Technology Whitepaper* (2015).

Alliance, HomePlog. "Homeplug™ Av2 Technology." (2007).

Alliance, Open Mobile. *Device Management Architecture*: OMA-AD_DM-V1_0-20050530-D (2016).

———. "Lightweight Machine to Machine Architecture." *Draft Version* 1 (2012): 1–12.

Basagni, Stefano, et al. "Carp: A Channel-Aware Routing Protocol for Underwater Acoustic Wireless Networks." *Ad Hoc Networks* 34 (2015): 92–104.

Brandt, A, and J Buron. *Transmission of Ipv6 Packets over Itu-T G. 9959 Networks.* (2015).

Bush, S. "Dect/Ule Connects Homes for IoT." *Electronics Weekly,* February 6 (2015): 2017.

Geetha, A., and K. Jamuna. "Smart metering system." *2013 International Conference on Information Communication and Embedded Systems (ICICES)* (2013). IEEE.

Chang, Zhuoqing, et al. "A Survey of Recent Advances in Edge-Computing-Powered Artificial Intelligence of Things." *IEEE Internet of Things Journal* 8.18 (2021): 13849–75.

Culler, David, and Samita Chakrabarti. "6LoWPAN: Incorporating IEEE 802.15.4 into the IP Architecture." White paper (2009).

Dujovne, Diego, et al. "6TiSCH: Deterministic IP-Enabled Industrial Internet (of Things)." *IEEE Communications Magazine* 52.12 (2014): 36–41.

Evanczuk, S. "Ant/Ant+ Solutions Speed Low-Power Wireless Design." (February, 2013).

Gerdes, Stefanie, et al. "An Architecture for Authorization in Constrained Environments." *IETF Draft, October* 22 (2018).

Gomez, Carles, Joaquim Oller, and Josep Paradells. "Overview and Evaluation of Bluetooth Low Energy: An Emerging Low-Power Wireless Technology." *Sensors* 12.9 (2012): 11734–53.

Group, IEEE 802 Working. "IEEE Standard for a Convergent Digital Home Network for Heterogeneous Technologies." (2013).

Group, OM. "Data Distribution Service (Dds)-V1. 4." (April, 2015).

Hahn, Jim. "The Internet of Things (IoT) and Libraries." *Library Technology Reports* 53.1 (2017): 5–8.

Haqiq, Nasreddine, et al. "AIoT with I4.0: The Effect of Internet of Things and Artificial Intelligence Technologies on the Industry 4.0." *ITM Web of Conferences.* (2022). EDP Sciences.

Hardt, D. "The OAuth 2.0 Authorization Framework: IETF RFC 6749." (2012).

Hasan, Anum, and Kashif Naseer Qureshi. "Internet of Things Device Authentication Scheme Using Hardware Serialization." *2018 International Conference on Applied and Engineering Mathematics (ICAEM).* (2018). IEEE.

Hassan, Wan Haslina. "Current Research on Internet of Things (IoT) Security: A Survey." *Computer Networks* 148 (2019): 283–94.

Hong, Yong-Geun, et al. "IPv6 over Constrained Node Networks (6lo) Applicability & Use Cases." *IETF Internet Draft* (2017).

Hoymann, Christian, et al. "LTE Release 14 Outlook." *IEEE Communications Magazine* 54.6 (2016): 44–49.

Hui, Jonathan, and Pascal Thubert. *Compression Format for IPv6 Datagrams over IEEE 802.15. 4-Based Networks.* (2011).

ISO—ISO/IEC. "Information Technology–Security Techniques–Guidelines for Security and Privacy in Internet of Things (IoT)." CD 27030. [online] Available: https://www.iso.org/standard/44373.html. (Mar. 2020).

ISO. "Information Technology—Future Network–Problem Statement and Requirements—Part 9: Networking of Everything." *TR 29181-9:2017,* (Apr. 2017).

ISO/IEC, ISO/IEC. "Information Technology—Data Structure—Unique Identification for the Internet of Things." (Aug. 2016): 29161:2016.

ISO/IEC/IEEE. "Software, Systems and Enterprise—Architecture Evaluation Framework." *42030:2019.* (Jul. 2019).

Karagiannis, Vasileios, et al. "A Survey on Application Layer Protocols for the Internet of Things." *Transaction on IoT and Cloud Computing* 3.1 (2015): 11–17.

Kianmajd, Parisa, Jeff Rowe, and Karl Levitt. "Privacy-Preserving Coordination for Smart Communities." *2016 IEEE Conference on Computer Communications Workshops (INFOCOM WKSHPS).* (2016). IEEE.

Kim, Anna N., et al. "When Hart Goes Wireless: Understanding and Implementing the Wirelesshart Standard." *2008 IEEE International Conference on Emerging Technologies and Factory Automation.* (2008). IEEE.

Kim, Eunsook, Dominik Kaspar, and JP Vasseur. *Design and Application Spaces for IPv6 over Low-Power Wireless Personal Area Networks (6lowpans)* 2012.

Kiyani, Faisal, et al. "ISDA-BAN: Interoperability and Security Based Data Authentication Scheme for Body Area Network." *Cluster Computing* (2022).

Kshetrimayum, Rakhesh Singh. "An Introduction to UWB Communication Systems." *IEEE Potentials* 28.2 (2009): 9–13.

Kumar, Sathish Alampalayam. "Security in Internet of Things: Challenges, Solutions and Future Directions." *2016 49th Hawaii International Conference on System Sciences (HICSS).* 2016. IEEE.

Lee, Euijong, et al. "A Survey on Standards for Interoperability and Security in the Internet of Things." *IEEE Communications Surveys & Tutorials* 23.2 (2021): 1020–47.

Lee, Juho, et al. "LTE-Advanced in 3GPP Rel-13/14: An Evolution toward 5G." *IEEE Communications Magazine* 54.3 (2016): 36–42.

Lodderstedt, Torsten, Mark McGloin, and Phil Hunt. *Oauth 2.0 Threat Model and Security Considerations* 2013.

Logvinov, Oleg, et al. "Standard for an Architectural Framework for the Internet of Things (IoT) IEEE P2413." *IEEE-P2413 Working Group. Technical Report* (2016).

Ludwig, Seitz, et al. "Use Cases for Authentication and Authorization in Constrained Environments." (2016). No. rfc7744.

Malar, K., and N. Kamaraj. "Development of Smart Transducers with IEEE 1451.4 Standard for Industrial Automation." *2014 IEEE International Conference on Advanced Communications, Control and Computing Technologies.* (2014). IEEE.

Mandza, Yann Stephen, and Atanda Raji. "Iotivity Cloud-Enabled Platform for Energy Management Applications." *IoT* 3.1 (2021): 73–90.

Melnikov, Alexey, and Kurt Zeilenga. *Simple Authentication and Security Layer (SASL)* 2006.

Mirzoev, Timur. "Low Rate Wireless Personal Area Networks (LR-WPAN 802.15. 4 Standard)." *arXiv preprint arXiv:1404.2345* (2014).

Montenegro, Gabriel, et al. *Transmission of IPv6 Packets over IEEE 802.15. 4 Networks* (2007).

Nieminen, Johanna, et al. *IPv6 over Bluetooth (R) Low Energy.* (2015).

Nobre, Marcelo, Ivanovitch Silva, and Luiz Affonso Guedes. "Routing and Scheduling Algorithms for WirelessHART Networks: A Survey." *Sensors* 15.5 (2015): 9703–40.

Park, Minyoung. "IEEE 802.11 Ah: Sub-1-Ghz License-Exempt Operation for the Internet of Things." *IEEE Communications Magazine* 53.9 (2015): 145–51.

Phan, Vu Hien, et al. "An IoT System and Modis Images Enable Smart Environmental Management for Mekong Delta." *Future Internet* 15.7 (2023): 245.

Poole, I. "Weightless Wireless—M2M White Space Communications-Tutorial." (2014).

Qureshi, Kashif Naseer, Gwanggil Jeon, and Francesco Piccialli. "Anomaly Detection and Trust Authority in Artificial Intelligence and Cloud Computing." *Computer Networks* (2020): 107647.

SA, IEEE. "The IEEE Standards Association—Home." [online] Available: https://standards.ieee.org/. (Mar. 2020).

Saint-Andre, Peter. *Extensible Messaging and Presence Protocol (XMPP): Core.* (2011).

Serizawa, Yasutaka, et al. "Reliable Wireless Communication Technology of Adaptive Channel Diversity (ACD) Method Based on ISA100.11a Standard." *IEEE Transactions on Industrial Electronics* 64.1 (2016): 624–32.

Singh, Meena, et al., "Secure MQTT for Internet of Things (IoT)." *2015 Fifth International Conference on Communication Systems and Network Technologies.* (2015). IEEE.

Standard, OASIS. "MQTT Version 3.1.1." http://docs.oasis-open.org/mqtt/mqtt/v3.1 (2014): 29.

———. "Oasis Advanced Message Queuing Protocol (AMQP) Version 1.0." *International Journal of Aerospace Engineering Hindawi www.hindawi.com* 2018 (2012).

Stusek, Martin, et al. "Remote security of Intelligent Devices: Using Tr-069 Protocol in IoT." *2016 39th International Conference on Telecommunications and Signal Processing (TSP).* (2016). IEEE.

Tasatanattakool, Pinyaphat, and Chian Techapanupreeda. "Blockchain: Challenges and Applications." *2018 International Conference on Information Networking (ICOIN).* (2018). IEEE.

Tschofenig, Hannes, and Thomas Fossati. *Transport Layer Security (TLS)/Datagram Transport Layer Security (DTLS) Profiles for the Internet of Things.* (2016).

Vangelista, Lorenzo, and Marco Centenaro. "Worldwide Connectivity for the Internet of Things through LoRaWAN." *Future Internet* 11.3 (2019): 57.

Winter, Tim, et al. *RPL: IPv6 Routing Protocol for Low-Power and Lossy Networks.* (2012).

Z-Wave. "Z-Wave Protocol Overview." (April 2006).

Zigbee. "Zigbee Resource Guide." (2016).

CHAPTER 5

AIoT as New Paradigm for Distributed Network

Sheetal Harris, Hassan Jalil Hadi, Yue Cao

School of Cyber Science and Engineering, Wuhan University, Wuhan 430000, China

Kashif Naseer Qureshi

Department of Electronic & Computer Engineering, University of Limerick, V94 T9PX Limerick, Ireland

5.1 INTRODUCTION

In 1956, John McCarthy coined the phrase Artificial Intelligence (AI) in a symposium at Dartmouth College. He is credited with starting current AI research and a new scientific field. The advancement in the years that followed is surprising. The researchers concentrated on automated reasoning and utilized AI for algebraic problem-solving and mathematical theorems. The computer software *Logic Theorist* proved many sophisticated theorems in Principia Mathematica (McCorduck and Cfe. 2004). These achievements filled AI pioneers with unbridled hope and supported their conviction that AI was here to stay and flourish. They soon discovered, however, that much work remained to be done before machines could exhibit intellect comparable to that of humans. The logic-based programs were unable to solve many significant tasks. The lack of computational resources to solve ever-more complex issues was another difficulty. As a result, organizations and funding sources ceased sponsoring these underwhelming AI efforts.

In the 1980s, several research-focused organizations and colleges developed an AI systems those compiles significant basic principles from expert knowledge, which further assisted non-experts in making predictions and extrapolations. The systems were widely known as expert systems: for example, Stanford University designed MYCIN and the Carnegie Mellon University designed XCON. Expert knowledge was used to develop logical rules which were then implemented in real-world situations. The information that made computers "smarter" lies at the heart of this era's AI research. There were certain drawbacks, for example adaptability, privacy, high maintenance costs, low versatility, etc. Meanwhile, the Fifth Generation Computer Project, supported and funded by the Japanese government, fell short of the majority of its initial objectives. This resulted in the refusal

DOI: 10.1201/9781003430018-6

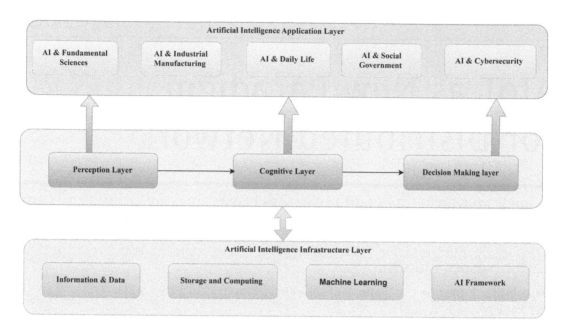

FIGURE 5.1 General framework of AI.

and rejection of further aid for AI research once again, and the field was in its second-lowest position ever. Figure 5.1 shows the general AI framework.

Authors LeCun, Bengio, and Hinton proposed a method for developing deeper neural networks and a strategy to prevent gradients from disappearing during training. As a result, Deep Learning (DL) algorithms have emerged as a significant field in AI research. Machine Learning (ML) enables an Information Security (IS) and applications to learn and develop intelligence and make predictions without human interaction. DL, a subset of ML, is based on many layers of neural networks with representation learning. Therefore, "learn" is the essential phrase for AI research currently. Big data technologies and the increase in processing power have further developed the effectiveness of information and feature extraction from large datasets.

To enhance the learning capability of DL and its applications, various advanced network architectures and training techniques have been established. For a selected dataset related to a problem, Computer Vision (CV), Natural Language Processing (NLP) and DL techniques match and surpass human skills. In every sphere of life, AI technologies have had tremendous success. They have also demonstrated their worth as the foundation of scientific inquiry, real-time processing, and applications. ML has a significant broad impact across various areas of the pure sciences, social science, technology, and science within AI. This is because ML methods perform data analysis and classification tasks, and their predictions and decisions are based on evidence. It is more convenient to train a classifier or a model by giving it examples of desirable input-output behavior than to manually program it by anticipating the intended response for every possible input.

The overwhelming majority of IoT allows wider proliferation in healthcare, transportation, manufacturing, and other industries. With the explosion of the number of IoT devices and sensors connected over the internet, interconnected devices have restrained the distributed sensor network infrastructure that has spread everywhere. Therefore, the prerequisite of intelligent techniques and emerging technologies is to ease the strain on the existing demands. AIoT emanated from the emergence of new demands and effective responses to IoT development and proliferation. It aims to ensure efficacious human-machine interactions, IoT operations, quick response mechanisms from loads of data, and sophisticated data management (Phan et al. 2023). The impetus to adopt AIoT applications and widespread integration has attracted researchers and industry. In addition, AIoT applications require extensive computing resources for real-time processing using ML and DL algorithms. The design and implementation of AIoT devices and applications to accomplish Quality-of-Service (QoS) requirements for resource-constrained (communication, computation, and storage) IoT devices are challenging.

The AIoT paradigm avails itself of the ML approach and the edge computing paradigm for sensing and Device layer, such as Transfer Learning (TL) (Shao, Zhu and Li. 2014), Active Learning (AL) (Qian, Sengupta and Hansen. 2019), and Federated Learning (FL) (Hao et al. 2019). The pre-trained models are used to ensure high performance and predictions that are created at the edge servers by using TL. The random data across the IoT network are controlled by using AL techniques. Lastly, FL offers the required level of privacy for information processing. The AIoT paradigm can benefit from recently developed communication networks and technologies, such as 5G/6G cellular communications and Software-Defined Networking (SDN) at the communication and Network layer (Iqbal et al. 2021).

Due to the complexity of AIoT networks, security is one of the challenges. AIoT networks are extremely vulnerable to security attacks because of the diverse devices and heterogeneous nature of the network. To secure the data in these networks is also challenging due to devices' mobility, networks topologies, and open systems. AIoT networks are based on 5G standards and offer high speed, low latency, and enormous bandwidth. These advantages also open many doors for attackers in the network. Therefore, they can easily access the Personal Identifiable Information (PII) of a customer during an attack (Khalid et al. 2023). Traditional security measures, particularly those that address rising security risks, are ineffective at resolving security challenges in these networks. The security solutions are now more effective and efficient because of the integration of AI technologies with IoT (Kiyani et al. 2023). AIoT general layer architecture, shown in Figure 5.2, consists of three layers: a Sensor and Device layer, a Communication and Network layer, and an Application layer.

AIoT applications can be widely used in planning smart urban cities, smart home appliances, and automobiles. Smart home appliances and medical devices with sensors and intelligence learn a user's behaviors through smart TVs, lighting, thermostats, refrigerators, wearables, and connected spirometers. The intelligence is best utilized to automate households and organize assistance for routine tasks, such as reducing energy consumption, at home and in offices. The sensors for face recognition restrict access and are widely used for access control management (Sodhro et al. 2020). The innovative paradigm for resource allocation and task offloading has been established for intelligent driving using AIoT and edge computing. It highly increases sensors efficacy to perform offload jobs as instructed.

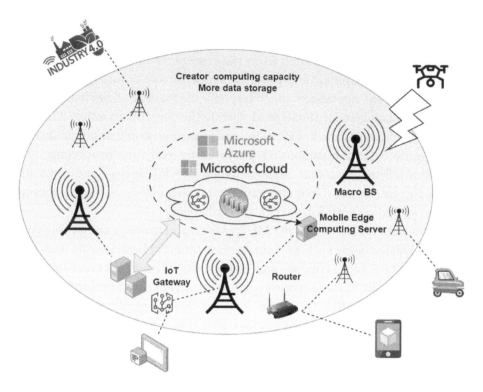

FIGURE 5.2 AIoT architecture and layers.

5.2 THE CONFLUENCE OF METHODS, PLATFORMS, AND ARCHITECTURES FOR AIOT

The confluence of platforms, methods, and architectures for AIoT can be viewed from two perspectives: AIoT architecture based on fog, edge, and Mobile-Edge Computing (MEC) architectures, and ML training methods. A method for resource-efficient edge computing, called ThriftyEdge, is proposed by X. Chen et al. 2018. An effective topology sorting-based task graph partition algorithm is provided as part of a device-centric approach to edge computing in order to reduce the consumption of cloud resources and meet QoS criteria. To fulfil QoS requirements and reduce edge resource occupancy of AIoT devices, the Virtual Machine (VM) selection method is also determined. To use the graph partition algorithm, VM types are sorted, rated, and designated according to their ranking.

By using the computational power of a MEC server installed on an Unmanned Aerial Vehicle (UAV), for data communication as suggested in Gong et al. 2020, is an AI-MEC architecture for IoT applications. Based on a game-theoretic model, this study developed the best offloading tactics for the UAV MEC servers. The theory of submodular games is used to discover the Pure Nash Equilibrium (PNE) strategies. The performance and operational properties of the models were shown by their experimental findings. Another method, known as Intelligent Cooperative Edge (ICE) is presented by Gong et al. 2020. Their method involves redesigning AI computations from the cloud and running on edge devices. Lightweight pipelines for edge reconstruction and cloud compression are used as the distribution strategy. The study and prototype suggested that the method

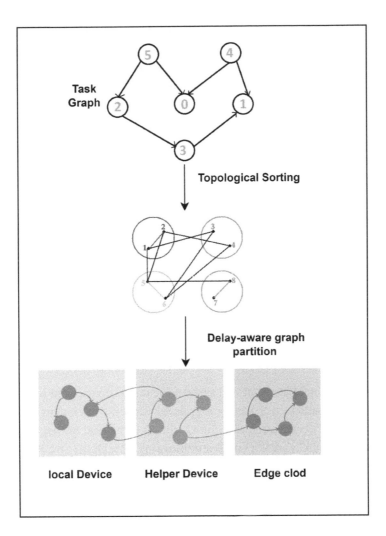

FIGURE 5.3   Task graph for topological sorting.

could make it possible to combine AI with edge computing in beneficial ways as shown in Figure 5.3.

The efficient distribution of computing tasks remains the limitation of a DL system. The study by Zhou et al. 2019 introduced a technique known as accelerating AIoT and distributes inference computation. Using this method, data is gathered, processed at the first layer, and transmitted to the subsequent device. This method is revised for each device, and the outcome is transmitted back to the initial device. Each layer's actions are based on the outcomes of the layer before it.

5.3 NEW ML AND TRAINING METHODS FOR AIoT

AIoT aims to escalate and accentuate the training method for devices by using ML and DL for an AIoT environment. A hierarchical training framework called HierTrain was presented by Liu et al. 2020 and has the potential to apply deep neural network training tasks on the Mobile-Edge-Cloud Computing architecture effectively.

The HierTrain framework is divided into three phases: profiling, optimization, and hierarchical training stages. The first stage profiles processing time for various layers on the cloud, edge, device, or relevant computing models. Secondly, the optimal partition model is selected that evaluates the training data for the devices and relevant servers. In the third stage, the samples are sent to the relevant servers, respectively. The implementation of the method on a hardware prototype collectively demonstrates that HierTrain could achieve a better performance speed, i.e., 6.9 times faster than the cloud-based approach.

For Industrial Internet of Things (IIoT) applications, the study of Liu et al. 2020 suggested a combined Federated Active Transfer Learning (FATL) model. The suggested FATL model aims to accelerate the learning process of the models by using ML approaches that limit the amount of labelled data used for training. TL is used for the pre-trained Artificial Neural Network (ANN), and FL is used for scheduling various devices over the edge IIoT architecture. Lastly, AL is used for end devices. The suggested FATL architecture provided high performance and simulation results.

The potential of AIoT for practical applications lies in additional research on the development of MEC architectures, edge, and fog computing. Future research directions, in terms of AIoT architectures and methodologies, are as follows:

- The creation of architectures that will sustain the use of distributed ML algorithms and methods in AIoT would be a crucial prerequisite for the advancement of AIoT. The study by Savaglio et al. 2019 evaluated the implementation method of dispersed data mining on edge devices, whereas authors in Teerapittayanon, McDanel and Kung proposed the method for deploying distributed deep neural networks over cloud and edge devices.

- The development and growth of AIoT architecture, strategies, and platforms depend upon the security and robust response to an adversarial attack on AIoT (Guin, Cui and Skjellum. 2018). Utilizing Blockchain technology to safeguard against duplicate, counterfeit nodes or devices, and the need for confirmation of validity would be an intriguing research direction.

- The creation of methods and tools for data mining and data collection within the AIoT would be a third area of attention. This is crucial for the AIoT, which includes diverse nodes and devices.

- Creating methods and tools for data mining and data collection on heterogeneous nodes and devices of AIoT would be the fourth area of future research.

5.4 THE CONFLUENCE OF DEVICES, ENERGY, AND SENSORS METHODS FOR AIoT

Various AI-based devices, sensors, sensing methods, and other methodologies are required to support AIoT which is the combination of IoT and AI. The study of Mukhopadhyay et al. 2021 provided an analysis of AI-based sensors and their implementation for future applications. The combination of sensors, devices, and sensing methods for AIoT is discussed in this section with an emphasis on two key perspectives. Firstly, AIoT computing, scalable sensing, and management, and secondly, energy harvesting methods and Wireless Power Transfer (WPT) are contemplated.

With the rapid expansion and geographically widespread use of IoT devices, the flexibility requirement for IoT sensing, computing, and administration is a crucial challenge. Quality of Experience (QoE) with the benefits of the AIoT paradigm is offered to consumers. However, challenges remain in instability and sluggish convergence with the present computation offloading using ML and DL techniques. The study by Lu et al. 2020 determined a method for offloading computation by using DRL (Lu et al. 2020). To solve the mentioned problems for DRL while providing consumers with a higher degree of QoE, the authors suggested a method based on Double-Dueling Deterministic Policy Gradients (D3PG). Various proposed features, such as task success rate, efficient energy, and computation consumption, can be integrated into models to address the issues.

A prospective solution for energy-efficient AIoT sensors is provided by Compressive Sensing (CS) methods. There are certain limitations of this method, such as analysis in the remote server and the overhead of signal reconstruction constraints. For implantable neural decoding, the study of Xu et al. 2020 leverages a compressive sensing architecture through DL. The proposed approach aims to moderate overheads with enhanced wireless transmission efficiency. A two-stage classification process with a coarse-grained screening module and a fine-grained analysis module is also propounded. The front-end classification task is carried out by the screening module for fine-grained analysis, which transfers compressed data to a remote server.

The study by Xu et al. 2020, suggested a method for managing decentralized IoT applications that makes use of the Edgence platform, i.e., an edge computing platform with Blockchain support. In the Edgence platform, there are many master nodes, and each master node is made up of a complete Blockchain node and a collateral. Edgence's administration of decentralized AI training also updates AI models through feed-propagation and back-propagation. The first layers are trained by using a user dataset, and the later layers are trained at a remote cloud centre.

5.5 AUTOMOBILES, SMART TRANSPORT, AND AIoT

Vehicles and transportation have benefited greatly from the use of AI algorithms and methodologies incorporated into AIoT. Autonomous or self-driving cars are one example of this application. Future modern self-driving automobiles will be equipped with a variety of sensing devices (such as radar, LIDAR, and cameras) and produce enormous volumes of data (up to 120 GB ps) (Zhang and Letaief. 2019). An important problem that needs to be overcome is the safe and timely dispensation of device data for an effective reply mechanism to multifaceted scenarios like avoiding obstructions and velocity adaptation. Potential solutions include federated ML, safe trust models, and AIoT organized at the network edge. A method for leveraging Blockchain in intelligent driving edge systems has been proposed (Xiao et al. 2020). In order to maximize edge computing user and service provider satisfaction, a double auction method was used. The test results of Xiao et al. 2020 demonstrated that the strategy might provide greater resource use.

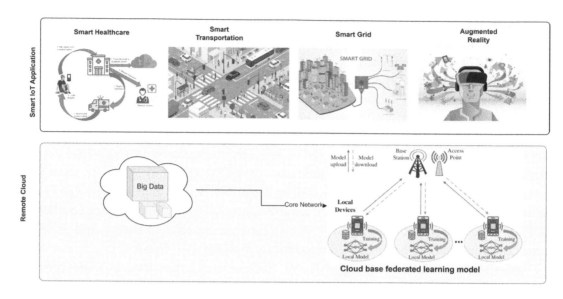

FIGURE 5.4   Endogenous Trusted Network (ETN) AIoT.

To assess the reliability of data produced by an intelligent transportation system based on IoT, there are sensor nodes involved. Authors in Dass, Misra and Roy presented the T-Safe trust evaluation scheme. Decision virtualization is a technique that is used by the safety-as-a-services architecture to offer end users safety-related information based on data produced by the sensing nodes. The authors assumed that the privacy of the identifying nodes, security, and reliability of data transmission determine the accuracy and effectiveness of such information. Figure 5.4 shows the Endogenous Trusted Network (ETN) for AIoT.

To solve this issue, the authors created a model for evaluating trust. To update trust measures on each node regularly, they made use of direct and indirect trust mechanisms. The trust of each data item created by the network is then assessed by using the trust measures. The authors developed an Integer Linear Programming (ILP) model to get the best information for making decisions while minimizing the impact of illegal nodes. The proposed system outperforms current techniques.

5.6 SMART HEALTHCARE AND AIoT

The data created by the Internet of Medical Things (IoMT) have been managed and processed using AIoT (Sun et al. 2020). An intelligent architecture was presented by Yang, Liang and Ji to handle visual data obtained from health systems, assisted by IoT, for which a processing method is required. Three modules make up their architecture: a cloud administration module, an edge control module, and an end processing module. The study of the sensor, machine, and human attributes produced intelligence on the other side. An intelligent measuring approach that the authors proposed is used to determine the intelligence on the edge and cloud sides. The proposed strategy could perform better than the current methods, as determined by their experimental findings. An IoT system based on AI is suggested by Mustafa et al. 2020 for identifying and categorizing stress. Their method involved measuring the physiological features by using a wearable device that is fitted with a variety of sensors. The user's mobile device is used to send the physiological data collection to the cloud. The data is analyzed by using an AI technique to determine the stress level. A mobile phone notifies the user of the anticipated stress level. The user's doctor would be notified in a circumstance with a high level of stress so the doctor may take the appropriate measures. Regarding real-time sensor data, their system achieved a binary classification performance accuracy of 97.6%.

5.7 ECOLOGICAL, SMART FARMING, AND AIoT

Smart agriculture, food processing, and environmental condition optimization have been the main areas of research using AIoT technology to boost food output. RiceTalk, an AIoT-based method for detecting rice blast illness is proposed by W.L. Chen et al. 2019. The plan is built on an IoT platform for soil cultivation. IoT sensors for agriculture are utilized to collect data, which the AI system automatically learns and analyzes in real time. Hyperspectral image or non-image data has been used in previous research to identify plant illnesses; however, these studies required human labor to take the photos and collect the data for analysis. The AI model is managed and treated as an IoT device by RiceTalk. This dramatically reduces the cost of running the platform to provide real-time training and prediction. The test results demonstrated that RiceTalk gives an accuracy of 89.4% for predicting rice blast.

5.8 AUTOMATION AND COMPUTER VISION IN AIoT

Robotics and computer vision applications have benefited greatly from AIoT. With the use of sensors and AI algorithms, robots can now collect and learn from data, becoming more intelligent. This has enabled robots to replace human expertise in healthcare, manufacturing, and other industries to complete jobs at a faster pace and cheaper cost (Velasco-Montero et al. 2019). Drones with AIoT capabilities are employed in smart cities for a variety of surveillance tasks, including real-time traffic monitoring. The speed limits and timing of the traffic signals are automatically adjusted based on the transmission, analysis, and usage of traffic data to help make decisions about the best method to relieve congestion (Dilshad et al. 2020). In order to respond to crisis circumstances when it is impractical to send workers, Lee and Chien 2020 built an AIoT architecture to manage surface, underwater, and aerial robots. The robots are used to gather information from a catastrophe scene and are connected to an IoT network. The data are sent from the field information systems to the cloud where a DL model is being trained over the IoT network. Once the model is trained and verified, the model is sent back to the robots via the field workstations so that item categorization may continue there. This will allow the robots to decide how to respond as they repeatedly validate their identification with the environment. For an AIoT setting, Kim et al. 2020 suggested a technique called Continuous Virtual Emotion Detection System (CONTVERB). IoT devices have wireless signal capabilities that allow them to deliver a signal to a person within their range and to catch the signal's reflection. There are at least four main types of human emotion, melancholy, joy, pleasure, and rage, that may be extracted from the reflected signal by the IoT devices through employing respiration procedures and a series of heartbeat segmentations. The effectiveness of the suggested system was demonstrated through simulations and implementations.

In a smart city, parking space occupancy can be detected using an intelligent edge computing approach (Ke et al. 2020). To spread out the compute load, edge AI and IoT are used. The amount of data that would be broadcast is intended to be minimal in order to accommodate bandwidth issues brought about by the real-time processing of video data. A Single Shot Detector For Mobile Networks (SSD-MobileNet) detector is implemented on IoT devices by using Tensorflow Lite, which is trained using the MIO-TCD dataset. On the server end, a tracking system is implemented to track cars in parking garages. During its three-month test period in a real-world setting, the system had a 96% accuracy rate.

A method which can be used for flaw identification in massive solar plants was put forth by Li et al. 2020. The flaw identification process was carried out using edge computing and UAVs in their method. In this study, the authors created a method for deployment on edge devices with limited resources that combines DL and text mining with data augmentation. In the network, methods were also employed to condense the model's parameters and size. The literature contains several other instances of AIoT for computer vision and robotics utilizing different methodologies. An approach to forecasting the performance of CNNs on vision-based AIoT devices was put forth by Li et al. 2020 Systems that offer AIoT video-based services presented a distributed learning strategy.

5.9 CYBER-SECURITY IN AIoT

A crucial component of AIoT is security. The research demonstrates that AIoT enables IoT devices to learn and make prompt responses in the presence of an anomaly or abnormal activity patterns (Wu et al. 2020). The proposed architecture for the IoT-enabled smart city that uses AI to prevent various current and imminent cyber-threats is proposed by Chakrabarty and Engels. A diverse, sizable, and complicated smart city system has a wide attack surface thanks to the widespread deployment of IoT in smart cities. Authors in Suresh and Madhavu suggested an Intrusion Detection System (IDS) with parallel processing and self-adaptation for an SDN network. The self-adaptive energy Bat Algorithm (BAT) is used for developing the AI-based IDS. The software layer analyzes incoming traffic packets in the early stages of their design process and selects features. Then the system categorizes the packets, and if an attack is proven, it controls and takes appropriate measures regarding network limits such as traffic management, routing, and resource allocation. The KDD CUP 99 dataset is used by the authors for training, while data from a real-time IoT platform are used for testing. In comparison to the swarm intelligence-based BAT algorithm, AI-based IDS performs better in the identification of significant features with minimum time requirement as a response mechanism along with a significant reduction in computational time and energy prerequisite.

Pass ban is the name of an intelligent anomaly-based IDS that is suggested by Eskandari et al. 2020. The system's deployment on affordable IoT devices and capacity for platform independence makes it unique. The authors wanted to make sure that data are harvested extremely close to data sources, protected, and could be evaluated for anomaly detection. IDS training is conducted by using a typical network flow. The trained model is stored in the internal memory of the gateway after training and utilized to identify attacks in incoming network traffic. The efficiency of the system is tested against prevalent cyber threats such as brute force attacks, port scanning, and Synchronization (SYN) flood assaults.

5.10 CONCLUSION

The convergence of AIoT, which is the incorporation of sophisticated machine-learning algorithms into resource-constrained IoT sensors and devices enabling broad and complicated sensor deployments in IoT infrastructures, is discussed in this chapter. The subject includes sensors and devices, communication, networking, and AIoT applications, among other levels and features of AIoT. This chapter also looks at using cutting-edge technologies to speed up the adoption of AIoT, including edge, fog, MEC computing, SDN, and 5G and 6G cellular networks. In order to enable the practical implementation of AIoT in increasingly varied and complex situations, the obstacles and concerns that must be handled are highlighted in this chapter.

REFERENCES

Chakrabarty, Shaibal, and Daniel W. Engels. "Secure Smart Cities Framework Using IoT and AI." *2020 IEEE Global Conference on Artificial Intelligence and Internet of Things (GCAIoT).* (2020). IEEE.

Chen, Wen-Liang, et al. "RiceTalk: Rice Blast Detection Using Internet of Things and Artificial Intelligence Technologies." *IEEE Internet of Things Journal* 7.2 (2019): 1001–10.

Chen, Xu, et al. "ThriftyEdge: Resource-Efficient Edge Computing for Intelligent IoT Applications." *IEEE Network* 32.1 (2018): 61–65.

Dass, Prajnamaya, Sudip Misra, and Chandana Roy. "T-Safe: Trustworthy Service Provisioning for IoT-Based Intelligent Transport Systems." *IEEE Transactions on Vehicular Technology* 69.9 (2020): 9509–17.

Dilshad, Naqqash, et al. "Applications and Challenges in Video Surveillance Via Drone: A Brief Survey." *2020 International Conference on Information and Communication Technology Convergence (ICTC).* 2020. IEEE.

Eskandari, Mojtaba, et al. "Passban Ids: An Intelligent Anomaly-Based Intrusion Detection System for IoT Edge Devices." *IEEE Internet of Things Journal* 7.8 (2020): 6882–97.

Gong, Chao, et al. "Intelligent Cooperative Edge Computing in Internet of Things." *IEEE Internet of Things Journal* 7.10 (2020): 9372–82.

Guin, Ujjwal, Pinchen Cui, and Anthony Skjellum. "Ensuring Proof-of-Authenticity of IoT Edge Devices Using Blockchain Technology." *2018 IEEE International Conference on Internet of Things (iThings) and IEEE Green Computing and Communications (GreenCom) and IEEE Cyber, Physical and Social Computing (CPSCom) and IEEE Smart Data (SmartData).* (2018). IEEE.

Hao, Meng, et al. "Efficient and Privacy-Enhanced Federated Learning for Industrial Artificial Intelligence." *IEEE Transactions on Industrial Informatics* 16.10 (2019): 6532–42.

Iqbal, Saleem, et al. "Automised Flow Rule Formation by Using Machine Learning in Software Defined Networks Based Edge Computing." *Egyptian Informatics Journal* 23 (2021).

Ke, Ruimin, et al. "A Smart, Efficient, and Reliable Parking Surveillance System with Edge Artificial Intelligence on IoT Devices." *IEEE Transactions on Intelligent Transportation Systems* 22.8 (2020): 4962–74.

Khalid, Bushra, et al. "An Improved Biometric Based User Authentication and Key Agreement Scheme for Intelligent Sensor Based Wireless Communication." *Microprocessors and Microsystems* 96 (2023): 104722.

Kim, Hyunbum, et al. "CONTVERB: Continuous Virtual Emotion Recognition Using Replaceable Barriers for Intelligent Emotion-Based IoT Services and Applications." *IEEE Network* 34.5 (2020): 269–75.

Kiyani, Faisal, et al. "ISDA-BAN: Interoperability and Security Based Data Authentication Scheme for Body Area Network." *Cluster Computing* 26.4 (2023): 2429–42.

LeCun, Yann, Yoshua Bengio, and Geoffrey Hinton. "Deep Learning." *Nature* 521.7553 (2015): 436–44.

Lee, Min-Fan Ricky, and Tzu-Wei Chien. "Artificial Intelligence and Internet of Things for Robotic Disaster Response." *2020 International Conference on Advanced Robotics and Intelligent Systems (ARIS)* (2020). IEEE.

Li, Xiaoxia, et al. "Edge-Computing-Enabled Unmanned Module Defect Detection and Diagnosis System for Large-Scale Photovoltaic Plants." *IEEE Internet of Things Journal* 7.10 (2020): 9651–63.

Liu, Deyin, et al. "HierTrain: Fast Hierarchical Edge AI Learning with Hybrid Parallelism in Mobile-Edge-Cloud Computing." *IEEE Open Journal of the Communications Society* 1 (2020): 634–45.

Lu, Haodong, et al. "Edge QOE: Computation Offloading with Deep Reinforcement Learning for Internet of Things." *IEEE Internet of Things Journal* 7.10 (2020): 9255–65.

McCorduck, Pamela, and Cli Cfe. *Machines Who Think: A Personal Inquiry into the History and Prospects of Artificial Intelligence.* CRC Press, 2004.

Mukhopadhyay, Subhas Chandra, et al. "Artificial Intelligence-Based Sensors for Next Generation IoT Applications: A Review." *IEEE Sensors Journal* 21.22 (2021): 24920–32.

Mustafa, Areej, et al. "Stress Detector System Using IoT and Artificial Intelligence." *2020 Advances in Science and Engineering Technology International Conferences (ASET).* (2020). IEEE.

Phan, Vu Hien, et al. "An IoT System and Modis Images Enable Smart Environmental Management for Mekong Delta." *Future Internet* 15.7 (2023): 245.

Qian, Jia, Sayantan Sengupta, and Lars Kai Hansen. "Active Learning Solution on Distributed Edge Computing." *arXiv preprint arXiv:1906.10718* (2019).

Savaglio, Claudio, et al. "Data Mining at the IoT Edge." *2019 28th International Conference on Computer Communication and Networks (ICCCN).* (2019). IEEE.

Shao, Ling, Fan Zhu, and Xuelong Li. "Transfer Learning for Visual Categorization: A Survey." *IEEE Transactions on Neural Networks and Learning Systems* 26.5 (2014): 1019–34.

Sodhro, Ali Hassan, et al. "Toward Convergence of Ai and IoT for Energy-Efficient Communication in Smart Homes." *IEEE Internet of Things Journal* 8.12 (2020): 9664–71.

Sun, Lanfang, et al. "Edge-Cloud Computing and Artificial Intelligence in Internet of Medical Things: Architecture, Technology and Application." *IEEE Access* 8 (2020): 101079–92.

Suresh, Geethu M., and Minu Lalitha Madhavu. "AI Based Intrusion Detection System Using Self-Adaptive Energy Efficient Bat Algorithm for Software Defined IoT Networks." *2020 11th International Conference on Computing, Communication and Networking Technologies (ICCCNT).* (2020). IEEE.

Teerapittayanon, Surat, Bradley McDanel, and Hsiang-Tsung Kung. "Distributed Deep Neural Networks over the Cloud, the Edge and End Devices." *2017 IEEE 37th International Conference on Distributed Computing Systems (ICDCS).* (2017). IEEE.

Velasco-Montero, Delia, et al. "On the Correlation of CNN Performance and Hardware Metrics for Visual Inference on a Low-Cost CPU-Based Platform." *2019 International Conference on Systems, Signals and Image Processing (IWSSIP).* (2019). IEEE.

Wu, Hui, et al. "Research on Artificial Intelligence Enhancing Internet of Things Security: A Survey." *IEEE Access* 8 (2020): 153826–48.

Xiao, Kaile, et al. "DAER: A Resource Pre-allocation Algorithm of Edge Computing Server by Using Blockchain in Intelligent Driving." *IEEE Internet of Things Journal* 7.10 (2020): 9291–302.

Xu, Jinliang, et al. "Edgence: A Blockchain-Enabled Edge-Computing Platform for Intelligent IoT-Based dApps." *China Communications* 17.4 (2020): 78–87.

Yang, Zheming, Bing Liang, and Wen Ji. "An Intelligent End–Edge–Cloud Architecture for Visual IoT-Assisted Healthcare Systems." *IEEE Internet of Things Journal* 8.23 (2021): 16779–86.

Zhang, Jun, and Khaled B Letaief. "Mobile Edge Intelligence and Computing for the Internet of Vehicles." *Proceedings of the IEEE* 108.2 (2019): 246–61.

Zhou, Jingyue, et al. "AAIot: Accelerating Artificial Intelligence in IoT Systems." *IEEE Wireless Communications Letters* 8.3 (2019): 825–28.

II

Data Communication Systems for AIoT Networks

CHAPTER 6

Networking and Protocols for AIoT Networks

Saleem Iqbal

Department of Computer Science, Allama Iqbal Open University, Islamabad, Pakistan

Syed Amad Hussain Shah, Saqib Majeed, Saud Altaf

University Institute of Information Technology, PMAS-Arid Agriculture University, Rawalpindi, Pakistan

6.1 A BLEND OF IoT AND ARTIFICIAL INTELLIGENCE

A network of interconnected physical devices having sensors and other embedded systems involving individuals and workflows is referred to as Internet of Things (IoT). These devices establish communication and exchange information with one another through the Internet, establishing a cohesive and interconnected system (Sung et al. 2021). The IoT has brought about a paradigm shift in engagement with the tangible realm and is capable of reshaping sectors like healthcare, production, transportation, and farming. The IoT enables enhanced automation and efficacy, increased safety and security, and elevated customer experiences. However, there are certain challenges that also come into play such as considerations that surround data privacy and security, as well as interoperability across diverse and converged networks. With the increasing proliferation of such interconnected devices, it becomes imperative to tackle these obstacles and necessary to establish standardized protocols to ensure the complete realization of IoT advantages while mitigating associated risks.

Artificial Intelligence (AI) grants machines the capability to execute tasks that conventionally require human engagement, encompassing aspects like acquiring knowledge from the surroundings, rationalizing decision-making processes, resolving problems based on accumulated information, and perceiving and comprehending specific scenarios (Fanibhare and Sarkar. 2021). The design process incorporates AI and its input into the computer through programs capable of scrutinizing and deciphering intricate scenarios, recognizing patterns, and potentially rendering decisions based on the resulting analysis (Nozari, Szmelter-jarosz and Ghahremani-nahr. 2022). AI finds utility in sectors like healthcare, finance, transportation, and manufacturing. A visual depiction of a standard IoT configuration is presented in Figure 6.1

DOI: 10.1201/9781003430018-8

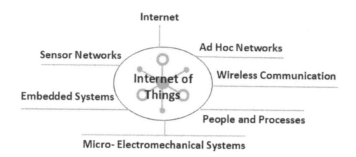

FIGURE 6.1   Elements composing the IoT.

AIoT represents the fusion of two compelling technologies, AI and IoT (Naseem et al. 2022). The making of AIoT includes diverse AI algorithms which are incorporated into embedded devices in order to elevate their intelligence and effectiveness (Seng and Ang. 2022). AIoT holds vast potential for diverse sectors encompassing the following:

a. **Intelligent Residences:** AIoT enables the development of smart homes capable of automatically adapting lighting, temperature, and other configurations in accordance with user preferences and behavioural patterns (Nandyala and Kim. 2016).

b. **Healthcare:** AIoT finds application in monitoring the real-time health of patients through wearable devices equipped with sensors, aiding in the early identification of health concerns, and delivering timely interventions. Additionally, it facilitates the automation of administrative responsibilities, such as fixing patients' appointments and issuing them timely reminders (Anwar et al. 2017).

c. **Manufacturing:** In this sector, AIoT presents opportunities for improving manufacturing processes by obtaining and analyzing data from sensors and machinery to forecast potential failures and proactively schedule maintenance. This aids in minimizing manufacturing plant downtime and enhancing overall system efficiency (Qureshi et al. 2020).

d. **Agriculture:** Monitoring crop health conditions and soil quality, automating irrigation systems, and forecasting weather patterns are some of the areas of the agriculture sector in which AIoT can play its role. These applications empower producers to optimize their crop yields while conserving water and other resources.

e. **Energy Management:** In most countries, especially underdeveloped and developing, energy management is one of the main challenges. The power of AIoT could be utilized for energy consumption monitoring within buildings or cities and could optimize its usage based on factors like occupancy or weather conditions. This supports the reduction of energy expenses and promotes sustainable practices.

f. **Transportation:** A good transportation system in any country is considered the backbone that pushes the economy toward the fast track. The AIoT offers possibilities for optimizing traffic flow, enhancing safety, and mitigating congestion (M. Ali et al. 2023).

6.2 AIoT NETWORKING STACK

The structure of AIoT networking can be broadly classified into four tiers: the initial tier is the Device layer, connected with the Network layer, followed by the Cloud layer, and finally the Application layer. The layers are built upon the preceding ones to form a cohesive framework as shown in Figure 6.2.

6.2.1 Device Layer

This layer is the base tier within AIoT, encompassing tangible devices, sensors, or actuators employed for collecting data from the physical environment (Lu et al. 2021). The sensors are capable of measuring various factors, including but not limited to temperature, pressure, humidity, motion, and light.

- **Sensing:** Data acquisition in the Device layer of AIoT entails gathering information from sensors integrated within IoT devices. These sensors have the capacity to perceive and quantify multiple physical aspects, including temperature, humidity, pressure, acceleration, and sound. Subsequently, AI algorithms analyze the collected data, discerning patterns, and deviations.

- **Partial Processing:** At the Device layer of AIoT, local processing involves conducting data processing and analysis directly within the networked devices, contrary to the usual practice of forwarding the data to the cloud for further processing.

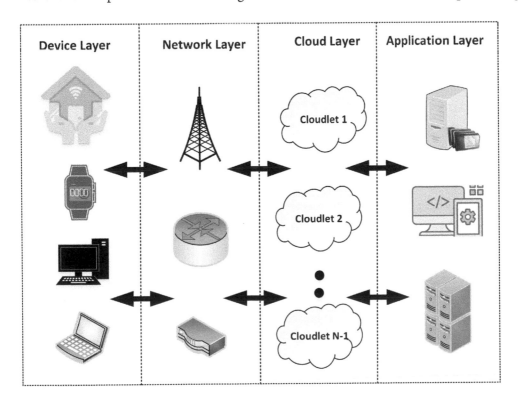

FIGURE 6.2   Networking stack architecture for IoT.

This optimizes the AIoT-based systems by minimizing the latency involved in between the data collection and decision-making phases, facilitating instant actions, and also lowering the dependence on cloud-based resources.

- **Transmission:** For the exchange of data from AIoT devices to either the cloud or edge computing devices, a proper transmission mechanism is required. Transmitting data within the Device layer of AIoT can present difficulties given the constrained bandwidth and computational capabilities of IoT devices, alongside the imperative of low latency and unwavering reliability. To tackle these hurdles, a range of techniques can be employed, including data compression and edge caching mechanisms. The Device layer encompasses an extensive array of components, spanning from basic sensors and actuators to sophisticated entities such as machines, Unmanned Aerial Vehicle (UAVs), and self-directed vehicles. These entities utilize diverse wireless and wired communication protocols to establish connectivity within the network, including but not limited to Wi-Fi, ZigBee, Bluetooth, Long Range Wide Area Network (LoRaWAN), and Narrowband IoT (NB-IoTs).

In the context of AIoT, the Device layer performs a core function in the acquisition of data and forwarding it to the Cloud layer for processing and deep analysis. The dependability and precision of the data acquired from these devices are imperative for making valuable decisions and gaining practical information, which can subsequently be harnessed to optimize functional operations, heighten efficiency, and curtail expenses. Consequently, the Device layer acts as a fundamental building block of AIoT, and the selection of appropriate protocols for the devices becomes paramount in developing a successful AIoT-enabled system.

6.2.2 Network Layer

The Connectivity (Network) layer in AIoT refers to the stratum facilitating the linkage among devices and enabling reliable communication among them. This layer incorporates various networking protocols and technologies, not only facilitating data transmission between devices but also transmitting data to the Cloud layer for further processing and analysis. There are different interacting technologies that find applicability within the Network layer of an AIoT system, including the following:

- **Mesh Networks:** Mesh networks are a famous networking technology that finds utility within AIoT systems. In this network, several devices collaborate to establish a network infrastructure capable of relaying data between devices, thereby extending the network's range. In a Mesh network (Hameed et al. 2022), each device enables data transmission and reception with other nodes. This attribute empowers Mesh networks to cover expansive areas and renders them valuable for diverse applications. Mesh networks have the capability to operate utilizing diverse wireless communication protocols, with ZigBee being a notable example as a protocol of choice for establishing Mesh networks within AIoT systems owing to its low-power consumption and capacity to support a substantial number of nodes. Additionally, Mesh networks can be employed for device control purposes, such as managing smart home lighting or overseeing industrial machinery in factory settings.

The major benefit of these networks in AIoT environments lies in their inherent self-healing capability. Should a node within the network experience a failure, other nodes can reconfigure data routing paths through alternative paths and nodes in order to ensure successful data delivery to its intended destination. This characteristic endows Mesh networks with enhanced resilience and reliability.

- **Cellular Networks:** The Cellular networks are considered best for ubiquitous coverage; these networks leverage mobile communication technologies like 4G or 5G to facilitate the transmission of data across extensive distances, rendering them well-suited for deployment in remote areas or for devices necessitating the requirement of high bandwidth. Additionally, Cellular networks are employed for device control purposes, enabling remote activation or deactivation of equipment and adjustment to device settings from a distant location. An inherent strength of Cellular networks within AIoT systems lies in their expansive coverage area. Cellular networks possess the capacity to span vast geographical regions, making them highly advantageous for applications involving precision agriculture, ecological monitoring, and smart automation. Another key benefit offered by Cellular networks pertains to their robust security features. Advanced encryption technologies are employed to ensure the confidentiality and integrity of transmitted data within Cellular networks. This attribute assumes particular significance within AIoT systems, where data privacy and security hold the utmost importance. Employing Cellular networks in AIoT systems does present certain limitations. A primary constraint is the potential costliness associated with utilizing Cellular networks, especially in big industries.

- **Wi-Fi Networks:** Wireless networks, like Wi-Fi networks, are also considered a compelling technology that finds applicability within AIoT systems. These networks establish connections among devices as well as facilitate their connectivity to the Internet (Famitafreshi and Afaqui. 2022). By leveraging Wi-Fi networks, data collection from sensors and other devices becomes achievable, subsequently allowing for the transmission of such data to the Cloud layer for further processing. In the realm of AIoT systems, Wi-Fi networks find application in a diverse range of scenarios, encompassing smart homes, healthcare, and retail domains. Notably, Wi-Fi networks offer the advantage of high-speed data transmission capabilities. Furthermore, they present ease of setup and versatility, enabling deployment in various environments ranging from residential settings to commercial establishments to public spaces. A key benefit associated with the utilization of Wi-Fi networks within AIoT systems pertains to their extensive adoption and widespread availability. Wi-Fi networks have achieved ubiquitous status, being pervasive in most households and public areas. This ubiquity renders them a readily accessible and cost-effective option for device connectivity. Moreover, Wi-Fi networks possess the capacity to accommodate a substantial number of devices concurrently, thereby making them well-suited for applications necessitating multiple device connections.

However, there exist certain limitations when employing Wi-Fi networks in AIoT systems. One such constraint is their restricted coverage range, which may render them unsuitable for extensive deployments or deployment in remote areas. Additionally, Wi-Fi networks may be susceptible to interference and signal deterioration within specific settings, such as densely populated public spaces or structures featuring thick walls.

- **Low-Power Wide-Area Networks:** The Low-Power Wide-Area Networks (LPWA) refer to communication links planned to enable low power devices connectivity across extensive distances while conserving energy. These networks also lend themselves to device control, allowing remote operations such as activating or adjusting equipment settings from a distant location. A notable advantage of LPWA networks in AIoT schemes lies in their energy efficiency. Furthermore, LPWA networks offer impressive long-range capabilities, enabling data transmission over substantial distances (Z. Ali et al. 2023). This characteristic renders them suitable for applications in remote or geographically dispersed locations. LPWA networks employ various wireless communication protocols, including LoRaWAN, Sigfox, and NB-IoT. However, it is important to acknowledge certain limitations when employing LPWA networks in AIoT systems. For instance, these networks may exhibit limited bandwidth, which could render them unsuitable for applications requiring high-speed data transmission.

- **Ethernet Networks:** Within AIoT systems, they serve as a means to link physical devices, such as cameras. These networks facilitate high-speed data transmission, enabling real-time processing and analysis of applications. The key advantage of incorporating Ethernet networks into AIoT systems lies in their substantial bandwidth. By accommodating high-speed data transmission, Ethernet networks prove advantageous in domains like video surveillance. An additional notable benefit of these networks is their trustworthiness. In comparison to Wireless networks, Ethernet networks demonstrate enhanced resilience against interference and signal degradation, rendering them a more dependable and stable choice for mission-critical applications.

However, there exist certain constraints associated with employing Ethernet networks in AIoT systems. One such limitation pertains to their physical restrictions whereby the installation of physical cables between devices becomes a necessity. Consequently, compared to wireless networks, the implementation and maintenance of Ethernet networks are more challenging and costly. Furthermore, Ethernet networks exhibit limitations in the way of the reporting zone, as the cable size impacts the maximum distance achievable between devices.

6.2.3 Cloud Layer

In the territory of AIoT networking, this layer typically refers to the infrastructure of cloud computing, which supplies connected devices (specifically IoT devices) with computing resources and services for the determination of fact execution and storage (Okafor et al. 2017). Additionally, this layer may encompass machine learning and AI algorithms capable of executing actions based on the amalgamated data from the source, extracting invaluable insights, and discerning patterns. Additionally, this layer possesses the capacity to facilitate instantaneous communication and harmonization among devices, thereby enabling them to collaborate seamlessly toward a shared objective. This layer undertakes the responsibilities of managing and monitoring IoT devices, administering software and firmware updates, as well as ensuring the security and confidentiality of data transmission (Raj. 2020). Such functionalities hold significant relevance, particularly within AIoT applications such as smart homes, where multiple devices must work in concert to deliver a smooth and integrated user experience. All in all, the Cloud layer within AIoT networking assumes a pivotal role by provisioning the requisite calculating assets, loading capabilities, and services essential for the computing of substantial data flows conveyed by network nodes.

6.2.4 Application Layer

The Application layer in AIoT systems serves as the repository of decision-making and intelligence capabilities (Upadhyaya et al. 2022). It undertakes the task of processing data acquired from lower layers, subjecting it to analysis through diverse algorithms and models, and subsequently furnishing meaningful insights and actionable outcomes based on the findings. Overall, the Application layer assumes a pivotal function within the AIoT network by supplying invaluable facilities and discernments to end users, capitalizing on the synergistic potential of AI and IoT technologies to amplify productivity, efficiency, and overall excellence of life span (Perwej et al. 2019). Networking represents an indispensable facet of AIoT, facilitating seamless data exchange and communication among AIoT devices and also with the back-haul infrastructure (typically in the cloud contemporary scenarios).

6.3 AIoT COMPUTING LAYERS

Edge computing pertains to the processing of data in close proximity to the network's edge, specifically at the level of devices or sensors. Edge computing proves valuable in situations where the utmost importance is placed on minimal latency and immediate processing. An illustrative example is the utilization of edge computing to handle data derived from sensors within autonomous vehicles, as any delays in processing could potentially result in hazardous incidents.

Fog computing pertains to the processing of data at the network's periphery, in close proximity to the source of the data rather than the cloud. This approach proves especially beneficial when dealing with data generated by a multitude of devices, where the data volume exceeds the capacity for edge processing. Fog computing serves to minimize network latency and enhance data privacy by locally processing the data. An instance where fog computing can be applied is in processing data from intelligent grids, where a vast array of sensors is employed to monitor energy usage. The concept of cloud computing revolves around handling data on remote servers located on the internet. Cloud computing proves notably advantageous in scenarios where substantial processing and storage capacities are indispensable. Its frequent application lies in analytics, deep learning, addressing situations, and machine learning where considerable data capacities necessitate processing. This computing may be harnessed to analyze data from smart cities, wherein an extensive array of sensors is deployed for monitoring traffic, air quality, and various environmental parameters.

6.4 AIoT PROTOCOLS

In the domain of AIoT, a group of methodologies has been adopted to elevate decision-making processes (Nozari, Szmelter-jarosz and Ghahremani-nahr. 2022). A few instances usually used are the following.

6.4.1 Machine Learning Algorithms

These algorithms play a pivotal role in scrutinizing data gleaned from AIoT devices and sensors, enabling the identification of patterns and making predictions. Additionally, Machine Learning (ML) aids in enhancing the precision of predictive maintenance and quality control efforts. In the realm of AIoT, one can find an array of ML algorithms in use (Dia, Ahvar and Lee. 2022), Here are a few examples of the commonly employed ones:

a. **Regression Analysis**: Regression Analysis (RA) finds practical application in predictive maintenance, anomaly detection, and trend analysis (Yuhao Wang et al. 2022). Below are a few instances showcasing how regression analysis serves AIoT:

- **Predictive Maintenance:** It enables foreseeing equipment failure through the examination of historical data. By scrutinizing device data (Zhang and Tao. 2020), encompassing pressure, temperature, and vibration, RA adeptly identifies arrangements indicative of a possible disaster.

- **Anomaly Detection:** Benefits from the implementation of regression analysis enables the identification of anomalies within sensor data. Through a comparison of present sensor data with historical records, RA proficiently detects unforeseen alterations in the data (Cook, Fan and Member. 2019).

- **Trend Analysis:** It offers a means to detect trends within sensor data as it evolves over time. Through the scrutiny of historical data, RA adeptly discerns patterns and trends that may elude a straightforward visual inspection. By analyzing historical data, RA can identify patterns and trends that may not be visible with a simple visual inspection. Generally, regression analysis is a powerful tool in AIoT for identifying patterns and relationships in data, and for making predictions about future outcomes. However, it requires a good understanding of statistical concepts and data analysis techniques to use them effectively.

b. **Random Forest**: It provides an ML technique that can be deployed in the domain of AIoT to enhance decision-making based on data collected from IoT devices and sensors (Thaseen, Priya and Xiaochun. 2022). The algorithm operates by utilizing diverse chunks of accessible data and structures. Every trained tree is on a distinct portion of data and features, with the outcomes amalgamated to form the ultimate prediction.

By employing different trees for different decisions, this algorithm yields more precise and resilient prognostications (Apat et al. 2022). Below are a few instances exemplifying how Random Forest finds application in AIoT:

- **Energy Optimization:** Benefits from the potential of Random Forest include offering an avenue to fine-tune energy consumption within intelligent buildings (Adli et al. 2023). Through the analysis of sensor data gathered from diverse rooms and appliances, Random Forest adeptly identifies the most effective configurations and dynamically adjusts them as needed (Forest et al. 2018).

- **Crop Yield Prediction:** It finds effective implementation with the use of Random Forest, enabling accurate projection of crop yields by analyzing environmental data, including temperature, precipitation, and soil quality (Kumar et al. 2022). Random Forest proves to be a formidable resource in AIoT for making predictions using intricate and erratic data. Its proficiency extends to managing substantial datasets and feature spaces of elevated dimensions, rendering it suitable for diverse applications. Nevertheless, achieving optimal performance necessitates meticulous calibration of the hyper parameters, and its computational cost may escalate for extensive datasets.

c. **Support Vector Machines (SVM):** SVM stands out as a well-liked ML algorithm deployed within AIoT for both classification and regression analysis. SVMs prove particularly beneficial in addressing intricate challenges within feature spaces of elevated dimensions (Padmaja et al. 2022). Their versatility extends to handling linear and nonlinear classification quandaries, and they find utility in both binary and multi-class categorization tasks. Below are a few instances illustrating the application of SVMs in AIoT:

- **Quality Control:** In the domain of quality control, SVMs serve to categorize products according to their attributes, encompassing size, weight, or colour.

- **Predictive Maintenance:** Benefits from the competency of SVMs include the fact that they can forecast equipment failure by analyzing sensor data. Through the examination of historical data, SVMs adeptly recognize patterns and correlations indicative of an impending failure. SVMs emerge as a formidable asset in AIoT, adept at addressing intricate classification challenges within feature spaces of elevated dimensions. They excel in managing non-linear associations among variables and exhibit considerable resilience to outliers.

d. **Neural Networks:** These are a form of ML algorithm integral to the realm of AIoT, encompassing forecasting and governance (Mania. 2012). Each neuron undertakes a basic calculation, akin to a subjective aggregation of ideas succeeded by a non-linear activation mechanism. Below are a few instances showcasing the deployment of Neural Networks within AIoT:

- **Predictive Maintenance:** Neural Networks have the potential to anticipate equipment failure by leveraging sensor data analysis. Through the examination of historical data, Neural Networks adeptly assimilate intricate associations between sensor readings and the probability of an impending malfunction.

- **Energy Optimization:** It finds a means of valuable implementation with Neural Networks, as they offer the means to fine-tune energy consumption in intelligent buildings (Himeur et al. 2020). Through the scrutiny of sensor data from diverse rooms and appliances, Neural Networks can acquire insights into energy usage patterns and make adaptive adjustments to the settings accordingly.

- **Object Recognition:** Object Recognition proves to be a domain where Neural Networks excel, as they can be harnessed to identify substances within videos or pictures acquired by IoT devices. Neural Networks stand as a formidable resource in AIoT, adept at resolving intricate and varied challenges (Liu et al. 2021).

6.4.2 Deep Learning Algorithms

Deep Learning (DL) algorithms make up a subset of ML algorithms that prove remarkably effective in addressing complex challenges within the domain of AIoT. DL algorithms are tailored to assimilate multiple layers of data representations, thus enabling them to encapsulate intricate connections and intricate patterns embedded within the data. Some examples are provided below of DL algorithms frequently deployed in AIoT applications:

a. *Convolutional Neural Networks (CNNs)*: The layers that exhibit full connectivity are accountable for the ultimate classification or prognostication. Below are a few instances exemplifying the application of CNNs in the realm of AIOTs:

- **Object Recognition:** Object recognition finds practical application with CNNs (Yadava and Chouhan. 2022), enabling the identification of objects within videos or pictures acquired by IoT strategies like scrutiny cameras or UAVs.

- **Medical Image Analysis:** Medical image analysis benefits significantly from CNNs, as they offer the means to examine medical images like X-rays or MRI scans for the detection of irregularities or disease diagnosis. Through training the network on an extensive collection of labelled medical images, CNNs acquire the expertise to discern subtle patterns and attributes that may signal the presence of a disease or medical condition.

- **Autonomous Vehicles:** In self-driving vehicles, CNNs showcase their ability to identify and categorize substances in the surroundings of a self-directed vehicle, including other walkers, traffic signs, and automobiles. In scrutinizing pictures obtained from diverse devices, CNNs furnish the vital data essential for the vehicle to execute judicious and precise actions.

CNNs serve as a potent asset in AIoTs for resolving intricate image and video recognition challenges. Their capacity to assimilate vast datasets and adapt to novel scenarios renders them well-suited for broad applications. Still, achieving optimal performance may entail the availability of substantial training data and meticulous tuning of the hyper parameters.

b. ***Recurrent Neural Networks (RNNs)***: By retaining an inner state that encodes the setting of prior inputs, RNNs excel in apprehending temporal relationships within the data Recognition. Their inherent ability to handle sequences of varying lengths renders them compatible with deployment in AIoTs. Below are a few instances exemplifying how RNNs can prove their benefits for AIoT networks:

- **Speech Recognition:** In the territory of speech recognition, this algorithm emerges as a formidable resource, enabling the identification of speech emanating from IoT devices like voice assistants or smart speakers.

- **Natural Language Processing:** In the domain of natural language processing, RNNs demonstrate their prowess by catering to an extensive array of tasks, encompassing emotion scrutiny (Sehovac, Member and Grolinger. 2020). By taking the text as input of an arrangement of characters or words, RNNs attain the ability to grasp intricate connections and arrangements inherent in the language.

- **Anomaly Detection:** RNNs are capable of detecting anomalies in time series data, including sensor data from IoT devices. RNNs can spot deviations from expected behaviour and trigger alerts or perform remedial steps by combining the data's usual patterns and linkages.

RNNs serve as a potent asset in AIoTs, excelling in handling evolving data and capturing temporal relationships within the data. Their capacity to undergo extensive training on substantial data volumes and adapt to novel scenarios renders them highly suitable for such applications.

c. ***Generative Adversarial Networks (GANs)***: GANs are a type of DL with potential application in AIoT scenarios for synthesizing lifelike and assorted facts (Dutt. 2021). The Generator Network is instructed to fabricate authentic data samples, such as sensor data, audio, or images from casual noise as input. Below are some instances showcasing the application of GANs in AIoT:

- **Data Augmentation:** It gains from GANs as they serve to fabricate synthetic data samples, amplifying the training dataset for ML models (Wickramaratne and Mahmud. 2021). This augmentation aids in elevating the models' precision and resilience, particularly in scenarios where the availability of training data is constrained.

- **Image and Video Generation:** The domain of image and video generation benefits from GANs since they excel in producing lifelike images and videos, proving valuable in diverse applications like autonomous driving and video surveillance. Through training, GANs acquire the ability to create novel samples that visually resemble genuine data.

- **Anomaly Detection:** The domain of GANs involves the creation of synthetic data samples that closely resemble normal data, facilitating the identification of real data anomalies that markedly differ from the synthetic counterparts. Such a method finds utility in detecting uncommon events or malfunctions in sensor data originating from IoT devices. On the other hand, training GANs can present challenges and necessitates meticulous calibration of the hyper parameters.

Within AIoT, DL algorithms prove to be formidable assets, capable of resolving intricate challenges entailing the handling of vast and intricate datasets. Nevertheless, they entail significant computational demands and may necessitate substantial training data and meticulous fine-tuning of the hyper parameters.

6.4.3 Reinforcement Learning

Reinforcement Learning (RL) operates on feedback signals. AIoTs can effectively incorporate RL algorithms, allowing AIoT devices to acquire knowledge and dynamically adjust to their surroundings as time progresses (Moerland, Broekens and Jonker. 2018). Here are some examples of RL algorithms used in AIOTs:

- **Q-learning:** A widely utilized RL algorithm, Q-learning finds application in AIoT settings by empowering devices in learning ideal policies for jobs, resource distribution, power controlling, and path routing. In the context of Q-learning, the agent acquires decision-making capabilities by continuously keeping informed of a Q-table that holds probable prizes for various state-action pairs. The Bellman equation is employed to iteratively update the Q-table, thus recursively enhancing the Q-function's value in light of the anticipated future rewards. These adjustments expand the horizons of Q-learning, enabling its application in diverse AIoT scenarios, such as automated grid controlling and manufacturing devices.

- **Deep Reinforcement Learning (DRL):** Deep Reinforcement Learning merges as a confluence of DL and RL strategies, proving valuable in AIoT applications to authorize IoT devices to acquire ideal policies amidst intricate and ever-changing surroundings (Yichuan Wang et al. 2021). In DRL, the agent acquires decision-making capabilities by leveraging a Neural Network, as encountered in RL algorithms. Deep Reinforcement Learning's set of rules demonstrates its versatility in managing high-dimensional state and action spaces, rendering them well-suited for diverse presentations like industrial automation. These algorithms are adept at decision-making even in environments with delayed rewards, showcasing adaptability to environmental changes over time. However, one of the challenges encountered with DRL is the computational expense involved in training deep Neural Networks on vast datasets. In AIoTs, RL algorithms serve as a potent asset, empowering devices to learn and evolve in sync with their surroundings as time progresses.

6.4.4 AIoT Communication Protocols

AIoT elevates Communication Protocols to a higher level by integrating AI and ML proficiencies into devices and networks. Below are a few of the frequently employed protocols in AIoT frameworks:

- **MQTT:** It stands for Message Queuing Telemetry Transport, an agile messaging protocol meticulously crafted for IoT gadgets and other networks with restricted resources. AIoT applications frequently embrace MQTT due to its adeptness, expandability, and minimal encumbrance. It relies on Transmission Control Protocol/Internet Protocol (TCP/IP) as its foundation and incorporates attributes like Quality of Service (QoS) grades, message resiliency, and session administration. In the territory of AIoT scenarios, MQTT can serve as a facilitator for inter-device and inter-service communication within a network. To illustrate, consider a smart home setup wherein MQTT fosters seamless communication among diverse devices like lights, thermostats, and security cameras. This interaction extends to a central AI hub. On the whole, MQTT garners significant popularity in the domain of AIoT applications due to its adaptability, efficiency, and adeptness in managing substantial data volumes in real time.

- **CoAP (Constrained Application Protocol):** It stands as a lightweight protocol crafted for IoT's resource-constrained devices and networks. It operates at the Application layer, leveraging User Datagram Protocol (UDP) as the underlying transport protocol, boasting simplicity, efficiency, and ease of implementation (Karagiannis et al. 2015). Within the domain of AIoT, CoAP finds relevance in facilitating communication between resource-constrained devices and cloud-based or edge services. Its suitability in AIoT applications arises from its adeptness in handling low-power, low-bandwidth networks, and devices, as well as its ability to offer secure communication via Datagram Transport Layer Security. CoAP serves as a pivotal protocol in AIoT, catering to diverse use cases like device control, fact gathering, and device-to-device messaging. For instance, CoAP finds application in controlling home automation smart devices, such as beams and sensors, while simultaneously gathering data from temperature and moisture sensors. Generally, CoAP's significance in the context of AIoT lies in its ability to enable efficient and secure communication among resource-constrained devices and other networked services.

- **AMQP (Advanced Message Queuing Protocol):** It stands as another frequently employed messaging protocol within AIoT applications. Similar to MQTT, it exhibits lightweight and efficient characteristics, yet it boasts advanced functionalities like message queuing, routing, and transactions. AMQP operates as a binary protocol with a client-server architecture, enabling seamless message exchange across devices and services within a network (Agyemang et al. 2022). It encompasses vital attributes such as message acknowledgments, directing, and filtering. Within the domain of AIoT, AMQP finds utility across diverse applications, including UDP streaming, result-driven schemes, and intricate scattered architectures. For instance, an industrial robotics setup with AMQP to govern the data stream among devices, controllers, and actuators, facilitating simultaneous switch and intensive care of industrial processes. This protocol's progressive capabilities render it well-suited for complex AIoT scenarios, where dependability, scalability, and security assume paramount importance. While it may entail more intricate implementation compared to MQTT, AMQP emerges as a potent resource for constructing refined scattered systems.

- **DDS (Data Distribution Service):** It stands as a widely employed communication protocol within AIoT presentations, mainly in organizations that necessitate more dependability and less delay. It is purposefully intended to facilitate real-time facts integration and distribution among devices and systems, employing a Distribute-Subscribe Model. DDS protocol that adopts a facts-centric methodology for messaging, prioritizing seamless data exchange among various modules of a scheme. This protocol also boasts progressive functionalities like data straining, caching, and QoS strategies. DDS emerges as a potent and powerful procedure for AIoT deployments, contributing progressive functionalities and extraordinary consistency that render it well-suited for critical real-time organizations. Whereas its implementation may require increased complexity compared to other protocols like CoAP, this protocol offers a level of accuracy and control that proves indispensable in certain requests.

6.5 CONCLUSION

AIoT has changed the traditional IoT network process by using advanced AI methods to manage the interactive devices and sensor nodes for data communication. Routing is one of the main requirements for data communication in these networks and provides the interconnection facilities among edge, cloud-based and AIoT networks to enhance user experiences through both wired and wireless mediums. This chapter discussed the existing communication standards, protocols and existing challenges posed by complex AI-enabled services and massive data processing in such types of networks. This chapter also discussed the prerequisites for AIoT networks, revealing data center networks, specialized mining networks, and protocols and communication standards for edge-based analytics networks. The findings of this chapter suggested the potential usage and improvements needed in existing protocols and standards for better services for AIoT networks.

REFERENCES

Adli, Hasyiya Karimah, et al. "Recent Advancements and Challenges of AIot Application in Smart Agriculture: A Review." *Sensors* 23.7 (2023): 3752.

Agyemang, Justice Owusu, et al. "A Lightweight Messaging Protocol for Internet of Things Devices." *Technologies* 10 (2022): 1–21.

Ali, Maisam, et al. "Decision-Based Routing for Unmanned Aerial Vehicles and Internet of Things Networks." *Applied Sciences* 13.4 (2023): 2131.

Ali, Z., et al. "Delay Optimization in LoRaWAN by Employing Adaptive Scheduling Algorithm with Unsupervised Learning." *IEEE Access* 11 (2023): 2545–56.

Anwar, Muhammad, et al. "Wireless Body Area Networks for Healthcare Applications: An Overview." *ELKOMNIKA (Telecommunication Computing Electronics and Control)* 15.3 (2017): 1088–95.

Apat, Shraban Kumar, et al. "The Robust and Efficient Machine Learning Model for Smart Farming Decisions and Allied Intelligent Agriculture Decisions." *Journal of Integrated Science and Technology* 10.2 (2022): 139–55.

Cook, Andrew, Zhong Fan, and Senior Member. "Anomaly Detection for IoT Time-Series Data: A Survey." *IEEE Internet of Things Journal* 7.7 (2019): 6481–94.

Dia, Issa, Ehsan Ahvar, and Gyu Myoung Lee. "Performance Evaluation of Machine Learning and Neural Network-Based Algorithms for Predicting Segment Availability in AIoT-Based Smart Parking." *Network* 2.2 (2022): 225–38.

Dutt, Niladri Shekhar. "Effect of Regularity on Learning in GANs." *Proceedings of the 2021 2nd International Conference on Control, Robotics and Intelligent System*. 2021: 163–68.

Famitafreshi, Golshan, and Muhammad Shahwaiz Afaqui. "Enabling Energy Harvesting-Based Wi-Fi System for an E-Health Application: A Mac Layer Perspective." *Sensors* 22.10 (2022): 3831.

Fanibhare, Vaibhav, and Nurul I. Sarkar. "A Survey of the Tactile Internet: Design Issues and Challenges, Applications, and Future Directions." *Electronics* 10.17 (2021): 2171.

Forest, Random, et al. "Hybrid Short-Term Load Forecasting Scheme Using." *Energies* 11.12 (2018): 3283.

Hameed, Shahzad, et al. "Connectivity of Drones in FANETs Using Biologically Inspired Dragonfly Algorithm (DA) through Machine Learning." *Wireless Communications and Mobile Computing* 2022 (2022): 1–11.

Himeur, Yassine, et al. "A Novel Approach for Detecting Anomalous Energy Consumption Based on Micro-Moments and Deep Neural Networks." *Cognitive Computation* 12 (2020): 1381–401.

Karagiannis, Vasileios, et al. "A Survey on Application Layer Protocols for the Internet of Things Research Motivation." *Transaction on IoT and Cloud Computing* 3.1 (2015): 11–17.

Kumar, Sachin, et al. "Sensor Network Driven Novel Hybrid Model Based on Feature Selection and SVR to Predict Indoor Temperature for Energy Consumption Optimisation in Smart Buildings." *International Journal of System Assurance Engineering and Management* 13.6 (2022): 3048–61.

Liu, Shicheng, et al. "Applied Sciences Application of Artificial Neural Networks in Construction Management: Current Status and Future Directions." *Applied Sciences* 11.20 (2021): 9616.

Lu, Zhao-xia, et al. "Application of Ai and IoT in Clinical Medicine: Summary and Challenges." *Current Medical Science* 41 (2021): 1134–1150.

Management, Residential Demand-side. "A Smart Home Energy Management System Using Two-Stage Non-Intrusive Appliance Load Monitoring over Fog-Cloud Analytics Based on Tridium 'S Niagara Framework for Residential Demand-Side Management." *Sensors* 21.8 (2021): 2883.

Mania, Khamis Al-mahallawi Jacky. "Using of Neural Networks for the Prediction of Nitrate Groundwater Contamination in Rural and Agricultural Areas." *Environmental Earth Sciences* 65 (2012): 917–28.

Moerland, Thomas M., Joost Broekens, and Catholijn M. Jonker. *Emotion in Reinforcement Learning Agents and Robots: A Survey*. Vol. 107: Springer US, 2018.

Nandyala, Chandra Sukanya, and Haeng-kon Kim. "From Cloud to Fog and IoT-Based Real-Time U-Healthcare Monitoring for Smart Homes and Hospitals." *International Journal of Smart Home* 10.2 (2016): 187–96.

Naseem, Shahid, et al. "Artificial General Intelligence-Based Rational Behavior Detection Using Cognitive Correlates for Tracking Online Harms." *Personal and Ubiquitous Computing* 27.1 (2022): 119–137.

Nozari, Hamed, Agnieszka Szmelter-jarosz, and Javid Ghahremani-nahr. "Analysis of the Challenges of Artificial Intelligence of Things (AIoT) for the Smart Supply Chain (Case Study: FMCG Industries)." *Sensors* 22.8 (2022): 2931.

Okafor, K. C., et al. "Leveraging Fog Computing for Scalable IoT Datacenter Using Spine-Leaf Network Topology." *Journal of Electrical and Computer Engineering* 2017 (2017): 1–11.

Padmaja, M., et al. "Grow of Artificial Intelligence to Challenge Security in IoT Application." *Wireless Personal Communications* 127.3 (2022): 1829–45.

Pawlyta, Magdalena, et al. "Deep Recurrent Neural Networks for Human Activity Recognition During Skiing." *Man-Machine Interactions 6: 6th International Conference on Man-Machine Interactions*, ICMMI 2019, Cracow, Poland, October 2–3, 2019. Springer International Publishing, 2020.

Perwej, Yusuf, et al. "An Extended Review on Internet of Things (IoT) and Its Promising Applications." *Communications on Applied Electronics (CAE), ISSN* (2019): 2394–4714.

Qureshi, Kashif Naseer, et al. "A Novel and Secure Attacks Detection Framework for Smart Cities Industrial Internet of Things." *Sustainable Cities and Society* 61 (2020): 102343.

Raj, Jennifer S. "A Novel Information Processing in IoT Based Real Time Health Care Monitoring System." *Journal of Electronics and Informatics* 2.3 (2020): 188–96.

Sehovac, Ljubisa, Student Member, and Katarina Grolinger. "Deep Learning for Load Forecasting: Sequence to Sequence Recurrent Neural Networks with Attention." *IEEE Access* 8.Ml (2020): 36411–26.

Seng, Kah Phooi, and Li Minn Ang. "Artificial Intelligence Internet of Things: A New Paradigm of Distributed Sensor Networks." *International Journal of Distributed Sensor Networks* 18.3 (2022): 15501477211062835.

Sung, Tien-wen, et al. "Editorial Artificial Intelligence of Things (AIoT) Technologies and Applications." *Wireless Communications and Mobile Computing* 2021 (2021): 1–2.

Thaseen, Sumaiya, Ikram V. Priya, and B. Anbarasu Xiaochun. *Prediction of IIoT Traffic Using a Modified Whale Optimization Approach Integrated with Random Forest Classifier.* Vol. 78: Springer US, 2022.

Upadhyaya, Animesh, et al. "Applications and Accomplishments in Internet of Things as the Cutting-Edge Technology: An Overview Abstract: Introduction." *Brainwave: A Multidisciplinary Journal* 3 (March 2022): 1–11.

Wang, Yichuan, et al. "Deep Learning Data Privacy Protection Based on Homomorphic Encryption in Aiot." *Mobile Information Systems* 2021 (2021): 1–11.

Wang, Yuhao, et al. "Real-Time Water Quality Monitoring and Estimation in AIoT for Freshwater Biodiversity Conservation." *IEEE Internet of Things Journal* (May 2021).

Wickramaratne, Sajila D., and Shaad Mahmud. "Conditional-GAN Based Data Augmentation for Deep Learning Task Classifier Improvement Using fNIRS Data." *Frontiers in Big Data* 4 (2021): 659146.

Yadava, Anil Kumar, and Vijay Chouhan. "A Study of the Progress, Challenges, and Opportunities in Artificial Intelligence of Things (AIoT)." *International Journal of Health Sciences* (May 2022): 2550–6978.

Zhang, Jing, and Dacheng Tao. "Empowering Things with Intelligence: A Survey of the Progress, Challenges, and Opportunities in Artificial Intelligence of Things." *IEEE Internet of Things Journal* 8.10 (2020): 7789–817.

CHAPTER 7

Novel Machine, and Deep Learning, and Training Techniques for AIoT

Muhammad Saidu Aliero

School of Information Technology, Monash University, Subang Jaya 47500, Malaysia

Yakubu Aminu Dodo

Architectural Engineering Department College of Engineering, Najran University, 66426, Najran, Saudi Arabia

Kashif Naseer Qureshi

Architectural Engineering Department College of Engineering, Najran University, 66426, Najran, Saudi Arabia

7.1 INTRODUCTION

Today, several research fields have combined the advantage of advanced Artificial Internet of Things (AIoT) techniques and Machine Learning (ML) to provide efficient and cost-effective functionalities. The evaluation and actuation functions aid in the creation of diverse practical solutions. Smart building is one of the AIoT network sectors that has gained a lot of interest, primarily for energy saving and individual comfort. In addition, smart buildings can help prevent and mitigate major and minor disasters within the building. Despite the fact that the majority of governments have special organization units that manage disasters such as earthquakes and fires, these disasters take an enormous toll on the scale of both resources and life (Muhammad S. Aliero et al. 2022). When this occurs, there are significant expenditures associated with building, equipment, recruiting, preservation, and learning. In the last few decades, many approaches for occupancy prediction have been presented. The majority of the research relies on past time series occupancy data to build prediction models. In general, the proposed approaches for occupancy prediction are divided into two types: statistical methods and ML methods. The statistical approaches use historical data to generate probabilistic models that estimate and assess the occupancy status of the number of people in the building.

DOI: 10.1201/9781003430018-9

The AI methods have adopted techniques, such as data mining approaches, that use occupancy prediction-related time series to determine the comparable nature of trend sequences for occupancy in the building. A decision tree is used to understand occupancy behavior trends and anticipate room occupancy levels (Zhou et al. 2020). Furthermore, a Random Forest (RF) is used to assist facility managers in improving building occupancy prediction (J. Zhang et al. 2021). Support Vector Machine (SVM) is used with an appropriate data extraction strategy to forecast the occupancy prediction in buildings (Tsai, Leu and You. 2016). Artificial Neural Networks (ANNs) are created for a variety of applications, including predicting building occupancy. The underlying properties of data retrieved from the Deep Learning (DL) algorithm's weakest to most advanced levels are far more accurate than those of the typical deep neural network. As a result, advanced architectures have significantly increased efficiency for modeling, classification, and visualization issues, and they have several implications.

7.2 CLASSIFICATION BASED ON SMART HOME TECHNOLOGIES

The smart home is one of the areas of AIoT networks where the smart system is used to manage the energy and usage of appliances and improve energy efficiency (Muhammad Saidu Aliero et al. 2021). Advanced AI methods are used to convert traditional homes into energy-aware systems, allowing programmed home management and processes that offer high energy savings potential and improve indoor occupants' comfort level. The AI smart home and building systems are classified into different technologies as follows:

- **Smart Heating, Ventilation, and Air Conditioning (HVAC) Systems:** These systems use a variety of sensors to track and control interior airflow. This technology's main objective is to analyze data from multiple sensors to improve the functioning of the HVAC system to increase occupant comfort and reduce wasteful energy use. Optimal energy usage and satisfactory interior comfort are the main aims of smart HVAC systems. On the basis of the data utilized as input to manage HVAC energy use, this technology is categorized into three groups including temperature and humidity, infrared camera, and carbon dioxide sensors (Muhammad Saidu Aliero et al. 2022; Qureshi et al. 2021). Smart HVAC systems perform better thanks to sophisticated ML and DL control algorithms that take into account both ambient temperatures and individual energy patterns (Iqbal et al. 2022; Naseem et al. 2022). However, the majority of the first category's solutions can't accurately capture the experience of thermal comfort, which leads to increased discomfort and energy use. In order to support the first category, the second and third categories were created. These categories estimate the total number of indoor occupants and then modify the airflow level in line with the number of people present, with the goal of keeping conditions at a comfortable level and preventing ventilation of empty space.

- **Smart Lighting:** Through the use of demand-response programs, wireless controls, and schedule control systems, smart lighting uses complex controls that combine occupancy with lighting and sophisticated dimming features to decrease overlighting and prevent unnecessary lighting of spaces. Every day, there is a growing need for smart lighting, particularly for impending rapid Light Emitting Diode (LED) projects for smart buildings and cities. Several smart lighting solutions (Qurat ul et al. 2018; Lin et al. 2021; Sambandam

Raju, Mahalingam, and Arumugam Rajendran. 2019) are available right now to demonstrate various fascinating gestures and emotions while emitting relevant colours. For instance, Philips Hue-Hue Go and the Logitech POP smart button offer ambiance and elegant colours to the home while also lighting it up, calming the atmosphere, and conserving energy. The attributes of the device type affect how smart lighting works. To prevent lighting up empty space, all devices still have infrared capabilities and brightness features. The sophistication of modern smart lighting technology is now at an all-time high.

- **Smart Plug:** It includes a wide variety of auxiliary and transportable home and office furnishings in building projects utilizing smart plug loading. In commercial buildings, almost all of the smart plug loads are managed via non-predictive control that relies on precise control. Contrarily, the predictive appliance control for residential buildings makes use of load detection or motion detection technologies to temporarily interrupt the energy supply to equipment that is not in use. By turning off tiny appliances when they are no longer needed, smart plugs significantly increase energy usage performance without requiring the user to be nearby or even at home. A portion of the current methods employ user behavior to determine how much energy is used. Smart plugs also utilized external information, such as energy prices, to determine how much energy is used by appliances.

- **Smart Window:** It uses intelligent window systems to regulate the amount of sunshine and solar heat that penetrates the building. Control mechanisms, such as active and passive window glazing that responds to changes in temperature or sunlight, as well as automated shade management that controls brightness throughout the day, are all examples of smart windows. Smart window solutions like those found in Zakirullin. 2020; Y. Wang et al. 2019; Dai, Liu and Zhang. 2020 can track a building's status and make decisions based on these updates to preserve suitable indoor comfort and save energy. However, only a small number of researchers consider how occupants' window opening habits affect interior ventilation and energy efficiency. The results show that smart windows employ ML to create occupant profiles in order to have a greater impact on energy savings.

- **Smart Energy Efficiency Application:** Smart energy efficiency application utilizes real-time data feedback in its intelligent energy efficiency technology. Studies in (D. Yang et al. 2018, Wang et al. 2019) used data that may be examined to estimate building energy performance and make proactive changes to minimize energy use, including occupancy behavior patterns, appliance energy profiles, weather forecasts, and various utility prices.

- **Human Operation:** Users may communicate with today's smart buildings using software displays that show building activity and energy utilization. On displays, the operator may monitor and assess all building data and receive warnings for any errors that the energy savings system detects (Zou et al. 2019; Vanus et al. 2017).

- **Distributed Energy Resources:** The technologies proposed in Barata and Silva use devices that supply power decentralized from the grid and autonomously create and store energy at the point of consumption. Examples include battery waste, rooftop solar photovoltaic systems, different grid technologies, integrated power and heat systems, and thermal storage.

7.3 CLASSIFICATION BASED ON AIoT DEVICE CONTROL APPROACHES

This section classifies the existing literature based on AIoT device control approaches.

- **Predictive Control:** This sort of control automates the handling of HVAC performance based on interior weather information gathered from sensors and occupant data to determine the likelihood that a room is occupied. Such occupancy information may be static or dynamic in real-time. In order to create an explicit controller for a group predictive control system, a model of the system is required (F. Wang et al. 2017). Typically, we would find such control by directly modeling the dynamics of the system or by using one of the parameter estimation techniques in system identification, and then construct a controller to meet the required design criteria. Using a smart grid or a timetable, predictive control relies on external warning signals that are supplied in advance. The current prediction algorithm in Muhammad S. Aliero et al. 2022; An et al. 2020 needs a scheduling system and predictive control values like cost, heat demand, or power generation to fulfill demand as cheaply as possible. This suggests that controllers must be aware of the proper input and analyze it in an effort to determine the ideal moment to use energy. Thus the control system must use the input data to get the best output possible from the process. A typical example that uses a more advanced controller which frequently uses inference rules is proposed by Aftab et al. 2017. The scheduling strategy often relies on precedents and practical resource restrictions to estimate job start and finish times, whereas rule-based strategies have specified membership functions and inference rules for control decision-making.

- **Non-Predictive Control:** This control uses research that heavily relies on occupancy-fixed timetables to create a model that predicts the likelihood that a building will be filled, and then uses that information to regulate HVAC operation. In a setting where occupation activities are carefully adhered to on a daily basis by a predetermined scheduling policy, this sort of control strategy may be useful. Commercial structures like offices, labs, and corporate environments are a fantastic illustration that fully utilized the control systems (Steyerberg and Harrell. 2016; Serra et al. 2014; Khalid et al. 2019; Lim, Song and Lee. 2016). This strategy, meanwhile, would not work well at a place where occupancy can skip or does not adhere to a set timetable. Most of the non-predictive control, such as that discussed in Brundu et al. 2017 and Cao et al. 2018, employed a binary algorithm that demonstrated that frequent OFF and ON tends to shorten the lifespan of electrical appliances. Because of this, more advanced (L. Yang et al. 2020) decision-control algorithms, such as fuzzy logic, were designed as improvements to binary algorithms with sets of values other than zeros and ones, giving context enabling additional choices for control to select.

These more advanced decision-control algorithms allow better control of vague and confusing information so that decisions may be made naturally. Many of the techniques are based on fuzzy logic-based intelligence computing in the smart building sector that uses thermal sensors to regulate the room temperature. The thermal patterns of the occupants were established based on guidelines suggested by the occupants to autonomously optimize energy use. Similarly, the principles of cost prediction and occupant satisfaction employ fuzzy logic to decide how to plan the usage of appliances based on several factors, including occupancy, external temperature, price of any sort, thermal comfort, modified schedules, and preferences.

- **Shiftable Appliances:** Are those appliances whose energy consumption demand may be postponed or stopped whenever the electricity price is at its highest. It is rarely possible that the expense of a shiftable strategy will be greater than the benefit of enhanced controls. To determine the control signal, traditional control methods, established programs and schedules, and rule-based approaches are employed. Having quick access to power grid voltage or rate stabilization is an excellent example of shiftable control employing model-based control. To secure the reliability of the power flow, internal forecasting command employs rules and processes that users install in a manner comparable to model-based control (Muhammad Saidu Aliero et al. 2021) Some non-predictive controls utilize data that travels over the barrier from the outside to the inside; however, this data mostly comes from cloud AIoT solutions, like IoTfy solutions applications to control information for prediction. Demand response is one example of such control (Aswani et al. 2012).

- **Non-shiftable Appliances:** These are appliances whose energy consumption demand cannot be planned or interrupted. Televisions, computers, and lighting systems are examples of non-shiftable equipment. One strategy used in the residential sector to prevent high electricity costs while demand is at its highest is the use of energy scheduling. With this system, occupants may postpone or delay power usage to certain times when the anticipated power demand is less. The schedule-based technique developed by Z. Zhang et al. 2019, Zhai et al. 2019, D. Yang et al. 2018, and Shakeri et al. 2017 is used to reduce energy costs and prevent the usage of appliances during times of high demand. For instance, it is possible to schedule accessible standby equipment to utilize energy when energy costs are lower so that other appliances in the house may use the energy that is kept within this appliance. Both runtime and a static technique may be used to provide this control.

In a static method, the rules for an occupant thermal comfort profile would be modeled using the weather and the user inside's activities. When the threshold of energy can be sold at a cheaper price, these methods enable smart energy regulation, which subsequently lowers the cost of energy use. By taking into account the demand for family economic satisfaction, these systems also have a tendency to minimize the local level of electricity output. For this purpose, a static timetable is an ideal choice for residents in a single building. The runtime technique creates occupant profiles for energy use based on weather forecasts and previous days' usage patterns. Conversely, a non-shiftable algorithm focuses on how control behavior is generated from the existing system state. Predictive algorithms, on the other hand, may be categorized according to the values that are projected and how a job schedule is managed. Since no forecast is ever accurate, handling assumptions might be crucial. Presently non-shiftable control is used for the majority of household appliance energy optimization. Real-time sensor data, such as that from PV power generation, temperature sensors, grid voltage, and cost data, can be utilized in estimating control decisions for energy-efficient controls. When projections are either insufficient or unable to provide more helpful information, this strategy is typically adopted.

7.4 METHODOLOGY

To train and test the proposed model in this chapter, datasets acquired in residential building settings are required. However, the recommended technique may also be used in commercial buildings, with the exception of chemical-based labs, where the quality of the indoor environment measurements and analytical settings are completely different from the scope of the research. The dataset utilized in this study was collected in a living room with year-round average temperatures of 25°C to 30°C. The data collection does not reveal any identifying or obvious behavior of the inhabitants and is largely anonymous to them. Numerous sensor modules have been installed in the living room to monitor interior parameters including temperature, light intensity, relative humidity, and CO_2 concentration (see Table 7.1).

7.5 EXPERIMENT

When ML algorithms are used to generate forecasts on data to quantify their forecasting accuracy, datasets are often split into the training and test ratios throughout the model training process. It is a simple and efficient strategy that aids in evaluating the output of ML algorithms and selecting the method that best fits the model prediction challenge. The process involves dividing the initial dataset into training and test ratios, such as 70:30 (Figure 7.1). The model is matched using the first part, sometimes referred to as the training dataset. The second part, known as the test dataset, is fed into the model as input along with the variables dataset to test the prediction and assess the outcome of the prediction.

7.5.1 Candidate Model

To further explore the parameters in ML architecture for an estimate, five candidate models have been chosen. These models are well recognized and frequently used as indicators of performance despite being less intricate and exciting than a lot of recent breakthroughs

TABLE 7.1   The Various Sensor Data Sources

Sensor	Detail	Measurement	Duration
Humidity	compute indoor relative humidity	Percentage	60 seconds interval
CO_2	compute indoor CO_2 level	Parts Per Million (ppm)	60 seconds interval
Temperature	compute indoor temperature	Degree Celsius	60 seconds interval
Light	compute Luminance Indoor Light Levels	Lux	60 seconds interval

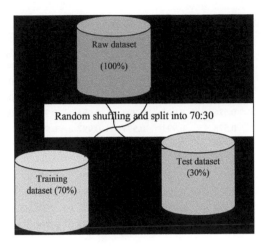

FIGURE 7.1   The ratio of training and test dataset.

in this field. These models also have the benefit of serving as the fundamental building blocks for many other applications than occupancy estimation, and as such, are currently extensively supported by machine learning libraries. The library documentation for the scikit-learn Python library, which is used in the configurations, contains information on the standard algorithm settings. This section's remaining paragraphs provide a high-level summary of the ML models that have been selected and their results for issues predicting occupancy in both binary and multi-class categories.

7.5.2 Random Forest

In order to forecast the behavior defined by training data, Random Forests (RF), the collection of different decision trees that are followed progressively from a root (parent) node to a terminal (or child) node, is used. This method offers a number of conditional rules that may be used simply as matching data samples based on shared characteristics by comparing sensor readings to a threshold. Bootstrap sampling, also known as bagging, is employed for each decision tree, using around two-thirds of the training samples for prediction and the remaining third to assess the accuracy of predictions for both deep and extremely deep trees. This suggests that while each RF tree is learning from different subsets of the training data, they are all working toward the same aim. The result of RF is presented in Table 7.2.

Table 7.2 shows how the RF classifier is assessed to confirm its efficiency forecast on fresh data. This is due to the fact that ML classifiers frequently perform well when evaluated against the original training dataset but strangely when assessed against a new dataset. As a result, the dataset record, divided into training and testing datasets, is stored in the scoring bin for accuracy. The binary prediction performance varies from 58.3% to 99.6%; for the F1 score, it ranges from 73.6% to 99.7%; for precision, it ranges from 58.3% to 99.9%; and for recall, it ranges from 97.8% to 100%.

7.5.3 Naïve Bayes Classification

Naive Bayesian (NB) is one of the most potent and successful classification methods. The Bayesian Theorem of Probability, which was initially put out by Reverend Thomas Bayesian

TABLE 7.2   RF Binary Occupancy Prediction Results Using CO_2 Data

Score Bin	Positive Rate	Negative Rate	Fraction Above Threshold	Accuracy	F1 Score	Precision	Recall	Negative Precision	Negative Recall	Cumulative AUC
(0.900,1.000)	1064	1	0.570	0.987	0.988	0.999	0.978	0.970	0.999	0.000
(0.800,0.900)	9	1	0.576	0.991	0.992	0.998	0.986	0.981	0.997	0.001
(0.700,0.800)	0	0	0.576	0.991	0.992	0.998	0.986	0.981	0.997	0.001
(0.600,0.700)	4	1	0.578	0.993	0.994	0.997	0.990	0.986	0.996	0.003
(0.500,0.600)	6	2	0.583	0.995	0.995	0.995	0.995	0.994	0.994	0.005
(0.400,0.500)	0	0	0.583	0.995	0.995	0.995	0.995	0.994	0.994	0.005
(0.300,0.400)	4	1	0.585	0.996	0.997	0.995	0.999	0.999	0.992	0.006
(0.200,0.300)	1	5	0.589	0.994	0.995	0.990	1.000	1.000	0.986	0.013
(0.100,0.200)	0	13	0.596	0.987	0.989	0.978	1.000	1.000	0.969	0.029
(0.000,0.100)	**0**	**755**	**1.000**	**0.583**	**0.736**	**0.583**	**1.000**	**1.000**	**0.000**	**0.999**

as foundation of the algorithm. According to the theorem, the probability of a hypothesis depends on current knowledge and previous information. It is a technique for assessing the impact of fresh evidence on the chance that a theory is correct. It has been applied to a variety of situations. The majority of machine learning algorithms focus on learning in an ongoing feature set in a real-world application. However, a number of classification tasks include continuous characteristics that must first be discretized in order to be addressed. The result of NB is presented in Table 7.3.

Table 7.3 shows that the RF classifier marginally outperformed the NB classifier in terms of accuracy, F1 score, precision, and recall, with performance values ranging from 58.3% to 99.1% for accuracy, 73.6% to 99.2% for precision, and 58.3% to 99.9% for recall.

7.5.4 Support Vector Machine

Unlike the Linear Discriminant Analysis (LDA) model, the Support Vector Machine (SVM) algorithm does not make the same assumptions while making predictions. Finding the border that maximizes the difference between the groups to be separated is how this method works, and it is always possible to do so in a high-dimensional space. By analyzing the connection between surrounding data samples and a selected kernel function, the

TABLE 7.3   NB Binary Occupancy Prediction Results Using CO_2 Data

Score Bin	Positive Rate	Negative Rate	Fraction Above Threshold	Accuracy	F1 Score	Precision	Recall	Negative Precision	Negative Recall	Cumulative AUC
(0.900,1.000)	950	1	0.510	0.926	0.932	0.999	0.874	0.850	0.999	0.000
(0.800,0.900)	44	0	0.533	0.950	0.955	0.999	0.914	0.893	0.999	0.000
(0.700,0.800)	30	0	0.549	0.966	0.970	0.999	0.942	0.925	0.999	0.000
(0.600,0.700)	28	0	0.564	0.981	0.983	0.999	0.968	0.957	0.999	0.000
(0.500,0.600)	16	0	0.573	0.989	0.991	0.999	0.983	0.976	0.999	0.000
(0.400,0.500)	18	15	0.591	0.991	0.992	0.985	0.999	0.999	0.979	0.019
(0.300,0.400)	1	20	0.602	0.981	0.984	0.968	1.000	1.000	0.954	0.045
(0.200,0.300)	0	45	0.626	0.957	0.964	0.931	1.000	1.000	0.896	0.103
(0.100,0.200)	0	42	0.648	0.934	0.946	0.898	1.000	1.000	0.842	0.156
(0.000,0.100)	**0**	**656**	**1.000**	**0.583**	**0.736**	**0.583**	**1.000**	**1.000**	**0.000**	**0.999**

TABLE 7.4   SVM Binary Occupancy Prediction Results Using CO_2 Data

Score Bin	Positive Rate	Negative Rate	Fraction Above Threshold	Accuracy	F1 Score	Precision	Recall	Negative Precision	Negative Recall	Cumulative AUC
(0.900,1.000)	4	1	0.578	0.993	0.994	0.997	0.990	0.986	0.996	0.003
(0.800,0.900)	6	2	0.583	0.995	0.995	0.995	0.995	0.994	0.994	0.005
(0.700,0.800)	0	0	0.583	0.995	0.995	0.995	0.995	0.994	0.994	0.005
(0.600,0.700)	4	1	0.578	0.993	0.994	0.997	0.990	0.986	0.996	0.003
(0.500,0.600)	6	2	0.583	0.995	0.995	0.995	0.995	0.994	0.994	0.005
(0.400,0.500)	12	0	0.583	0.995	0.995	0.995	0.995	0.994	0.994	0.005
(0.300,0.400)	18	15	0.591	0.991	0.992	0.985	0.999	0.999	0.979	0.019
(0.200,0.300)	1	20	0.602	0.981	0.984	0.968	1.000	1.000	0.954	0.045
(0.100,0.200)	0	45	0.626	0.957	0.964	0.931	1.000	1.000	0.896	0.103
(0.000,0.100)	0	42	0.648	0.934	0.946	0.898	1.000	1.000	0.842	0.156

border is found. Examples of kernels include sigmoid, radial, linear, and polynomial basis functions. The radial basis function will serve as the kernel in this method. The advantage of this strategy is that judgments may be made without having to cover the complete dataset since SVM just uses the data samples that are closest to the edge. The result of SVM is presented in Table 7.4.

Data from Table 7.4 show that the SVM classifier suffered when compared to RF and NB classifiers, with accuracy outcomes ranging from 58.3% to 86.7%, F1 score efficiency results from 73.6% to 87.7%, precision efficiency results from 58.3% to 99.9%, and recall efficiency results from 72% to 100%.

7.5.5 Artificial Neural Networks

Artificial Neural Networks (ANNs) are biologically inspired structures created for modeling estimates of modeling problems. During training, a variety of variables are predicted using sample data. The model in charge of the data in the neural net scheme is learned via the use of a number of dependent and independent variables. Each neuron makes up one of these networks. Typically, precise learning algorithms are used to determine the weights of connections between neurons. A neural network with two hidden layers and an identical combination of neuron numbers in each layer was tested using the dataset. The network mistake is carried backward from the output layer to the input layer using the backpropagation technique. The result of ANN is presented in Table 7.5.

The efficiency results for ANN vary from 58.3% to 99.5% for accuracy, 73.6% to 99.6% for F1 score, 58.3% to 99.9% for precision, and 95.3% to 100% recall (see Table 7.5). ANN classifier also outperformed NV.

7.5.6 Logistic Regression

With a variable that is dependent that has two possible values results and one or many independent variables, Logistic Regression (LR) estimates a dependent variable in logistic settings. In order to determine which independent variable is acceptable for forecasting based on the variable, the independent variables are assessed using the dataset and often

TABLE 7.5   ANN Binary Occupancy Prediction Results Using CO_2 Data

Score Bin	Positive Rate	Negative Rate	Fraction Above Threshold	Accuracy	F1 Score	Precision	Recall	Negative Precision	Negative Recall	Cumulative AUC
(0.900,1.000)	1036	1	0.556	0.972	0.976	0.999	0.953	0.938	0.999	0.000
(0.800,0.900)	8	0	0.560	0.976	0.979	0.999	0.960	0.948	0.999	0.000
(0.700,0.800)	12	0	0.566	0.983	0.985	0.999	0.971	0.962	0.999	0.000
(0.600,0.700)	5	0	0.569	0.986	0.987	0.999	0.976	0.968	0.999	0.000
(0.500,0.600)	4	0	0.571	0.988	0.989	0.999	0.980	0.973	0.999	0.000
(0.400,0.500)	9	3	0.578	0.991	0.992	0.996	0.988	0.984	0.995	0.004
(0.300,0.400)	9	1	0.583	0.995	0.996	0.995	0.996	0.995	0.994	0.005
(0.200,0.300)	1	5	0.586	0.993	0.994	0.991	0.997	0.996	0.987	0.011
(0.100,0.200)	1	17	0.596	0.984	0.987	0.976	0.998	0.997	0.965	0.033
(0.000,0.100)	**2**	**752**	**1.000**	**0.583**	**0.736**	**0.583**	**1.000**	**1.000**	**0.000**	**0.999**

using a maximum-likelihood computation. When there are no or few interaction factors and variable transformations are used, there is a limited potential for model complexity in logistic regression. Overfitting is less of an issue in this case. Variable selection is a technique for decreasing the variability of a model and, hence, the risk of overfitting, but it may also reduce the model's adaptability. Table 7.6 displays the results analysis of the LR for binary occupancy prediction.

Finally, the results in Table 7.6 for the LR classifier show that while it performed better than the SVM classifier prediction, it performed poorly when compared to RF, NB, and ANN classifiers. The results for performance ranged from 58.3% to 96.6% for accuracy, 73.6% to 97.1% for F1 score, 58.3% to 99.9% for precision, and 67% to 100% recall.

7.6 MODEL VALIDATION

In contrast to binary occupancy prediction, which employs a single variable parameter (CO_2) to determine whether the room is filled or not, this section deals with the multi-class occupancy estimate problem utilizing five distinct ML techniques. Table 7.7 presents their performance analysis findings.

TABLE 7.6   LR Binary Occupancy Prediction Using CO_2 Data

Score Bin	Positive Rate	Negative Rate	Fraction Above Threshold	Accuracy	F1 Score	Precision	Recall	Negative Precision	Negative Recall	Cumulative AUC
(0.900,1.000)	9	3	0.578	0.991	0.992	0.996	0.988	0.984	0.995	0.004
(0.800,0.900)	9	1	0.583	0.995	0.996	0.995	0.996	0.995	0.994	0.005
(0.700,0.800)	1	5	0.586	0.993	0.994	0.991	0.997	0.996	0.987	0.011
(0.600,0.700)	1	17	0.596	0.984	0.987	0.976	0.998	0.997	0.965	0.033
(0.500,0.600)	9	3	0.578	0.991	0.992	0.996	0.988	0.984	0.995	0.004
(0.400,0.500)	9	1	0.583	0.995	0.996	0.995	0.996	0.995	0.994	0.005
(0.300,0.400)	1	5	0.586	0.993	0.994	0.991	0.997	0.996	0.987	0.011
(0.200,0.300)	0	139	0.727	0.855	0.890	0.801	1.000	1.000	0.653	0.344
(0.100,0.200)	0	105	0.783	0.799	0.853	0.744	1.000	1.000	0.519	0.479
(0.000,0.100)	0	404	1.000	0.583	0.736	0.583	1.000	1.000	0.000	0.998

TABLE 7.7   Five ML Prediction Results on Multi-class Occupancy Estimation Using Different Evaluation Metrics

Parameters	SVM	RF	ANN	LR	NB
Mean Absolute Error	0.99722211	0.997222	0.98778	0.113427	0.987781
Relative Absolute Error	0.11342742	0.022869	0.113427	0.010241	0.010789
Coefficient of Determination	0.982471709	0.994745	0.982472	0.814167	0.814133
Precision	0.999062	0.997222	0.999062	0.999006	0.999065
Recall	0.814167433	0.98989	0.979761	0.924563	0.982521
F-Score	0.11342742	0.022869	0.113427	0.010241	0.010789
AUC	0.982471709	0.994745	0.982472	0.814167	0.814133
Average Log Loss	0.999062	0.997222	0.999062	0.999006	0.999065

The accuracy of the model decreases as the number of occupants in the room grows since the multi-class occupancy estimation classifier employs five variable parameters to predict the number of people present in the space. It is crucial to verify the model and compare the assessment findings to determine whether the approach is suitable for solving the multi-class occupancy estimation issue in order to make sure the model generates trustworthy results on fresh datasets. Since the accuracy metric frequently falls short of meeting this decision-making need, other metrics are taken into account as explained in this section.

7.7 CONCLUSION

The development of AIoT technical ideas intended to lower excessive energy usage in buildings is the smart home energy management system. Researchers have put forth a variety of methodologies and tactics to forecast whether building occupants will be able to prevent needless HVAC in unoccupied spaces. This chapter reviewed articles on smart buildings. Current research emphasis is focused on employing algorithms that work best in commercial buildings with a fixed schedule for the occupants but perform poorly in residential structures. This research also demonstrates that the most effective methods for bridging the gap between HVAC energy-saving and acceptable interior thermal comfort levels are camera-based imaging and video processing methodologies. Additionally, this chapter also used interactive learning approaches and a rule-based classifier to merge the data from the camera and environmental sensing with other sensors, actuators, and analytical data methods. With over 40,000 records and the most realistic and difficult setting available for building occupancy prediction right now, this research created a brand-new, complete public collection of training datasets. To the best of our knowledge, this work is also the first to consider a multimodal input to a single output regression model through the mining and mapping of feature significance, which has advantages over statistical techniques, and to achieve a robust occupancy count in AIoT smart home systems. The suggested approach is examined using a prototype system in a living room.

REFERENCES

A, J. Chandramohan, et al. "Intelligent Smart Home Automation and Security System Using Arduino and Wi-Fi." *International Journal of Engineering and Computer Science* 6.3 (2017): 20694–8.

Aftab, Muhammad, et al. "Automatic HVAC Control with Real-Time Occupancy Recognition and Simulation-Guided Model Predictive Control in Low-Cost Embedded System." *Energy and Buildings* 154 (2017): 141–56.

Aliero, Muhammad S, et al. "Non-Intrusive Room Occupancy Prediction Performance Analysis Using Different Machine Learning Techniques." *Energies* 15.23 (2022): 9231.

Aliero, Muhammad Saidu, et al. "Smart Home Energy Management Systems in Internet of Things Networks for Green Cities Demands and Services." *Environmental Technology & Innovation* 22 (2021): 101443.

An, C., et al. "Machine Learning Prediction for Mortality of Patients Diagnosed with Covid-19: A Nationwide Korean Cohort Study." *Scientific Reports* 10.1 (2020): 18716.

Aswani, A., et al. "Reducing Transient and Steady State Electricity Consumption in HVAC Using Learning-Based Model-Predictive Control." *Proceedings of the IEEE* 100.1 (2012): 240–53.

Barata, Filipe A., and R. N. Silva. "Distributed Model Predictive Control for Housing with Hourly Auction of Available Energy." *Technological Innovation for the Internet of Things: 4th IFIP WG 5.5/SOCOLNET Doctoral Conference on Computing, Electrical and Industrial Systems, DoCEIS 2013*, Costa de Caparica, Portugal, April 15–17, 2013. Proceedings 4. Springer Berlin Heidelberg, 2013.

Brundu, Francesco Gavino, et al. "IoT Software Infrastructure for Energy Management and Simulation in Smart Cities." *IEEE Transactions on Industrial Informatics* 13.2 (2017): 832–40.

Cao, Ningyuan, et al. "Smart Sensing for HVAC Control: Collaborative Intelligence in Optical and IR Cameras." *IEEE Transactions on Industrial Electronics* 65.12 (2018): 9785–94.

Dai, Xilei, Junjie Liu, and Xin Zhang. "A Review of Studies Applying Machine Learning Models to Predict Occupancy and Window-Opening Behaviours in Smart Buildings." *Energy and Buildings* 223 (2020): 110159.

Iqbal, Saleem, et al. "Automised Flow Rule Formation by Using Machine Learning in Software Defined Networks Based Edge Computing." *Egyptian Informatics Journal* 23.1 (2022): 149–57.

Khalid, Rabiya, et al. "Fuzzy Energy Management Controller and Scheduler for Smart Homes." *Sustainable Computing: Informatics and Systems* 21 (2019): 103–18.

Lang, Bo, Jinmiao Wang, and Zhenhai Cao. "Multidimensional Data Tight Aggregation and Fine-Grained Access Control in Smart Grid." *Journal of Information Security and Applications* 40 (2018): 156–65.

Lim, Jin-Sun, Ki-Il Song, and Hang-Lo Lee. "Real-Time Location Tracking of Multiple Construction Laborers." *Sensors (Basel)* 16.11 (2016): 1869.

Lin, Jing, et al. "Thermo and Light-Responsive Strategies of Smart Titanium-Containing Composite Material Surface for Enhancing Bacterially Anti-Adhesive Property." *Chemical Engineering Journal* 407 (2021).

Naseem, Shahid, et al. "Artificial General Intelligence-Based Rational Behavior Detection Using Cognitive Correlates for Tracking Online Harms." *Personal and Ubiquitous Computing* (2022): 119–37.

Qurat ul, Ain, et al. "IoT Operating System Based Fuzzy Inference System for Home Energy Management System in Smart Buildings." *Sensors (Basel)* 18.9 (2018): 2802.

Qureshi, Kashif Naseer, et al. "Trust Aware Energy Management System for Smart Homes Appliances." *Computers & Electrical Engineering* (2021): 107641.

Sambandam Raju, P., M. Mahalingam, and R. Arumugam Rajendran. "Design, Implementation and Power Analysis of Pervasive Adaptive Resourceful Smart Lighting and Alerting Devices in Developing Countries Supporting Incandescent and Led Light Bulbs." *Sensors (Basel)* 19.9 (2019): 1–20.

Serra, Jordi, et al. "Smart HVAC Control in IoT: Energy Consumption Minimization with User Comfort Constraints." *Scientific World Journal* 2014 (2014): 161874.

Shakeri, Mohammad, et al. "An Intelligent System Architecture in Home Energy Management Systems (Hems) for Efficient Demand Response in Smart Grid." *Energy and Buildings* 138 (2017): 154–64.

Steyerberg, E. W., and F. E. Harrell, Jr. "Prediction Models Need Appropriate Internal, Internal-External, and External Validation." *Journal of Clinical Epidemiology* 69 (2016): 245–7.

Tsai, Kun-Lin, Fang-Yie Leu, and Ilsun You. "Residence Energy Control System Based on Wireless Smart Socket and IoT." *IEEE Access* 4 (2016): 2885–94.

Vanus, Jan, et al. "Monitoring of the Daily Living Activities in Smart Home Care." *Human-centric Computing and Information Sciences* 7.1 (2017): 1–34.

Wang, Fulin, et al. "Predictive Control of Indoor Environment Using Occupant Number Detected by Video Data and CO_2 Concentration." *Energy and Buildings* 145 (2017): 155–62.

Wang, Yu, et al. "Tungsten-Doped VO_2/Starch Derivative Hybrid Nanothermochromic Hydrogel for Smart Window." *Nanomaterials (Basel)* 9.7 (2019): 970.

Yang, Dan, et al. "Passive Infrared (PIR)-Based Indoor Position Tracking for Smart Homes Using Accessibility Maps and A-Star Algorithm." *Sensors (Basel)* 18.2 (2018): 332.

Yang, Lijian, et al. "Independent Control of Temperature and Humidity in Air Conditioners by Using Fuzzy Sliding Mode Approach." *Complexity* 2020 (2020): 1–12.

Zakirullin, Rustam S. "A Smart Window for Angular Selective Filtering of Direct Solar Radiation." *Journal of Solar Energy Engineering* 142.1 (2020): 011001.

Zhai, Shaopeng, et al. "Appliance Flexibility Analysis Considering User Behavior in Home Energy Management System Using Smart Plugs." *IEEE Transactions on Industrial Electronics* 66.2 (2019): 1391–401.

Zhang, Jin, et al. "Data Augmentation and Dense-LSTM for Human Activity Recognition Using WiFi Signal." *IEEE Internet of Things Journal* 8.6 (2021): 4628–41.

Zhang, Zhisheng, et al. "Optimal Scheduling Model for Smart Home Energy Management System Based on the Fusion Algorithm of Harmony Search Algorithm and Particle Swarm Optimization Algorithm." *Science and Technology for the Built Environment* 26.1 (2019): 42–51.

Zhou, Xiaokang, et al. "Deep-Learning-Enhanced Human Activity Recognition for Internet of Healthcare Things." *IEEE Internet of Things Journal* 7.7 (2020): 6429–38.

Zou, Han, et al. "Multiple Kernel Semi-Representation Learning with Its Application to Device-Free Human Activity Recognition." *IEEE Internet of Things Journal* 6.5 (2019): 7670–80.

CHAPTER 8

Role of Blockchain Models for AIoT Communication Systems

Ibrahim Tariq Javed

Blockchain@UBC, University of British Columbia, Vancouver Canada

Kashif Naseer Qureshi

Department of Electronic & Computer Engineering, University of Limerick, V94 T9PX Limerick, Ireland

8.1 INTRODUCTION

Artificial Intelligence of Things (AIoT) is an emerging field that has evolved in recent years as a result of the convergence of Artificial Intelligence (AI) with the Internet of Things (IoT) (Mohamed. 2020). This emerging paradigm blends the capabilities of AI with IoT technologies to create a dynamic ecosystem where intelligent devices, data-driven insights, and autonomous decision-making converge. As a result, industry and daily life have been transformed. AIoT systems create large volumes of data that devices can process and analyze to produce in-the-moment insights and proactive decision-making (Hansen and Bøgh. 2021). AIoT may anticipate user requirements, system faults, and trends using predictive analytics, resulting in smooth and customized experiences. Additionally, AIoT devices have cognitive capacities that allow them to learn from previous mistakes and modify their behavior in response to a variety of dynamic settings. AIoT systems encounter several significant issues that impede their efficient and secure functioning. To begin, building trust and guaranteeing security among AIoT devices are top priorities (Yang et al. 2021). First, traditional centralized systems may be vulnerable to cyber-attacks and data breaches, putting data integrity and user privacy at risk. Second, it is vital to ensure the accuracy and provenance of the massive volumes of data created by AIoT devices (Naseem et al. 2022). Without a visible and permanent record, tracking the origin and history of data becomes difficult, which can impede decision-making and impair the credibility of insights obtained from AIoT systems (Zhang and Tao. 2020). Additionally, obstacles to ensuring smooth data interchange and communication across AIoT components are presented by the compatibility of various devices, protocols, and data formats. Inefficiencies and poor teamwork may result from a lack of established communication channels. Last but not least, protecting user privacy in the face of huge data collection and processing by AIoT devices is a continuing worry that calls for strict adherence to data protection laws and privacy protection

DOI: 10.1201/9781003430018-10

mechanisms (Xiong et al. 2021). To fully utilize AIoT and ensure the reliable, secure, and effective operation of AIoT communication systems, these issues must be resolved.

Blockchain technology seems a possible remedy to these issues, providing special capabilities that help strengthen AIoT networks. Blockchain is a ledger technology distributed across multiple nodes to maintain immutable transactions to ensure high transparency and security (Guo and Yu. 2022). Since every node on the Blockchain network maintains a duplicate copy of the database, it is regarded as a decentralized database. Before storing a new transaction in the database, each node on the network verifies it. Transactions are grouped into a block that cannot be altered or deleted once added to the Blockchain (Rajasekaran, Azees and Al-Turjman. 2022). Therefore, all transactions remain visible to the network nodes, making it transparent and difficult to hide malicious activities. This makes Blockchain suitable technology to store and maintain data in various areas such as banking, healthcare, and supply chain management (Krichen et al. 2020). In addition, Blockchain technology has improved data security, transparency, accountability, and reliability in multiple applications. Stakeholders may improve the reliability of data transfers, encourage secure cooperation, and provide the groundwork for a more effective and decentralized AIoT ecosystem by incorporating Blockchain into AIoT communication platforms (Wang et al. 2019; Qureshi, Jeon and Piccialli. 2020). Blockchain technology is set to alter the way linked devices interact and communicate as it continues to develop, spurring innovation and defining the future of interconnected systems.

Blockchain technology is well-suited for usage in AI applications. It provides many advantages when utilized in combination with AI systems. Its primary use is to provide data accuracy to train AI models (Ekramifard et al. 2020). AI models are often only as good as the data on which they are trained. The final AI model will be flawed if the data is correct, biased, or complete (Whang et al. 2023). By using Blockchain to validate the legitimacy and integrity of the data needed to train AI algorithms, we can ensure that the resulting models are more accurate and reliable. Blockchain can enable AI models to be trained on decentralized trusted data sources to solve complex problems. Another advantage Blockchain can provide is a marketplace for AI services where developers can securely share their AI models. Finally, Blockchain might be used to incentivize data sharing in AI systems. By employing Blockchain to create a decentralized marketplace for data exchange, we can incentivize individuals and organizations to share their data with others. Consequently, the dataset will be more robust and diverse for training AI models.

In AIoT, Blockchain can provide significant benefits, including improved data integrity, decentralized systems, privacy, and incentivized data sharing (Mohanta et al. 2020). As these technologies evolve, we expect to see more innovative uses of Blockchain in AIoT applications. In this chapter, we look at the inherent characteristics of Blockchain technology that make it particularly well-suited for AIoT applications. Furthermore, we investigate how Blockchain contributes considerably to the growth of AIoT by concentrating on important topics such as Device Identity and Authentication, Data Exchange and Monetization, Smart Contracts and Automation, and Federated Learning. This chapter goes on to discuss the creation and deployment of numerous Blockchain initiatives targeted at aiding AI applications. The first project, called Ocean Protocol (McConaghy. 2022), is a platform for exchanging data on a Blockchain that is intended for AI applications. It encourages a cooperative environment for AI innovation by empowering data owners to safely and openly commercialize and share their data. SingularityNET (Liu et al. 2020), the second Blockchain technology, functions as a decentralized marketplace for AI models and services. It guarantees data protection and ownership while facilitating easy access to a range of AI capabilities. Fetch.ai (Simpson. 2023) is another project that aims to build a decentralized network that allows autonomous agent interactions to take place without human involvement. With the help of this collaborative and autonomous agent architecture, intelligent agents may carry out challenging tasks in a variety of IoT applications. The Oasis Protocol (Yu et al. 2018), a Layer 1 Blockchain protocol, emphasizes the development of privacy-focused apps. As a basic Blockchain layer, it contains cutting-edge privacy features and technologies to provide secure and private data management. Because it provides a context that safeguards privacy, the Oasis Protocol is a viable platform for privacy-sensitive AIoT use cases. It is especially well suited for AI applications where data privacy is critical. ORAIchain (Pasdar, Dong and Lee. 2021), the first AI oracle, seamlessly integrates Blockchain with AI services. It ensures that data are safely and reliably sent between the decentralized network and external sources, hence increasing the trustworthiness of AI-powered smart contracts. This cutting-edge technology opens up new avenues for monetizing AI services and fosters innovation across several industries.

8.2 BLOCKCHAIN's IMPACT ON AI: KEY FEATURES AND ADVANTAGES

Blockchain is a replicated database that utilizes a consensus mechanism and runs over a decentralized network of untrustworthy members. Blockchain can simply be described as a chronological succession of data stored in blocks that are managed by a cluster of interconnected nodes. Each block contains a collection of confirmed transactions. The immutability of the data is guaranteed by the fact that once a block is published to the Blockchain, it is almost impossible to modify. Each block is linked to the previous block by carrying a cryptographic hash of the preceding block's header. Because of this connection, it is computationally difficult to change the Blockchain's history, which creates an ordered chain in which every change to a prior block causes changes in subsequent blocks. Blockchain enables an open, decentralized, and secure framework for the management of data and transactions. To guarantee data integrity and immutability, it makes use of distributed consensus, cryptographic hashing, and an auditable chain of blocks (Rehman et al. 2022). For each node to agree upon the authenticity of the data record, a consensus protocol is used. Consensus protocols are essential to the functioning of Blockchain technology as they offer agreement and trust in distributed nodes. As the basis of Blockchain technology, two primary consensus mechanisms have emerged. The first is Proof of Work, which provides the authority to add new blocks depending on computing power given by miners. This competitive mining process protects the Blockchain's security and immutability, as changing previous transactions would take massive processing power. Proof of Stake (PoS), which was implemented to alleviate energy consumption concerns, eliminates the need for energy-intensive mining and decides the right to verify and add new blocks based on the stake held. A chain of blocks forms the foundation of the Blockchain data structure as shown in Figure 8.1.

Numerous Blockchain implementations, especially those employed in AI applications that need reliability, openness, and data integrity, have been shown to benefit greatly from

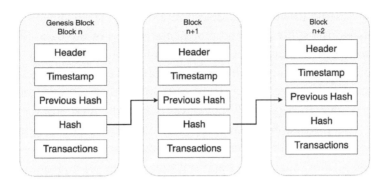

FIGURE 8.1   Blockchain architecture.

this design. Blockchain technology offers several features that can be beneficial for AI applications. Decentralization is the core feature of Blockchain technology that AI applications can benefit from (Qureshi et al. 2022). By decentralizing, single points of failures are countered by dispersing data among several nodes, providing continuous access to data and services. This high availability is critical for applications that require real-time or continuous processing. Decentralization improves AI system security by reducing the attack surface for potential security breaches. Because Blockchain-based AI systems are distributed, they offer more resistance to unwanted access and data manipulation. Decentralization also allows for collaborative decision-making by allowing various nodes to participate in AI model training and validation, fostering strong and varied models while respecting privacy and data ownership. Overall, Blockchain decentralization improves the dependability, security, resilience, and collaboration capacities of AI systems, limiting the risks associated with centralization and encouraging a more transparent, trustworthy, and efficient environment.

Blockchain data's integrity and dependability in AI applications are facilitated by its immutability and tamper-proof characteristics. Data is validated and verified by the consensus system, making it very difficult to change or modify it (Sunny, Undralla and Pillai. 2020). Because of this immutability, data provenance is guaranteed, which is essential for trustworthy machine-learning models. Blockchain data is crucial in delicate industries like healthcare, banking, and supply chain management because it offers transparency and traceability throughout the data lifecycle. The very difficult and immediately observable character of tamper-proof Blockchain data reduces hazards of data tampering and illegal adjustments. The immutability and tamper-proof nature of Blockchain data builds stakeholder trust, allowing for informed decisions and transparency in AI systems. Overall, these qualities can improve the accuracy of AI models, reduce the risks of data manipulation, and enable transparent, responsible decision-making.

Blockchain technology's transparency and auditability are essential features for the accountability and reliability of AI systems. By logging transactions and operations on a public, distributed ledger, Blockchain provides stakeholders with visibility into the activities and processes occurring within the system (Zarrin et al. 2021). The fairness and accountability of algorithms and decision-making processes are supported by transparency in AI systems, which makes it possible to audit and confirm the data sources used to train models.

This openness lowers the likelihood of discriminatory or biased outcomes by enabling stakeholders to assess the sufficiency and representativeness of the data. Blockchain data auditability ensures the immutability and time stamping of all transactions and updates, allowing stakeholders to trace and authenticate the history of data changes. It also makes it easy to detect any unauthorized or suspicious systemic activity. Because of openness and auditability, stakeholders in AI systems may have trust in the methods, data sources, and algorithms used. This transparency promotes accountability by encouraging meaningful debates, evaluations, and modifications to address any biases, mistakes, or ethical issues. Overall, the usage of Blockchain in AI applications establishes a strong basis for trust, accountability, and fairness, allowing stakeholders to validate decisions and processes, fostering responsibility and ethics in AI, and promoting transparency and bias reduction.

Smart contracts are a critical component of Blockchain technology that improves the functionality and efficiency of AI applications. These self-executing contracts, which are maintained on the Blockchain, enable transparency and immutability, allowing trust to be established and removing the need for middlemen or central authority. They reduce expenses and eliminate the danger of human error or manipulation by enabling the execution of transactions and agreements without the need for manual intervention (Hewa, Ylianttila and Liyanage. 2021). Additionally, smart contracts make it possible for AI systems to conduct automated business, such as trading AI models or services in a decentralized marketplace. They establish transaction terms, such as pricing, licensing, and usage rights, and automatically carry them out when specific conditions are met. They also have control over the sharing and use of data and AI models, such as in federated learning, ensuring an equitable and transparent allocation of contributions and benefits. Smart contracts used in AI applications may boost transparency, efficiency, and security while reducing the need for trust between parties and promoting dependable and seamless interactions. Smart contracts must be properly designed and audited to preserve their security and validity. Thorough testing and auditing techniques are required to ensure the validity of the contract's code. Overall, smart contracts in AI applications enable the automated, dependable, and effective implementation of agreements, transactions, and procedures, which increases the functionality and efficiency of AI systems as a whole.

Blockchain technology is an appealing approach for assuring data security in AI applications. It secures data and transactions using cryptographic algorithms, assuring secrecy and integrity (Deepa et al. 2022). Encryption is used to make stored data unreadable to unauthorized parties. Access control is made possible through private and public key cryptography, with each participant holding a unique pair of key. Decrypting encrypted data necessitates the use of the associated private key, which ensures that only authorized persons may access and decode it. Because Blockchain is decentralized, it is more resistant to assaults because data is distributed across several nodes. The immutability of data on the Blockchain makes it difficult to modify or tamper with, making the discovery of manipulation more likely. Blockchain technology provides a secure and transparent framework for storing and accessing data, building trust, and preserving sensitive information in AI systems by using cryptographic techniques, access control mechanisms, decentralized architecture, and data immutability.

By solving important challenges like data security, privacy, cooperation, and responsibility, Blockchain technology has the potential to transform the area of AI. Its capacity to improve data security and privacy through encryption and decentralization, assuring transparency and preventing unwanted access or manipulation, is one of its primary advantages. Smart contracts, which specify the terms and circumstances of data exchange, are another feature of Blockchain that makes it possible for numerous parties participating in AI projects to collaborate and share data securely and effectively. Additionally, Blockchain can provide an accurate history of data provenance and traceability, guaranteeing the reliability of data sources, which is especially useful in industries like supply chain management and medical research. Additionally, the technology can offer a decentralized framework for federated learning, enabling equitable participation and safe coordination among dispersed servers or devices. Additionally, markets for AI models and algorithms built on Blockchain technology can provide safe trading and exchange while defending intellectual property rights and allowing developer reputation systems. Blockchain technology promotes transparency and accountability in algorithmic decision-making, which helps with AI governance and accountability. It is now feasible to examine and evaluate the fairness, bias, and accountability of AI systems by documenting AI operations on Blockchain. While Blockchain has the potential to improve several AI-related features, its usage should be carefully assessed depending on the unique requirements and difficulties of each use case.

8.3 ROLE OF BLOCKCHAIN IN AI IoT APPLICATIONS

Despite the convergence of the IoT with AI, there are still difficulties to be handled in terms of trust, security, and effective data exchange. This is where Blockchain technology can be utilized. By combining Blockchain with AIoT applications, a new paradigm is formed that provides increased data integrity, safe device interactions, transparent data exchange, and improved automation. IoT devices may come to autonomous agreements thanks to Blockchain's decentralized and immutable ledger design, which also guarantees trust and data integrity. By empowering industries, reimagining supply chain management, enhancing privacy, and supporting innovative business models, the AIoT ecosystem may overcome barriers and fulfill the revolutionary promise of Blockchain. Blockchain technology will usher in a new era of efficiency, security, and trust when combined with AIoT applications. Blockchain technology can be integrated into AIoT applications to address specific challenges and enhance various aspects of the ecosystem. Here are some areas where Blockchain can be utilized.

- **Device Identity and Authentication:** IoT applications require safe and trustworthy device identity and authentication to enable dependable and secure interactions. Blockchain technology provides a secure identity management solution for IoT devices by assigning each IoT device a unique digital identity in the form of cryptographic keys. These keys are stored on the Blockchain for access control and authentication. Devices verify their identity by signing requests with their private key.

The Blockchain network gives access based on predefined access control settings after confirming the signature with the corresponding public key. Blockchain-based device identity and authentication solutions effectively stop spoofing and unauthorized access attempts. It is more difficult for criminals to invent or alter identity information because of the secure storage of digital identities, which also makes tampering and illicit modifications visible. Authenticated and granted access devices can safely connect to other authorized devices on the network. Data encryption and decryption are made possible by cryptographic keys, guaranteeing the secrecy and integrity of data while it is being transmitted. In general, Blockchain-based identity management systems reduce the risks of unauthorized access, data breaches, and device spoofing by offering a very secure and reliable environment for IoT applications.

- **Data Exchange and Monetization:** Blockchain-based systems improve data sharing and income creation in IoT applications by providing secure and transparent methods. Smart contracts, which automate and enforce data-sharing agreements, enable IoT devices to participate in direct peer-to-peer data exchanges while maintaining ownership and control over their data. The recording of all data transactions in this decentralized data market ensures the integrity and traceability of shared data. When two devices agree to send data, a smart contract is created that specifies the kind, quantity, pricing, and usage limits. Blockchain promotes data safety and privacy in the IoT ecosystem by allowing IoT device owners to retain ownership and control over their data. With reward systems in place where devices that give meaningful data receive tokens or digital assets, incentives are essential for increasing data sharing. By combining Blockchain technology and IoT data sharing, new business models are made possible, expenses are reduced, and effective income sharing between data sources and consumers is encouraged. Furthermore, by eliminating the chance of a single point of failure and unauthorized access, Blockchain enhances data privacy and security. Immutability and cryptographic techniques, which forbid tampering and unlawful alterations, safeguard data integrity. The IoT data economy may now reach its full potential thanks to the transformation of data sharing and monetization brought about by Blockchain technology in AI IoT applications.

- **Smart Contracts and Automation:** The primary innovation of Blockchain technology, smart contracts, enables the automation and self-execution of contracts in IoT applications. The programmable logic that specifies words, conditions, and actions allows for direct device-to-device interactions, which speeds up operations. Smart contracts function independently after they are set up on the Blockchain, continually monitoring the network and performing specified actions when specific conditions are met. This self-execution eliminates the need for manual intervention and allows IoT operations to be smoothly automated. Since the contract code and execution are available to all parties thanks to the Blockchain's decentralized nature, smart contracts also promote trust and transparency. This transparency removes the requirement for trust in a centralized authority by ensuring that agreed-upon operations are carried out precisely as indicated. By self-executing, delays, dependencies, and costs associated with third-party services are avoided. By automating interactions between IoT devices, smart contracts increase productivity and save expenses. They accomplish this by eliminating human procedures and allowing activities to be carried out quickly and practically instantaneously, hence boosting the responsiveness, accuracy, and dependability of IoT systems. Furthermore, smart contracts benefit from the consensus mechanisms built into Blockchain technology, which rely on the consent and validation of network participants. When smart contracts are implemented on the Blockchain, they safeguard the transparency and immutability of agreed-upon operations.

- **Federated Learning:** A unique approach to training AI models that emphasizes data security and privacy is federated learning. It enables distributed collaborative model training while protecting sensitive data and utilizing the combined knowledge of many individuals. With the potential to enhance privacy and guarantee participant fairness, Blockchain technology can handle the coordination, verification, and incentive components of federated learning. With smart contracts establishing the rules and protocols, Blockchain technology offers a decentralized and transparent platform for process coordination. Model updates and data contributions may be easily validated because of Blockchain's immutability and transparency, while incentives and rewards encourage participation and contribution. Private key management solutions, which ensure data confidentiality and integrity, boost privacy and security even further. Transparency and consensus-building procedures promote fairness and trust, removing the need for trust between unknown partners. The combination of privacy-preserving federated learning and the openness, security, and automation of Blockchain provides a powerful solution for collaborative AI model training while safeguarding data privacy and ensuring the quality of the learning process.

8.4 BLOCKCHAIN INTEGRATION WITH AI

The recent fusion of two ground-breaking technologies, Blockchain, and AI, has had a significant influence on several different businesses. Blockchain and AI together have created a fresh ecosystem that is defined by decentralization, transparency, and increased security, radically altering paradigms for data administration and consumption. This section explores cutting-edge Blockchain projects, such as Ocean Protocol, SingularityNET, Fetch.ai, Oasis Protocol, and ORAIchain.

8.4.1 Ocean Protocol

Ocean Protocol (McConaghy. 2022), is a Blockchain-based project that provides a decentralized marketplace for data that can be used for AI applications. It is built on the Ethereum blockchain allowing data providers, consumers, and AI service providers to exchange and use data securely. One of the major concerns the AI industry faces is the availability of high-quality data. Constructing accurate and dependable AI models without access to massive amounts of diverse and high-quality data can be difficult. Ocean Protocol seeks to address this issue by establishing a marketplace for data trading, analysis, and profit.

Ocean Protocol's major goal is to enable data sharing and monetization in a decentralized, safe, and private manner. It offers a framework for purchasing, selling, and transferring data assets while maintaining data privacy and access control. Ocean Protocol aims to establish new data-driven business models and inspire innovation across several industries by simplifying data sharing in a transparent and trusting way.

The Ocean Protocol is divided into many tiers, each with its own set of characteristics. The application layer is the top layer of the Ocean Protocol architecture, and it allows users to interact with the protocol. This layer includes applications like marketplaces, market integrators, and data service providers. Its primary goal is to simplify the sharing, purchasing, and selling of data assets. The Ocean Protocol architecture's intermediate layer is made up of middleware and software libraries, which programmers may use to construct applications that interface with the protocol. This layer has a variety of tools for dealing with concerns such as metadata, access control, data provenance, and data discovery. For example, the Ocean.js library, which offers a JavaScript Application Programming Interface (API) for interacting with the protocol, is one of these tools. The Ocean Protocol architecture is built on the smart contract layer, which outlines and upholds the protocol's governance and rules. The token contract, market contract, and staking contract are just a few examples of the Ethereum smart contracts that make up this layer and control how the protocol operates. The Ocean Protocol's native coin, Ocean Tokens, which are utilized for protocol transactions, is managed by the token contract. By staking their tokens to cast votes on proposals, token holders may take part in protocol governance thanks to the staking contract. A framework for purchasing and selling data assets on the system is provided by the market contract. The protocol's transactions must be secure, transparent, and auditable to function. The use of smart contracts, which ensure that protocol transactions are carried out automatically without the need for intermediaries or centralized control, also ensures high security and reliability.

Ocean Protocol makes it simpler to transfer data assets in a secure, decentralized, and advantageous way, which may considerably aid in the creation of AIoT applications. Data are an essential resource in AI that powers the creation of machine learning models. The design of Ocean Protocol ensures privacy and security while granting access to numerous high-quality data assets. Additionally, the Ocean Protocol's decentralized structure makes it easier to create cooperative and interoperable ecosystems, which boosts the efficiency and cost-effectiveness of AI research. The democratization of data and AI brought about by the Ocean Protocol can also encourage innovation and raise the level of competition in the AI market. Many Ocean Protocol characteristics might be highly useful for IoT applications. One of its primary characteristics is its decentralized data marketplace, which provides access to a diverse variety of data assets. This comprises information obtained from a variety of sources, such as government organizations, commercial enterprises, academic institutions, and people. This access to a diverse variety of data assets has the potential to improve the quality and accuracy of machine-learning models. Furthermore, Ocean Protocol provides safe and privacy-preserving data asset exchange, reducing the danger of data breaches and privacy violations. This allows for larger datasets and improves the accuracy and durability of machine-learning models.

Ocean Protocol's Blockchain provides a transparent and auditable framework for determining who owns and has access to which data assets. This ensures that data for AIoT applications is accurate and trustworthy. The formation of a decentralized marketplace for AI models is another major function given by Ocean Protocol. By making high-quality models accessible for purchase and use in AI applications, it encourages AI developers to create them. This promotes AI research and economic development while also offering a venue for AI developers to be recognized for their accomplishments. The interoperable infrastructure of Ocean Protocol enables the simple integration of data assets with diverse AI tools and platforms, enabling collaboration and innovation among AI developers. Ocean Protocol's decentralized data-sharing features can considerably improve the efficacy of AI development while lowering data-collecting costs. By removing the need for middlemen, decentralized data exchange reduces transaction costs for both consumers and data producers. Finally, the decentralized data exchange of the Ocean Protocol democratizes access to data assets and AI solutions, allowing individuals and smaller enterprises to engage in the AI sector. This fosters creativity and competition, which boosts the AI industry's economic growth.

By establishing a decentralized ecosystem for data and AI services, Ocean Protocol has the potential to be an essential part of AIoT applications. The platform enables data owners to monetize their data while simultaneously giving AI developers access to high-quality data and AI services. This creates a new, decentralized, transparent, and inclusive environment for AI creation. As the AI industry develops, the Ocean Protocol's role in democratizing access to data and services will become ever more important.

8.4.2 SingularityNET

SingularityNET (Liu, Yiming, et al. 2020), a decentralized, open-source network, seeks to facilitate the creation and deployment of AI applications using AI agents. These autonomous systems may learn from their interactions with the environment and are adaptive since they are built to execute certain tasks. SingularityNET's goal is to establish a marketplace where AI agents can be purchased and sold, allowing developers and enterprises to acquire the AI tools they want without having to build them from the ground up. SingularityNET also has a reputation system to maintain quality, a marketplace for AI agents, and a federated learning approach to allow AI agents to collaborate. The platform also gives developers a variety of tools and services to build and use AI applications. The decentralized approach of SingularityNET intends to democratize AI and make it available to everyone. SingularityNET's emphasis on building a decentralized AI network where many AI agents may connect and work together decentralized is another crucial aspect of the project. SingularityNET seeks to democratize AI development and deployment to increase accessibility. Figure 8.2 shows the singularityNET high-level architecture.

SingularityNET's architecture comprises four essential components: transactions, settlements, incentives, and governance. These components aid in the platform's decentralized operation. The platform users exchange value through transactions, which may include the exchange of data among AI agents or tokens for AI services. Smart contracts ensure that transactions are transparent, secure, and irreversible by eliminating the need for intermediaries and minimizing transaction costs. The use of escrow accounts

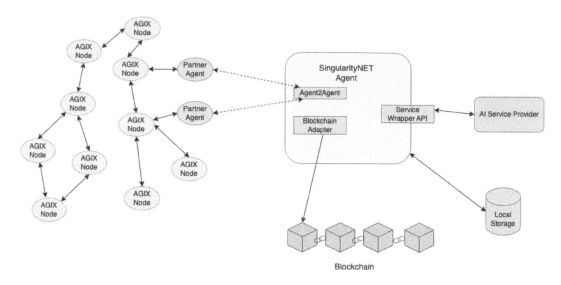

FIGURE 8.2   SingularityNET high-level architecture.

makes it simpler to ensure that everyone involved in a settlement receives the value to which they are entitled. This arrangement encourages all parties to keep their agreements and protects them from risk. Incentives are used to promote network-beneficial behaviors by rewarding high-quality AI services and penalizing low-quality services. A reputation system handles these incentives and penalties by allowing people to rate the efficacy of various AI bots. Last, governance refers to rules and laws regulating platform decision-making, such as incentive management and dispute resolution. The platform changes are proposed and decided by the community as part of SingularityNET's decentralized and community-driven governance structure. Parties come to decisions by working out an agreement. These tactics enable the interchange of AI services safely and efficiently while promoting cooperation and creativity in the creation of AI applications.

SingularityNET may be applied to AI applications in several different ways. With the help of the decentralized AI network created by SingularityNET, AI agents may interact with one another and work together to solve complex problems. This is especially useful in the context of the IoT, where several devices and sensors may work together to collect data and execute a task. For instance, a network of smart home devices may work together to optimize energy consumption using information from sensors placed around the house. Additionally, SingularityNET's AI agent marketplace may help companies and developers get the AI tools they need without having to build them from the ground up. This is crucial in the context of the IoT, where specialized AI agents could be required to carry out operations like image recognition, natural language processing, or data analysis. Businesses and developers may save time and money while focusing on developing apps that use AI to improve the performance of their IoT devices by acquiring AI agents through the SingularityNET marketplace.

Furthermore, AI bots may learn from one another in a decentralized way thanks to SingularityNET's federated learning strategy. When AI agents may need to learn from data gathered by numerous devices and sensors, this is especially helpful. Businesses and developers may design AI agents that can learn from several datasets, enhancing their accuracy and performance, using SingularityNET's federated learning technique. SingularityNET is a useful resource for developing and deploying AI applications for the IoT. Its federated learning approach, a marketplace for AI agents, and decentralized AI network may help companies and developers build and deploy IoT devices and apps that are more accurate, effective, and profitable thanks to AI.

8.4.3 Fetch.ai

Fetch.ai (Simpson et al. 2023) is a decentralized network that leverages Blockchain and AI to connect digital and real goods. The project aims to create an open-source ecosystem in which autonomous economic agents may interact with one another and the outside world safely and successfully. The platform is built on a revolutionary consensus approach known as "proof of useful work," which rewards nodes for doing beneficial computations that improve network functionality. Numerous use cases are supported by Fetch.ai such as supply chains, smart cities, etc. Advanced machine learning and AI technologies are used by Fetch.ai, to streamline user transactions and data sharing. The network is built to support a wide range of applications, including autonomous economic agents and distributed autonomous groups. The ultimate goal of the project is to use Blockchain and AI together to allow a more connected and intelligent future.

The Fetch.ai platform is divided into three layers: The Autonomous Economic Agent (AEA layer), the Open Economic Framework (OEF layer), and the Open Economic Ledger (OEL). The autonomous economic agents are found in the AEA layer. AEAs are computer programs that can represent people or organizations and communicate with other AEAs and digital and physical things in the real world. They can decentral negotiate contracts, make judgments, and carry out activities. The AEA layer is created to be flexible and modular, enabling customization and specialization to satisfy the requirements of particular use cases. The OEF layer provides the platform's architecture for coordination and communication. AEAs may find and connect with other agents and services on the network thanks to this decentralized search engine. Additionally, the OEF offers AEAs a messaging system for inter-AEA communication and a reputation system that helps ensure the dependability and quality of services offered by agents. The OEL layer is the foundation of Fetch.ai's technical stack. This decentralized ledger maintains track of all AEA transactions. The OEL ensures that the system is secure and impermeable and that all transactions are transparent and irreversible. Furthermore, it enables the creation of a decentralized marketplace where AEAs can trade value directly without intermediaries. Useful Proof of Work (PoW), a novel consensus technique, combines conventional proof of work with a framework of financial incentives to assure efficiency and security. Together, these three layers form the architecture of Fetch.ai, enabling the creation of decentralized and autonomous systems that can coordinate and collaborate securely and efficiently.

By offering a decentralized and intelligent architecture that can facilitate autonomous decision-making and effective resource allocation in IoT networks, Fetch.ai can play a vital role in AIoT applications. Managing, processing, and analyzing data effectively are some of the biggest issues facing IoT networks. By developing intelligent agents that can process and analyze data from IoT devices and make autonomous decisions based on the information they receive, Fetch.ai's AEAs can assist in solving this challenge. These agents can cooperate to enhance system performance and resource allocation. The lack of compatibility across various platforms and devices presents another difficulty for IoT networks. In the technological stack of Fetch.ai, the OEF layer offers a platform for data sharing and connectivity across various IoT systems and devices. This makes interoperability possible and makes it possible to build a decentralized IoT ecosystem where devices may communicate and work together to accomplish shared objectives. Another crucial component that might be very helpful to AIoT applications is Fetch.ai Smart Ledger. The integrity and transparency of AI applications are ensured by this high-performance Blockchain, which enables the secure and effective exchange of money and data among AI agents. Furthermore, with machine learning capabilities included in AI, AEAs may learn from their interactions and experiences to enhance their performance over time. The agents' ability to enhance their performance and adjust to changing circumstances continually can result in a rise in the accuracy and efficacy of AI applications.

8.4.4 Oasis Protocol

The Oasis Protocol (Yu, Shitang, et al. 2018) is a Layer 1 Blockchain platform for developing privacy-focused apps. It seeks to combine the benefits of Blockchain technology with secure, private data processing and scalability. Oasis aims to provide a robust and user-centric environment for conducting transactions, executing smart contracts, and utilizing the potential of decentralization. It maintains control over sensitive data by combining the benefits of Blockchain technology with privacy-preserving techniques such as secure enclaves. The Oasis Protocol stands apart from other layer 1 Blockchains by combining privacy, scalability, and developer-friendly features singularly. By including secure enclaves, it makes it possible to execute private smart contracts that safeguard sensitive data while still allowing for verification. ParaTime, a hybrid consensus system, enables parallel runtimes with programmable rules, enhancing developer freedom. The protocol stands out in part because it emphasizes privacy, offering a safe and secure environment. Oasis Protocol is an appealing option for creating privacy-focused apps on the Blockchain because of its emphasis on data protection, scalable speed, and extensive developer tools. Figure 8.3 shows the Oasis architecture with secure enclave.

One of the essential components of the Oasis Protocol's architecture is the Trusted Execution Environment (TEE) or the secure enclave. Secure enclaves offer a reliable execution environment for delicate data and calculations. These enclaves establish segregated areas inside a processor, ensuring that private information stays encrypted and off-limits to the public. One of the main advantages of secure enclaves is that they safeguard sensitive data from unwanted access, ensuring data privacy. Additionally, safe enclaves provide secure computing, enabling activities like data manipulation or cryptographic calculations that protect user privacy. Verifiability is another feature of the Oasis Protocol that enables third parties to check the precision of enclave operation without jeopardizing data privacy. Smart contracts can use secure enclaves to offer privacy-preserving features, ensuring that

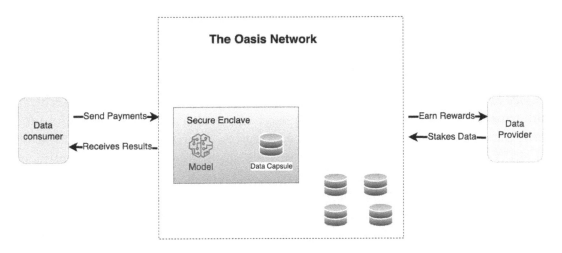

FIGURE 8.3   Oasis architecture with secure enclave.

inputs, outputs, and interim outcomes are shielded from the network. While preserving general privacy and security in the Oasis network, this privacy-focused method enables delicate financial transactions, secure calculations, and other private processes.

A key component of the Oasis Protocol is secret smart contracts, which allow for privacy and secrecy in Blockchain-based applications. These smart contracts in the Oasis Protocol run in trusted execution environments for sensitive calculations, such as Intel SGX secure enclaves. By hiding the contract's inputs and outputs from the network, confidential smart contracts offer privacy. To do this, cryptographic techniques are used to encrypt and secure the data while allowing for the validity of the contract to be checked without revealing sensitive information. The Oasis Protocol facilitates the secure processing of sensitive data and private computations while upholding the network's overall privacy and secrecy by executing smart contracts in secure enclaves. The Oasis Protocol is ideally suited for applications that need secrecy, such as private lending, decentralized finance (DeFi) transactions, and other use cases where data privacy is crucial.

For AI and IoT applications, the Oasis Protocol has certain clear advantages. Its confidentiality-preserving features, such as the usage of secure enclaves, guarantee the secure processing of sensitive data. The Oasis Protocol allows privacy by keeping inputs and outputs concealed from the network by executing private smart contracts within these enclaves. This guarantees that AIoT stakeholders may safely access data markets and maintain control over their data. A distributed network can efficiently compute AI algorithms because of the protocol's scalability and modular architecture, which can handle the massive amounts of data produced by IoT devices. The Oasis Protocol also encourages transparency and trust through cryptographic verifiability, enabling participants to confirm the precision of private smart contract execution. As a result, trust is built up inside the AI-IoT ecosystems, encouraging cooperation and accelerating the creation of safe marketplaces and rewards for data sharing and AI contributions. Overall, the Oasis Protocol offers a solid framework for AI-IoT applications by integrating privacy, scalability, and trust to support creative and safe deployments in this field.

8.4.5 ORAIchain

ORAIchain (Pasdar et al. 2021), a Blockchain-based oracle network that serves as a critical connection between smart contracts and real-world data, enables decentralized apps (dApps) to securely and reliably communicate with external data. Its primary job is to provide exact and validated data inputs to smart contracts, allowing them to be executed with trust. ORAIchain incorporates cutting-edge AI-based data validation algorithms to verify the validity and accuracy of external data sources, ensuring data dependability and tamper-resistant performance. The design of ORAIchain is committed to data privacy and encryption, using strong privacy-preserving measures to protect sensitive data and enabling authorized parties, such as smart contracts, to safely access specified information. It is a flexible and useful addition to the Blockchain ecosystem that facilitates cross-chain communication and data exchange thanks to its interoperability and scalability. The expanding demands of decentralized applications across many industries may be met thanks to ORAIchain's capacity to handle large numbers of data requests effectively. Overall, ORAIchain provides developers and companies looking for a trustworthy connection between their smart contracts and real-world data with a verified and trusted data source. Figure 8.4 shows the ORAIchain system architecture.

Users or smart contracts can submit requests by calling an Oracle script that is accessible through the ORAI gateway or marketplace. The Oracle script includes test cases, transaction costs, and data sources for AI for each request. A random validator is selected to acquire data from AI providers and run test scenarios when a request is made. To ensure the integrity of the data, requests are terminated if an AI provider fails to test. The ORAIchain Blockchain records the outcomes of successful queries, proving their execution and avoiding data manipulation. The API testing functionality of ORAIchain is special since it is built on test cases. Testing is essential to regulate the caliber of AI providers since ORAIchain focuses on AI APIs. To encourage AI providers to increase the accuracy of their AI models, test providers might suggest

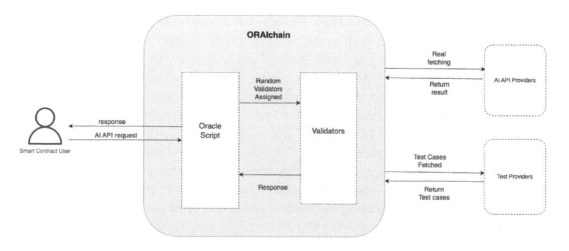

FIGURE 8.4 ORAIchain system architecture.

appropriate test cases. The ORAIchain community has the authority to rank validators' performances in raising the caliber of AI APIs. Tokens will be reduced as a punishment for improper behavior by validators, such as neglecting to run test cases or validate AI providers. However, a large number of validators must be recruited, and they must be encouraged to join and uphold the standard of their work in the ORAIchain network through block rewards and transaction fees to ensure scalability and high availability.

8.5 DISCUSSION

Blockchain technology, a distributed ledger, enables safe, open, and immutable record-keeping. AIoT has the potential to create vast amounts of data that may be exploited by AI applications to give services to users. Blockchain technology can play an essential role in AIoT applications by enabling decentralized AI models and ensuring secure data exchange. Blockchain's safe and transparent way of tracking data ensures that data are not exploited or altered. Blockchain can also help with monetization, allowing owners to sell their data directly to interested parties. This chapter examines the characteristics of Blockchain technology that make it especially applicable for applications related to the IoT, emphasizing its function in maintaining data security and transparency. Furthermore, this chapter explores the significant contribution that Blockchain technology makes to AIoT, highlighting crucial aspects such as Device Identity and Authentication, Data Exchange and Monetization, Smart Contracts and Automation, and Federated Learning. To facilitate AI applications, several Blockchain projects are being developed and implemented. The potential benefits of these Blockchain initiatives, namely Ocean Protocol, Fetch.ai, SingularityNET, Oasis Protocol, and ORAIchain, for advancing the creation and use of AIoT applications are also discussed in this chapter. Ocean Protocol aims to create a data economy where data can be shared and monetized in a privacy-preserving manner using Blockchain technology. Fetch.ai, on the other hand, allows intelligent agents to perform complex tasks by creating a decentralized AI network, whereas, SigularityNET allows the sharing of AI models while maintaining data privacy and ownership. The Oasis Protocol is a Layer 1 Blockchain platform for developing privacy-focused apps particularly suitable for AI applications. ORAIchain is the first layer 1 AI Oracle, facilitating connectivity between Blockchains and real-world applications with AI and data-driven smart contracts. The revolutionary effect of Blockchain on AIoT applications is highlighted in this chapter by looking at these aspects, with a focus on the development of a decentralized, secure, and trusted AIoT ecosystem.

8.6 CONCLUSION

The fusion of AI and the IoT into the domain of AIoT has provided a potential frontier for disruptive innovation across several sectors. Nonetheless, this rapid convergence of technologies faces several serious issues in terms of data security, openness, interoperability, and privacy. In response to these challenges, Blockchain technology appears as a compelling and practical alternative for fortifying the foundations and enhancing the capabilities of AIoT applications. The key features of Blockchain technology that make it particularly well-suited for integration inside AIoT applications have been carefully examined throughout this chapter. This chapter emphasizes the critical function of Blockchain technology in AIoT applications, presenting a variety of use cases that maximize its potential and capabilities in this area. We have also looked at several real-world Blockchain projects in this chapter that demonstrate how AIoT and Blockchain may work together to provide innovative new solutions. These efforts show the real-world impacts of Blockchain on the development of AIoT. They range from empowering data owners to safely share and monetize their data, to creating decentralized markets for AI services and models, to implementing cutting-edge privacy measures for data. These projects also fill the gap between Blockchain networks and real-world applications powered by smart contracts and AI.

REFERENCES

Deepa, Natarajan, et al. "A Survey on Blockchain for Big Data: Approaches, Opportunities, and Future Directions." *Future Generation Computer Systems* 131 (2022): 209–26.

Ekramifard, Ala, et al. "A Systematic Literature Review of Integration of Blockchain and Artificial Intelligence." *Blockchain Cybersecurity, Trust and Privacy* (2020): 147–60.

Guo, Huaqun, and Xingjie Yu. "A Survey on Blockchain Technology and Its Security." *Blockchain: Research and Applications* 3.2 (2022): 100067.

Hansen, Emil Blixt, and Simon Bøgh. "Artificial Intelligence and Internet of Things in Small and Medium-Sized Enterprises: A Survey." *Journal of Manufacturing Systems* 58 (2021): 362–72.

Hewa, Tharaka, Mika Ylianttila, and Madhusanka Liyanage. "Survey on Blockchain Based Smart Contracts: Applications, Opportunities and Challenges." *Journal of Network and Computer Applications* 177 (2021): 102857.

Krichen, Moez, et al. "Blockchain for Modern Applications: A Survey." *Sensors* 22.14 (2022): 5274.

Liu, Yiming, et al. "Blockchain and Machine Learning for Communications and Networking Systems." *IEEE Communications Surveys & Tutorials* 22.2 (2020): 1392–431.

McConaghy, Trent. "Ocean Protocol: Tools for the Web3 Data Economy." *Handbook on Blockchain*. Springer, 2022. 505–39.

Mohamed, Esraa. "The Relation of Artificial Intelligence with Internet of Things: A Survey." *Journal of Cybersecurity and Information Management* 1.1 (2020): 30–34.

Mohanta, Bhabendu Kumar, et al. "Survey on IoT Security: Challenges and Solution Using Machine Learning, Artificial Intelligence and Blockchain Technology." *Internet of Things* 11 (2020): 100227.

Naseem, Shahid, et al. "Artificial General Intelligence-Based Rational Behavior Detection Using Cognitive Correlates for Tracking Online Harms." *Personal and Ubiquitous Computing* 27.1 (2022): 119–137.

Pasdar, Amirmohammad, Zhongli Dong, and Young Choon Lee. "Blockchain Oracle Design Patterns." *arXiv preprint arXiv:2106.09349* (2021).

Qureshi, Kashif Naseer, Gwanggil Jeon, and Francesco Piccialli. "Anomaly Detection and Trust Authority in Artificial Intelligence and Cloud Computing." *Computer Networks* 184 (2020): 107647.

Qureshi, Kashif Naseer, et al. "A Blockchain-Based Efficient, Secure and Anonymous Conditional Privacy-Preserving and Authentication Scheme for the Internet of Vehicles." *Applied Sciences* 12.1 (2022): 476.

Rajasekaran, Arun Sekar, Maria Azees, and Fadi Al-Turjman. "A Comprehensive Survey on Blockchain Technology." *Sustainable Energy Technologies and Assessments* 52 (2022): 102039.

Rehman, M., et al. "A Cyber Secure Medical Management System by Using Blockchain." *IEEE Transactions on Computational Social Systems* (2022): 1–14.

Simpson, T., Sheikh, H., Hain, T., Ronnow, T., Ward, J. *Fetch: Technical Introduction. A Decentralized Digital World for the Future Economy [White Paper].* 2023.

Sunny, Justin, Naveen Undralla, and V Madhusudanan Pillai. "Supply Chain Transparency through Blockchain-Based Traceability: An Overview with Demonstration." *Computers & Industrial Engineering* 150 (2020): 106895.

Wang, Kai, et al. "Securing Data with Blockchain and AI." *IEEE Access* 7 (2019): 77981–89.

Whang, Steven Euijong, et al. "Data Collection and Quality Challenges in Deep Learning: A Data-Centric AI Perspective." *The VLDB Journal* 32.4 (2023): 791–813.

Xiong, Zuobin, et al. "Privacy Threat and Defense for Federated Learning with Non-IID Data in AIoT." *IEEE Transactions on Industrial Informatics* 18.2 (2021): 1310–21.

Yang, Chao-Tung, et al. "Current Advances and Future Challenges of AIoT Applications in Particulate Matters (PM) Monitoring and Control." *Journal of Hazardous Materials* 419 (2021): 126442.

Yu, Shitang, et al. "A High Performance Blockchain Platform for Intelligent Devices." *2018 1st IEEE International Conference on Hot Information-Centric Networking (HotICN)*. 2018. IEEE.

Zarrin, Javad, et al. "Blockchain for Decentralization of Internet: Prospects, Trends, and Challenges." *Cluster Computing* 24.4 (2021): 2841–66.

Zhang, Jing, and Dacheng Tao. "Empowering Things with Intelligence: A Survey of the Progress, Challenges, and Opportunities in Artificial Intelligence of Things." *IEEE Internet of Things Journal* 8.10 (2020): 7789–817.

CHAPTER 9

Big Data Analytics for AIoT Network

Faisal Rehman, Muhammad Anwar, Anees Ul Mujtaba, Hanan Sharif

Department of Information Sciences, Lahore Leads University, Lahore

Naveed Riaz

Department of Computer Science, National University of Science and Technology, Islamabad

9.1 INTRODUCTION

The pace at which data is being created in the digital world is amazing, and it's just becoming faster. Even though these "Big Data" have opened up innovative options to get a better understanding of public health, they still contain far more promise for study and clinical use. The increased number of Internet users producing an enormous volume of data is a direct consequence of the technological revolution that has recently taken place as a result of the growing usage of such gadgets. Specifically, distant sensors consistently create a large amount of heterogeneous data that might be organized or unstructured. Big Data is distinguished by three characteristics (a) the quantity and variety of the data; (b) the inability of the data to be organized inside conventional relational databases; and (c) the speed with which the data are created, recorded, and analyzed. Big Data has a lot of potential for commercial applications and is a fast-growing sector of the information technology industry. It has sparked a substantial amount of interest in a variety of industries, including the production of medical equipment, financial transactions, social networking, and satellite imagery (Ballin. 2016).

Researchers in the fields of decision-making, data sciences, commercial applications, and government are paying a significant amount of attention to technological breakthroughs and the availability of large volumes of data on the Internet. Researchers may make use of a wide variety of opportunities afforded by the vast amounts of data collectively referred to as "Big Data." However, using Big Data requires a significant investment of time and introduces great computing complexity (Che, Safran, and Peng. 2013).

AIoT edge computing satisfies the essential requirements in terms of application intelligence, real-time operations, and data and energy optimization. This is because of the demand for IoT devices, which is expected to last for an estimated 10 years, between 2018 and 2027. The Internet of Things (IoT) is a network of physical devices, cars, buildings, and

DOI: 10.1201/9781003430018-11

other items that are integrated with sensors, software, and connectivity, which enables them to gather and share data. These objects may also communicate with one another across the network (Silverio-Fernández, Renukappa, and Suresh. 2018). Edge computing is a model of distributed computing that moves processing and data storage closer to the devices and sensors that create and utilize data in IoT systems. Edge computing is also known as "edge analytics." Fog computing is a computer paradigm that extends the advantages of edge computing by adding a layer of intermediary nodes between the edge devices and the cloud, allowing efficient data processing and administration (Iorga et al. 2018). Blockchain is a distributed ledger technology that enables new business models and value propositions by providing a safe and transparent method for storing and exchanging data in IoT devices. Cybersecurity is the activity of securing IoT devices, networks, and data against unauthorized access, use, disclosure, interruption, modification, or destruction. Related terms include information assurance, network security, and data protection (Di Pierro. 2017).

With the advent of new networking technologies such as Bluetooth, Wi-Fi, and Long-Term Evolution (LTE), the IoT has expanded rapidly over the past twenty years. A wide variety of products, from smart cameras, lights, bicycles and electricity meters, to wearables, healthcare, smart grids, intelligent transportation (Qureshi and Abdullah. 2014), and smart homes (Qureshi, Alhudhaif, et al. 2021), are just a few examples of IoT networks. There are three levels of IoT networks including the "perception" layer, the "network" layer, and the "application" layer (Chiang and Zhang. 2016). The sensors, actuators, and other devices that make up the perception layer provide the foundation of the (IoT) architecture. Network layers are the backbone of the IoT's architecture, consisting of Local Area Networks (LANs) cellular networks, the Internet, and devices like hubs, routers, and gateways enabled by various communication technologies like Bluetooth, Wi-Fi, LTE, and fifth-generation mobile networks (5G). The top IoT layer is the application layer, which relies on cloud computing platforms as a means of individualized services to its end customers. In typical IoT implementations, sensors gather data, which is then sent to a network-based processing and analysis step in the cloud. The findings or instructions are sent to the end devices or actuators.

However, given the vast quantities of sensors deployed in different contexts, this centralized design presents substantial challenges. By 2025, there will be 50 billion IoT-connected devices, creating 79.4 ZB of data (Abiodun et al. 2021). High latency is the consequence of the transmission of this large volume of data, processing it in the cloud, and then delivering the findings back to end devices. To remedy the situation, Cisco introduced the concept of "fog computing," which involves moving data storage, processing power, and networking resources to the network's periphery (e.g., to scattered routers and other fog nodes). For IoT applications, fog computing provides low latency and high processing capability (Tordera et al. 2016). Edge computing entails increasing computing capability deployment on control devices near actuators and sensors (Zhang et al. 2019; Wang et al. 2019). It is worth noting that fog computing is often seen as a subset of edge computing or that the terms are used interchangeably.

Recent years have seen a revival in deep learning-enhanced AI. In recent years, Deep Neural Networks (DNNs) have seen widespread use, including retrained models that degenerate when examples are encountered in neither the label set nor the training set. In the manufacturing sector, for instance, equipment might lose its initial settings or alter its operation mode over time. Because of this inability to adjust to variation, models trained for the first mode suffer drops. There are many different types of Machine Learning (ML); few-shot-learning, zero-shot-learning, metal learning, unattended, semi-supervised, transfer, and domain adaptation are all related research topics in ML that address these same kinds of problems. Progress in these areas has been facilitated by Deep Learning (DL). This indicates that DL may be equally exploited to increase IoT system learning. Reasoning and behavior are also critical for an IoT system to interact with its surroundings and people. A smart parking system can infer about the available places in the area. The AI Chabot may then expose him to parking deals, auto maintenance services, and local eateries. Recent developments in causal inference and discovery, graph-based reasoning, Reinforcement Learning (RL), and voice recognition and synthesis techniques (Yang et al. 2020) may be useful in certain application situations. 5G networks and AI will pave the way for ubiquitous connectivity (Khan et al. 2022). This will usher in the AIoT age or the age when AI meets IoT. Numerous AIoT applications, which provide services and generate value, have been created thanks to substantial investment from both the academic community and the business sector. Therefore, we conducted a literature review of this developing field to show how AI technologies provide intelligence to inanimate objects and improve software (Ashfaq et al. 2022).

9.2 EXISTING RESEARCH ON AIoT NETWORKS

Research has often focused on a few aspects of the IoT networks, including but not limited to, computer systems, networks, programs, safety, security, and privacy (Un Nisa et al. 2022). These authors provided a useful overview of the IoT paradigm by describing it from three perspectives: the "things" perspective, the "Internet" perspective, and the "semantic" perspective, which correlate to devices networks, and data handling and analysis, respectively. The authors examined security and privacy issues that still need to be resolved. In addition, they examined the enabling technologies and IoT applications in several fields. Authors Contreras-Castillo, Zeadally, and Guerrero Ibáñez. 2017 provided an overview of IoT and highlighted current developments and obstacles. Authors summarized the various common IoT architectures, such as Software Defined Networks (SDN), Mobile First Design, and the IoT. They said that future IoT architecture will need to scale well, be adaptive, and properly integrate and manage large numbers of connected devices, both the traditional three-layer design (consisting of a "perception," "network," and "application" layers) and the more recent service-oriented design as discussed in Aslam, Michaelides, and Herodotou.

In Guan et al. 2017, various common IoT frameworks are discussed, such as the Mobile First Design, the Cloud Things framework, and other frameworks based on SDN networks. The authors argue that in the future, IoT designs need to be scalable, adaptive, interoperable, energy efficient, and secure to integrate and manage vast numbers of linked devices. The three-tier design consists of a service-oriented architecture: a perception layer, a network layer, and an application layer. Integration of cloud and fog/edge computing (Chiang and Zhang. 2016) is gaining attention as a key component of the IoT's computing architecture. We are interested in cloud, fog, and AI-enhanced

IoT, including edge computing designs for systems that can benefit from DL in the IoT. Multiple networking methods are required to carry data at scale and connect many devices to data centers. Edge analytics systems, cloud computing systems, and hyperconverged systems, for massively parallel mining, enable real-time analyses of enormous IoT data (Catarinucci et al. 2015). IoT also uses Wireless Sensor Networks (WSN) for monitoring external or physical influences. 5G mobile networks, which are now under development, may provide much more base station capacity and ultra-low latency. It is expected that 5G will accelerate the development of IoT software in addition to boosting the number of connected devices (Lamarre and May. 2019). Resource management has become a hot topic as the amount of traffic and the number of connected devices in IoT networks has exploded, with promising results from state-of-the-art deep learning algorithms.) IoT networks enable the transmission and storage of massive amounts of user data generated by pervasively connected devices. Faces, voices, and fingerprints are all examples of biometric data included in these records. Because of the potential for data leakage in the event of a cyberattack on an IoT system, data security, and privacy have emerged as pressing issues in IoT deployments. To ensure the safety and privacy of the IoT, researchers have recently analyzed the effectiveness of access control and trust management (Qureshi, Iftikhar, et al. 2020).

9.3 AIoT ARCHITECTURE

Computing-centric approaches like those discussed in Palomares et al. 2021, use a three-tiered architecture. The approaches are simplified by referring to the three tiers of computing as the cloud, the fog, and the edge. As discussed in Palomares et al. 2021, the edge computing layer may serve similar duties like cloud computing. In addition, the edge layer allows the management and operation of sensors and actuators. This layer's ultimate goal is to provide AIoT devices with enhanced perceptual and behavioral capabilities. Network elements like hubs, routers, and gateways are all examples of fog nodes, which embody the computational layer of fog networks. Similar to the application layer and the intelligent integration block, the cloud computing layer supports several application services. Due to their access to enormous amounts of information and extensive processing capabilities, AIoT systems greatly benefit from computers in the cloud and fog. Keep in mind that the cloud plays a major role in an AIoT network. In addition, edge devices and fog nodes move throughout the network.

1. **Stack in the Cloud:** Instead of investing in costly on-premises hardware for AIoT operations, businesses may leverage cloud computing to access computing resources digitally via the Internet. This access may enable a wide variety of AIoT applications by providing dependable, scalable, and adaptable computing, storage, and networking resources. Massive amounts of data from widely dispersed sensors and equipment are often sent via the Internet to a distant cloud center. This is where they are integrated, processed, and stored.

    Figure 9.1 shows the three-tier computing architecture of AIoT networks.

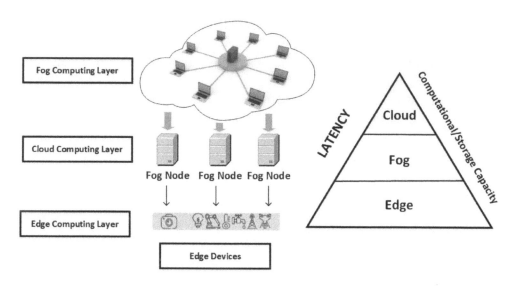

FIGURE 9.1   Diagram of three-tier computing architecture of AIoT.

The cloud makes it simple to set up a production environment for training and deploying DNNs for processing enormous volumes of data. This is thanks to ML tools and scalable computing capacity. Cloud computing's elastic computing resources on a pay-as-you-go basis are particularly well-suited to AIoT services, which see wildly varying volumes of user traffic. An additional benefit is that it is possible to utilize information gathered from all devices in a network in IoT applications. This helps to refine the representation and generalization skills of the deep models used in the application's training process.

1.1 **Fog Computing Layer:** Using fog computing, data may be stored, processed, and sent at the network's edge, right where the devices are. Fog nodes consist of a variety of devices, Wi-Fi access points, routers, switches, and gateways that contribute to a fog network. While comparable to cloud computing, fog computing's proximity to endpoints allows lower latency. Additionally, fog computing may provide service continuity independent of the Internet. This is particularly useful for some internet-dependent AIoT applications, such as those used in the agricultural, mining, and shipping industries. Since data may be stored locally on the LAN, fog computing also protects user information confidentiality and security. Due to their limited storage capacity and reliance on data from nearby devices, fog nodes are better suited to DNN deployment than training.

1.2 **Edge Computing Layer:** While edge computing and fog computing are synonymous in certain contexts (Zhang and Lu. 2021), alternatively, edge computing is used to refer to a more general idea that includes fog (Shi et al. 2020). However, for clarity, we will regard these two ideas as entirely separate throughout this chapter. We differentiate between cloud computing at the network's periphery (fog) and at device-level (edge) processing. Edge computing refers to the technique of putting sensors and actuators physically near computation nodes. The capacity of edge computing to turn data into compact, organized information locally, before transmission, is a significant advantage over fog and cloud computing, particularly for AIoT applications that make use of multimedia sensors. However, only lightweight DNNs can operate on edge devices because of their low processing power. This has led to a rise in interest in such areas of study as the creation of neural network architectures, the search for optimal network configurations in a mobile environment, and network pruning, compression, and quantification. To create an intelligent hybrid computing architecture, it is usual practice to deploy several models onto cloud platforms, fog nodes, and edge devices in an IoT system. It is anticipated that minimal latency may be achieved while exploiting deep learning capacities for processing vast volumes of data by intelligently offloading some of the computing effort from edge devices to the fog nodes and cloud. To identify vehicles in a live video feed, for instance, a lightweight model may be used on edge devices. It may be used as a switch to send keyframes to the cloud or fog nodes for processing.

9.3.1 Components and Programs

1. **Hardware:** The general-purpose Graphics Processing Unit (GPU) is a driving force in the deep learning revolution, alongside DNNs and large data, because of the tremendous computational power it transferred from its shading pipeline (e.g., for massive vector operations). Using GPUs to execute parallelly several of the network's operations, such as convolution, may significantly reduce the training and inference periods of neural networks. Google has unveiled a neural network ML application-specific integrated circuit. As a result of their efficiency and speed, Field-Programmable Gate Arrays (FPGAs) have also found widespread use to accelerate DNNs.

2. **Software:** Researchers and developers need streamlined processes for creating, deploying, training, and using DNNs. For this reason, several open-source deep learning frameworks have been created since its inception, ranging from those aimed at novices like Caffe1 and MatConvNet2 to the more advanced and widely used TensorFlow3 and PyTorch. Four convolutional neural networks may be implemented with MatConvNet, a MATLAB toolkit. Caffe is fast, written in C++, and accessible through Python and MATLAB, but it lacks distributed computing and mobile deployment. Caffe2 makes the necessary enhancements, which were ultimately included in PyTorch. TensorFlow and PyTorch's accessibility and popularity may be attributed to their user-friendly features, such as dynamic computation graphs and automated gradient calculation. By allowing hardware acceleration, quantization, and compressed models they also help when installing models on mobile devices. Moving models across frameworks is an important and helpful process. This is made possible by the open standard for expressing ML models such as ONNX5; TensorFlow and PyTorch both support this format. NCNN9 is a mobile device framework for inferring using neural networks; competing deep learning frameworks include MXNet, Theano, Paddle, and others.

9.4 EVALUATION OF BIG DATA IN AIoT

AI technology paves the way for IoT applications, with a specific emphasis on Deep Learning (DL). This section explores the DL perception, and AIoT systems' capabilities for cognition, reasoning, and behavior.

9.4.1 Observing

Understanding the environment via different devices is essential for AIoT systems. This understanding is only possible if objects are given the capacity to perceive their environments. Several interconnected themes emerge. This section focuses on image classification, object identification and tracking, semantic segmentation, and text spotting. Image classification is the act of assigning a broad category to an image. DNNs have been shown to outperform standard ML algorithms based on hand-crafted features on large-scale benchmark data sets like ImageNet, prompting a flurry of studies on DNN design including more recent models, such as Alex Net (Rehman et al. 2019) and ResNet. Figure 9.2 shows a conceptual map of AIoT perception-related issues.

To decrease network parameters and expand network depth, a stacked 33 convolutional layer has been developed; an 11 convolutional layer has been implemented to decrease feature dimension; residual connections have been implemented to prevent thick connections; and features have been created to recycle features from preceding layers and achieve gradient vanishing to increase network capacity. As the network depth and parameters increase, the top 1 ImageNet dataset misclassification error decreases. The network structure is also crucial. When compared to older networks like VGGNet, newer networks like ResNet and DenseNet perform better. They require fewer model parameters and less computing complexity. Artificial Neural Networks (ANNs) are preferred by AI applications that deploy them to edge devices. Networks like Mobile Net have been developed recently that make effective use of computing by using depth-wise convolutions, pointwise convolutions

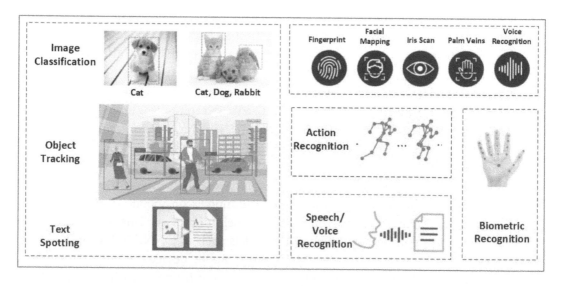

FIGURE 9.2   A conceptual map of AIoT perception-related issues.

(Jin et al. 2020), or binary operations (Rehman et al. 2019). Many AIoT applications may take advantage of image recognition. These include smart education tools and toys that employ cameras to aid and educate youngsters in exploring the world. Additionally, certain well-known smartphone apps that identify things like flowers, birds, foods, and calories benefit from these developments as well.

- **Object Detection:** Recognizing an item's category and position, also known as generic object detection, is a necessary crucial first step in the direction of many later household tasks, including expression recognition, person identification, posture estimation, and behavior analysis. DNNs have revolutionized photo-identification techniques. There are two types of cutting-edge techniques: those with two stages, and those with just one. While the former follows the standard "proposal detection" paradigm, indirectly evaluating all potential item candidates before delivering detection results, the latter does so directly. In other words, the former assesses detection through an intermediary evaluation of all potential candidates, while the latter directly provides detection results (Riaz, Shah, Rehman, and Gilani. 2019). An improved speed-accuracy trade-off has recently been suggested for onboard detection in AIoT applications via one-stage anchor-free detectors (Riaz, Gilani, et al. 2020) which describes item position substituting points or areas for anchors. Onboard detection in AIoT applications refers to the capability of performing detection and inference tasks directly on the edge devices or sensors without the need for external processing or cloud-based services. An extensive study into the identification of particular types of objects, like people, cars, road traffic signs, and certificate plates, is helpful for AIoT road traffic and public security monitoring, and self-directed driving. Many AIoT systems with optical sensors depend on object detection for video data structure. To achieve retrieval, verification, statistics, and analysis with minimal expenses related to transmission, storage, and computing.

- **Object-Tracking:** Traditional approaches to object-tracking fall into two categories: very original and selective. The former looks for a place most like the target, whereas the latter uses both the target and its surroundings to train a discriminative classifier online (Floridi et al. 2019). Among the DL techniques introduced later to enhance traditional techniques are end-to-end representation learning, multiresolution deep features, and Siamese networks. For AIoT applications, object trackers, which generally function substantially quicker than object detectors, might be used on edge devices like video surveillance and autonomous driving, where creating trajectories and predicting motion is necessary.

- **Semantic Segmentation:** *Predicting* an image's category label at the pixel level is known as "semantic segmentation" due to its ability to cascade convolution blocks while keeping spatial correlation. The encoder-decoder architecture of Convolutional Neural Network (CNN) has emerged as the standard method for semantic segmentation. To boost representational capacity and prediction accuracy, several deep models have been suggested: first, embedded in context, then increased resolution, and lastly, refined boundaries. Modules like the global context pooling component of Parse Net and the arousal-based spatial pyramid pooling are methods that successfully use context information to create more accurate feature representations are provided, such as the Deep Lab models and the pyramid pooling section of PSPNet. Increasing feature map resolution may improve prediction accuracy, especially for small things.

- **Text Spotting:** Text detection and identification are both components of the larger problem of text spotting. Although similar to generic object detection, text detection has its unique challenges. Text, unlike generic objects, may vary in length and form depending on the length and placement of the characters. Identical text can seem quite different depending on the font, style, and context in which it is shown.

- **Biometric Identifiers:** The study of biometric identifiers such as the human face, fingerprint, and iris has been ongoing for quite some time. We begin with a brief history of facial recognition technology. The four main phases of detection using a facial recognition system are alignment, representation, classification and verification. There is hope for the subfield of object detection known as face detection thanks to DL's recent triumph in general object recognition. The enormous gap between positive and negative recommendations, the incongruity between profile and front view, occlusion, and motion blur all call for more research. The Viola-Jones method is a well-known example of a classical algorithm; it forms the basis for modern facial recognition technology. Numerous DL methods model themselves after cascade classifiers (Jin et al. 2020).

- **Person Re-Identification:** Recognizing an individual from many disparate camera perspectives is called "person reidentification," a subfield of "image retrieval." Person reidentification is more difficult than face recognition in a controlled situation because of factors such as perspective, resolution, clothes, and background context which are out of one's control. Methods proposed to get around these problems include employing human posture and a parsing mask as guidance, deep metric learning with varying losses, integrating local features and context, and multitask learning with additional attribute annotations (Li et al. 2011). Generative Adversarial Networks (GANs) help bridge data that have recently been employed to produce style-transferred pictures. When existing biometric recognition methods cannot be used, such as in an uncontrolled and noncontact setting, there is a lot of potential for human reidentification to be used in IoT applications like smart security. Although more work is required to develop usable person reidentification systems with a human overseer, AI may accomplish remarkable feats with little human input. Initial proposal rating and filtering may be performed using the person reidentification model, for instance, before being passed on to human experts for ultimate determination.

- **Recognizing Human Gestures and Actions from Estimated Pose:** Estimating a person's posture from a single photograph is known as human key-point detection or pose estimate. Top-down and bottom-up approaches estimate human posture techniques. Although the latter immediately recognizes all key points from the picture and connects them with matching person instances, the former comprises two steps: person finding and key point finding. Top-down approaches are often slower than bottom-up approaches (Bonomi. 2011), even though they continue to top the scoreboard example, MS COCO10. The following points sum up the state of the art in this field today.

- **Crowd Counting:** Indoor and outdoor population counts are essential for avoiding congestion and accidents in video surveillance scenarios. WI-FI, Bluetooth, and camera-based solutions have been presented for real-world AIoT applications with crowd-counting capability (Riaz, Shah, Rehman. 2020, Gilani, et al. 2019). These techniques may roughly gauge how linked a mobile device is to a Wi-Fi hotspot or Bluetooth beacon. Although it is possible to estimate the size of a crowd by counting the number of visible faces or heads, this approach is limited by poor resolution and blurred individual instances in crowd images. Moreover, identifying a large number of individuals simultaneously is computationally inefficient. Since Gaussian density maps are used to construct the truth nodes, most CNN-based algorithms do a straight regression on the population density map.

- **Probable Depth/Location/SLAM:** *Camera-based* distance estimation has been studied for a long time (Macaulay, Buckalew, and Chung. 2015; Bonomi. 2015). Monocular cameras, stereo cameras, and Multiview camera systems are only some of the possible AIoT setups in the real world. In recent times, there has been a lot of focus on camera location estimation and depth estimation from monocular video when compared to methods that rely on manual matching and optimization. Unsupervised or self-supervised DL has several advantages in this field's current research. The standard optimization target includes matching error and photometric error. They build the self-supervisory signals using the re-projection Multiview's well-defined geometry which allows for precise measurements of light loss as a function of distance and camera orientation. Despite CNN's impressive representational prowess, it still faces obstacles including occlusions, moving objects, and the scale problem (per-frame ambiguity and temporal inconsistency). Both Visual Odometer (VO) and Visual-Inertial Odometer (VIO) (Chiang and Zhang. 2016) seek to estimate consecutive camera postures of a person or thing utilizing information from a camera and IMU sensor for camera posture estimation. Back-end Simultaneous Localization and Mapping (SLAM) systems use nonlinear optimization to estimate posture globally and drift-free. Of the pose graph, Front-end SLAM systems always use VO and VIO. In old-style methods like Oriented FAST and Rotated BRIEF Simultaneous Localization and Mapping (ORB-SLAM) (Lamarre and May. 2019), the front and back ends are treated as separate entities. A novel, adaptable design, a neural network optimizer, has just been developed for worldwide pose graph optimization. It provides a complete neural network implementation of SLAM by combining it with a local posture estimation model.

- **Image Enhancement:** To improve a single attribute of a picture, whether its brightness, contrast, or sharpness, is a job known as image enhancement. Images were taken with poor vision in dim light and blurred features because of inadequate incident light or underexposure. Based on the Retinex hypothesis a picture may be broken down into a reflectance map and an illumination map. After that, the illumination map may be improved to restore proper lighting to the initial dark picture. However, extracting the reflectance and illumination from a single picture is a classic example of an ill-posed task. Various low-light enhancement strategies based on either previous knowledge or learning have been suggested to solve this problem in recent research. To refine the initial estimate, LIME utilizes a structural prior for the illumination map, while (another method) employs a piecewise smoothness constraint. To estimate reflectance, light, and noise simultaneously, several strong Retinex models have been constructed (Tordera et al. 2016). This is necessary since low-light pictures often include noises that would be enhanced after using AI methods. The attenuation and scattering effects of the haze result in dimly lit images. It is also a difficult problem to recover a clear picture from a single foggy input, although this issue may be tackled using either prior-based or learning-based approaches. Authors (Bonomi. 2011) introduced the first deep CNN model for photo defogging, which uses the superior representation capacity of CNNs to beat conventional prior-based approaches to assess the transparency and realism techniques. Some methods, statistical priors, and DL have been used to offer options with comparable functionality, including Optimal Reflectance Prediction, Glow Separation, and Network Delay (ND-Net).

- **Correction and Stitching of Images:** Able to capture a wider area of the scene than narrow field-of-view cameras, wide-angle cameras like fisheye cameras have found widespread usage in a variety of AIoT applications, including surveillance cameras and self-driving cars. The acquired pictures are flawed, however, since they fail to conform to the expected perspective transformation. Correcting the problem upfront will make subsequent processes easier. Camera calibration and distortion model techniques are used in rectifying the problem. The former adjusts for perspective distortion through camera calibration for both internal and external factors. The formulation optimization constraints and loss functions in learning-based systems leverage geometric signals like lines and vanishing spots. If conditions are right, fisheye pictures may form panoramas.

- **Speech Recognition:** Automatic Speech Recognition (ASR), or voice recognition, a part of computational linguistics, attempts to automatically understand and translate spoken language into text. DNNs have transformed complete ASR analysis outside of a specialist's area. Conventional ASR models use the process of feature engineering, Hidden Markov Model (HMM) design, or an explicit reliance hypothesis based on the cepstral value and the Hidden Markov System (HMS). To represent long-range voice sequence relationships and decode text (Yang et al. 2020), Recurrent Neural Networks (RNNs) are often utilized. However, RNN analyzes data sequentially, rendering it inappropriate for parallel processing; additional work is required with preferment training sequences so that the classification loss may be assessed independently at each point in the sequence. The Connectionist Temporal Classification

(CTC) is proposed as a solution for the first issue since it can optimize the likelihood of the correct label sequence in an adaptable fashion. The other issue is solved by the transformer architecture's usage of scaled dot-product attention and multicolored attention.

- **Speaker Recognition:** In the same way that facial recognition attempts to identify a person based on his or her appearance, speaker recognition does the same thing by analyzing vocal characteristics. There are four main parts to a speech recognition system: voice input and output, the matching and classifying of patterns, the representation of features, and the selection of features. Previously, a framework for probabilistic linear discriminant analysis was based on an I-vector representation. Ani-vector is a technique for extracting low-dimensional speaker embeddings from adequate data. To outperform I-vector baselines, numerous comprehensive deep speaker identification models have been developed. Advances in deep metric learning, such as using both face recognition and voice identification, benefit from the use of large-scale data sets and the use of the loss functions of contrastive loss and triplet loss to train discriminative speaker embeddings. Speaker recognition has several potential applications within the realm of AI and the IoT, including automatic transcription systems for big meetings, customized recommendation systems driven by the use of audio forensics, and advanced speech recognition software. The development of voice recognition and facial recognition may be combined for use in door locks.

- **Machine Translation:** Automatic text translation from one language to another is another branch of computational linguistics called Machine Translation (MT). In recent years, deep learning-based neural MT (NMT) has made significant strides, outperforming more conventional statistical MT techniques and example-based MT approaches by using the former's potent representation capability and massive amounts of training data. The encoder-decoder architecture (Bonomi. 2011) is widely used in NMT. Later, at each stage of RNN decoding, an attention mechanism is employed to focus on either every single word in the source (known as the world is paying attention (or "global attention")), or on a small group of words (known as "local attention"). When it comes to joint alignment and translation, attention may be a useful tool for learning target-relevant context components, particularly for longer sentences. Unsupervised representation learning, using methods like BERT to train embeddings that are both context-aware and informative, has shown encouraging performance on several downstream language tasks. Unsupervised NMT, which can be trained with just monolingual corpora, has also been the subject of a recent study. NMT has demonstrated success utilizing BERT as contextual embedding by borrowing informative context from the retrained model. Many AIoT applications, including language instruction, autonomous integration of MT with voice recognition, and speech synthesis have the potential to revolutionize translation, transcription, and multilingual customer assistance.

- **Multimedia and Multimodal Analysis:** Multimedia content (containing text, audio, image, and video) is increasingly being created on a broad range of internet platforms, and keeping up with it is an expanding field of study. New studies on the topic of cross-media retrieval and matching use DL, particularly adversarial learning, to semantically align the two domains. However, learning representations are hampered by data that is unique to a certain modality. To solve this problem, researchers have suggested disentangled representation learning, which attempts to extract modality-independent features from shared feature embeddings across modalities. Cross-modal matching includes the generative tasks of both image/video captioning and text-to-image generation seeking to automate the process of creating a textual description of an image or video based on a supplied textual description. Additional data modalities, such as depth pictures, LiDAR point clouds, and thermal infrared images, may further help in scene interpretation by providing supplementary information to the components already mentioned. This diversified set of modalities enhances the richness of the data representation, enabling a more comprehensive and accurate understanding of the scene through the incorporation of depth, spatial details from LiDAR, and thermal information, thereby contributing to a more robust and context-aware interpretation. Using RGB pictures, several practical applications have begun to include cross-modal perception, such as scene parsing for autonomous driving object identification, tracking in low-light circumstances, and action recognition. There are three approaches to combining multimodal data: input-level fusion, feature-level synthesis, and output-level synthesis. The most typical approach is to combine information from several sources at the feature level, which may be further subdivided into early fusion, late fusion, and multi-layer fusion. This approach offers a multi-branch group fusion module to fuse features from RGB and thermal infrared images, taking into account the fact that semantic information and visual details vary at different levels. This ensures a comprehensive integration of both modalities, allowing for a more nuanced representation that captures the diverse characteristics present in RGB and thermal infrared data. Multimedia production and cross-modal analysis are useful in certain AIoT applications, such as speech-described TV show retrieval and recommendation, a teaching helper in the classroom, a Chabot's insight into the world of e-commerce via automated (custom) item description production, response to multimedia content, night-time object detection and tracking for smart security, and action recognition for rehabilitation monitoring and assessment. Multimedia coding is another area of study that is related to AIoT and has benefited from DL.

- **Network Compression and Neural Architecture Search (NAS):** To make DNNs more successful for AIoT applications where computing resources are limited, network compression is a practical option. Four main methods are used including pruning and quantizing networks, low-rank factorization, and distilling information. To prune a network, one must first train a big network, apply a pruning criterion, and then retrain the network in terms of pruning criterion Depending on the size of weights or responses shown, weight pruning, neuron pruning, and filter pruning are all examples of finer-grained forms of network pruning that adhere to the L1/L2 norm and channel pruning. Network quantization may drastically decrease memory utilization and float point operations while sacrificing just a small amount of accuracy by lowering the number of bits needed for each weight in the original network's representation. The network as a whole will typically follow a uniform precision quantization scheme, where each layer uses the same bit width. To make use of NAS's capabilities, a mixed-precision model quantization approach was recently presented (Macaulay, Buckalew, and Chung. 2015) in which each layer/channel uses a unique bit width. The goal of NAS is to eliminate the need for human network design by doing an automated search of the architecture within a finite area (Bonomi. 2011). There are three main types of NAS approaches: evolutionary, Reinforcement Learning (RL), and gradient-based. A population of neural network designs must be trained before evolutionary approaches may begin to develop them via recombination and mutation. In RL-based techniques, the architecture generation model (for instance, the RNN controller) is updated using RL algorithms, and the reward is the validation accuracy of the sampled network design. Both strategies are motivated by the brain architecture's reward or fitness system. When it comes to representing architecture, gradient-based approaches instead use continuous relaxation. Since gradient descent can be performed in a continuous space, this allows for much quicker optimization of neural architecture.

9.4.2 Learning

Since the actual world is always changing, AIoT systems that rely on a static model are likely to underperform. Therefore, giving objects the capacity to learn is crucial for AIoT so that it can adapt to new circumstances. Deep Unsupervised and Semi-Supervised Learning (USL) uses DNNs, such as deep autoencoders, deep belief networks, and GAN, to model probability distributions. Different GAN models have been presented recently, each capable of producing high-resolution, photorealistic pictures from a vector distribution. To represent the probability distribution of data, DNNs, like deep autoencoders, deep belief networks, and GAN, are used in deep USL. Different GAN models have been presented recently, each capable of producing high-resolution, photorealistic pictures from a vector distribution. As a result, the models should have picked up an abstract comprehension of the training data's semantics. Figure 9.3 shows an outline of AIoT learning-related concepts.

An encoder is used to train an input-to-latent space inverse mapping (Floridi et al. 2019); the most recent Big Bidirectional Generative Adversarial Network (BigBiGAN) model may acquire a discriminative visual representation with excellent performance transfer to downstream tasks. Completing predetermined pretext activities as a means of learning discriminative visual representation is another area of ongoing research (Chiang and Zhang. 2016).

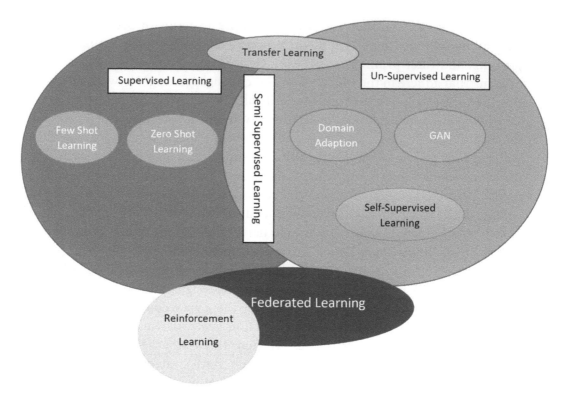

FIGURE 9.3   An outline of AIoT's learning-related concepts.

To fix target Task Learning (TL) with insufficient training data, TL applies what has been learned in the context of a similar source task. Importantly, unlike SSL, which requires that the source data distributions and the destination domains be similar, TL does not impose this constraint. For quicker convergence and greater generalization, it is common practice to fine-tune models that are retrained using ImageNet and then applied to new problems. This is particularly true for semantic segmentation and object recognition.

Significant empirical findings, such as which visual activities generalize easily to various goals, and reusing monitoring, are straightforward across comparable activities to minimize labeled data while maintaining performance. Study of Data Analysis (DA), which aims to transfer training of a model from one or more source domains to a target domain where it excels at the same task, is ongoing and closely connected to TL. Learning with Few or No Attempts is a kind of meta-learning (or "learning how to learn"). Few or No Attempts Learning (FSL) seeks to train itself using minimal annotated examples. Due to the limited size of the training set used for FSL, it is possible to make use of previously acquired information to handle the problematic empirical risk minimizer problem. Training data may be improved with the use of previous information in several ways. For instance, samples from the training set can be transformed using prior knowledge, or an additional weakly labeled/unlabeled data set can be employed. In addition, FSL is used to modify the search method in hypothesis space by imposing constraints on the range of possible hypotheses. Rare occurrences, such as a vehicle accident, cyber-attack, or machine malfunction, must be detected by AI models in practical AIoT applications. However, it is often challenging to gather and annotate such extensive case data. So, in these cases, FSL may be used to train appropriate models.

- **Major Learning Paradigms:** RL (Reinforcement Learning) uses an agent to interact with its environment to maximize cumulative reward. Deep Reinforcement Learning (DRL) has led to rapid advances. DNNs can acquire compressed and discriminative feature representations from high-dimensional image and video data, improving RL. A vast variety of AIoT applications employ DRL's capacity to offer inanimate things the ability to interact with and adapt to their surroundings Such applications include autonomous driving in smart transportation (Tordera et al. 2016), 3-D landmark identification of CT scans, robot control in smart healthcare, course recommendation in smart education, Real-Time Scheduling (RTS) for smart factories, load scheduling in smart grids, and plant monitoring. It has been shown that Federated Learning's (FL) privacy-friendly architecture can support DRL-based learning (Tordera et al. 2016).

- **Federated Learning:** The original motivation for FL was to solve the learning challenge of confidentially brought about with sharing data across numerous devices. When many data owners work together to train a model, that model should be as effective as one trained with all of the data at once. In most implementations of FL, a server (or collaborator) acts as the hub for a network of dispersed client devices. Each client generates its gradients from its data, which are then transmitted to the server to be aggregated (or concatenated) before being delivered back to clients to be used in updating their models.

9.4.3 Reasoning

Internet data, medical records, financial activities, etc., all include a wealth of information that may be utilized to infer patient cohorts or reason the answer to a query. As a species, we have the capacity for causal thinking, which includes processes like causal inference and discovery. For AIoT to make informed, auditable judgment calls, it must be endowed with this level of reasoning capability. We provide a comprehensive discussion of Knowledge Graph (KG) reasoning and causal reasoning here.

- **Knowledge Graph and Reasoning:** KGs are a structured method of representing knowledge in which nodes represent things and edges reflect relations (also known as triples) as a representation of information (Entity, Relationship, and Ending Entity). Knowledge reasoning has been employed in the development and implementation of several prominent KGs, including Word Net, Freebase, YAGO, and NELL. Deducing new information from old is called "knowledge reasoning," and it includes tasks like fixing errors, filling in blanks, finding answers to questions, and drawing conclusions.

Ontology languages, first-order predicate logic, and probability and route reasoning are some of the rule-based systems traditionally used in knowledge reasoning. KG embedding-based techniques have gained popularity in recent years (Palomares et al. 2021). These methods attempt to map a KG onto a continuous vector space, allowing for reasoning to be performed utilizing translational distance models and semantic matching models.

- **Causal Reasoning:** Causality is the relationship between an effect and its underlying cause, in which the cause partially accounts for the effect and the effect partially relies on the cause. To arrive at an estimate of causal impact, causal inference is a part of causal reasoning. In contrast, causal discovery is a part of causal reasoning that focuses on identifying causal relationships. Although expensive and time-consuming, randomized controlled trials are a standard means of arguing causality by comparing the results of a treatment group with those of a control group. There has been a lot of interest as of late (Riaz, Gilani, et al. 2019) in the concept of learning causality from observational data. Both the structural causal model and the prospective outcome framework are well-known causal models that may be used to learn about causality (a.k.a. Rubin Causal Model). Several strategies for causal inference using the POKER framework have been presented. These strategies include representation learning, multi-task learning, and mental earning.

9.4.4 Behaving

Whether an AIoT system is passively monitoring and reacting to changes in its surroundings, actively searching for relevant information, or somewhere in between, the ability to behave well is crucial. So, here we provide a quick overview of two areas associated with behavior in AIoT: control and interaction. Whether an AIoT system is passively monitoring and reacting to changes in its surroundings, actively searching for relevant information, or somewhere in between, the ability to behave well is crucial. Therefore, in this overview, we delve into two key areas associated with behavior in AIoT: control and interaction.

9.5 BIG DATA ANALYTICS FOR AIoT APPLICATIONS

There is significant promise in the development of AI to provide perceptual, learning, reasoning, and behavioral capabilities to the linked devices in AIoT networks. The ensuing AIoT systems have far-reaching effects on many facets of the economy and the places where we live, including transportation, healthcare, education, industry, energy, agriculture, and public safety. The Big Data sources encompass various networks that span different facets of the economy and the places we live. The purpose of intelligent safety is to safeguard offline and online environments via the use of different forms of AI/OT technology. Human-centric perception is one of the examples to identify people and evaluate their actions to deter criminal behavior. Cloud/fog computing and edge computing have made possible the deployment of facial recognition systems in public spaces like airports, train stations, and building entrances. Data security and privacy preservation are key concerns of these networks despite their usefulness. Person reidentification seeks to identify people and follow their trajectories in various cameras by using spatial and temporal human body traits (such as form and gait), in addition to biometric data identification based on facial features, fingerprints, and eyes.

AIoT-enabled smart transportation encompasses traffic components (such as smart Internet of Vehicle (IoV), transportation networks, and business uses. (e.g., smart, connected logistics). Self-driving cars are one common use of AI's ability to combine perception, learning, reasoning, and behavior. An autonomous vehicle's perception of its surroundings includes things like road and traffic sign detection, pedestrian and vehicle trajectory prediction, and traffic sign interpretation. In addition, SLAM should quantify the stance and placement of landmarks (such as traffic signs). This data informs the autonomous vehicle's driving policy and interactions with other vehicles on the road. Recently, deep RL has been utilized to directly take in visual information (such as front-facing pictures) to inform a driver's strategy. However, it is too expensive to put the training into practice in actual conditions. Monitoring, examination, surgery, and rehabilitation are just a few of the many areas that may benefit from AIoT systems in smart healthcare. Human activity recognition may be monitored using either cameras or wearable devices equipped with motion sensors. Semantic segmentation and 3-D landmark recognition in CT scans are only two examples of the medical image processing challenges to which deep learning has been applied to avoid the high computational cost and privacy concerns of utilizing public clouds. Hospitals generally deploy these models on their private cloud. Recent work on 2D orthotropic gauze has employed deep RL to control multilateral cutting. It has also been suggested that AIoT systems may be used to monitor and evaluate various forms of rehabilitation including, for example, stroke therapy and ankle rehabilitation. Patients in remote places may benefit from therapists' ability to evaluate the progress of their rehabilitation using the linked 3-dimensional augmented reality/virtual reality (3-D AR/VR) equipment. These days, it's possible to get quick answers to health questions and even get a second opinion from a robot doctor who works from home.

Children and students may benefit from AI technologies enabled by AIoT items by identifying new species, learning local or foreign languages, choosing customized learning materials, and learning through interactions with visually impaired individuals. This AIoT system allows instructors to command a Raspberry Pi to take pictures of the blackboard/whiteboard with a single, static hand gesture, then convert those pictures into an editable format that can be stored in a student's desktop. Applications are backed up to a private cloud where they may be accessed for additional modification or group work. Using voice speech-to-text production, recognition of languages, and translations, presents a solution for portable devices to do multilingual translation from written text to spoken word. This also has offline functionality and provides helpful grammatical information for other language students. Thanks to developments in AI technology like deep learning, numerous new mobile translation solutions that can translate dozens of languages have been introduced in time for the 2020 Consumer Electronics Show. Open online courses for many people at once, like Coursera, have emerged as a popular alternative to traditional classroom instruction. Students access the content via the cloud using their own devices.

Industry 4.0's smart factories may greatly benefit from digital twins, which are digital copies of physical systems that can be used for monitoring the production process, identifying problems, and avoiding downtime. Connected sensors and actuators may gather real-time data from production lines and communicate it to the digital twin running in the cloud, making AIoT a crucial component in implementing digital twins. In addition, AI technologies allow for sophisticated data analysis and aid in making sound judgments. Smart grid AIoT applications include cyber-threat detection, controlling and distributing workloads, and fault diagnostics. To classify and estimate the damage to electricity distribution poles, UAVs (unmanned aerial vehicles) are deployed and connected to the command center through the cellular network. Using images captured by UAVs and stored in the cloud, a CNN model can estimate the extent of collapse, damage, and burns. On top of that, certain so-called "industrial stethoscopes" are made to locate the origin of abnormal noises in visual environments using a combination of cameras and other sensors. Microphones, with the algorithm able to perform near-real-time monitoring on edge devices, enable efficient data processing and analysis directly at the source. Recently, an attention mechanism-equipped two-stream network for direct image-based sound source localization was suggested. Fault diagnosis has also been aided by AI technologies. For power transmission line fault detection using power and current information, for instance, a convolutional sparse auto encoder-based USL technique has been presented. Its low latency of 7 MS makes it suitable for use in practical settings. In addition, techniques for defect detection and effect causal analysis in the power grid are investigated, including knowledge representation and causal relationship identification. TL and deep RL algorithms are presented for load monitoring and charging scheduling of electric vehicles

Precision agriculture, which uses sensors, autonomous agricultural tools, and geographic information systems to monitor, measure, and react to crop variability, has gained traction in recent years as an example of the kind of "smart agriculture" made possible by the AIoT. Precision agriculture places a premium on issues like crop counting and production estimates. Images of crops and fruits taken with UVAs are sent to the cloud for tally purposes (Shi et al. 2020). Because fruits are tallied twice in neighboring frames, the entire yield cannot be calculated by adding together the counting results over many picture sequences. A detection tracking counting based approach is presented as a solution since it can filter out anomalies and avoid counting the same fruit again. By taking pictures of agricultural fields at regular intervals and aligning them in time, UAVs may likewise be utilized for continuous crop monitoring. The above-mentioned activities, which have been explored in the agricultural setting, rely heavily on UAVs' capabilities for self-localization and navigation.

"Smart" towns, houses, structures, and the smart industries just stated are connected to AIoT and may be fueled by the same kinds of AI technology. Here are a few instances that illustrate the point. One example of smart security is continuously identifying the speaker by programming smart home voice assistants to combine vibration cues from the speaker's body with the speech signals. Similar to this is how hand gesture recognition is utilized in smart home HMI systems (e.g., control television) and how circulation sign language recognition is used in smart transportation and in education.

9.6 OPPORTUNITIES AND CHALLENGES

Problems arise in AIoT systems while processing, sending, and storing multimodal heterogeneous data because the large numbers of sensors of varying types and characteristics provide a flood of data with unpredictable structure, volume, and timing. A more efficient encoding approach may reduce network congestion and increase data transmission rates. The video coding technique for machines is one such example of a technique for video encoding with the potential to streamline future computer vision projects. If compact and ordered representations of the data could be recovered, the transmission and storage requirements of the AI perception technologies would be significantly optimized. AIoT systems need deep CNN models placed on edge devices to manage data streams in real-time with low latency. However, edge devices can't do much due to their limited resources. Thus, developing or autonomously searching for lightweight, computationally efficient, and hardware-friendly DNN architectures is useful yet challenging. Quantization, compression, and pruning in networks are also crucial concepts to master.

AIoT architecture often makes use of cloud servers, fog nodes, and edge devices. Computational scheduling is a problem in real-world AIoT systems since certain intensive computing may need to be offloaded from edge devices to the fog node or cloud center. Data type and volume, network bandwidth, processing latency, performance accuracy, energy consumption, and data security and privacy are all important considerations when scheduling computation among multiple resources. Uneven data flow and fluctuating user needs might be accommodated by a flexible scheduling approach. There is a tremendous opportunity for DL to be applied to the large amounts of sensor data that permeate AIoT systems. Thanks to massive amounts of labeled data, deep-supervised learning algorithms have seen great success in several fields of perception. However, the vast majority of AIoT data is unlabeled, and it would be prohibitively costly and time-consuming to name them all. Future initiatives are likely to significantly use AIoT data, particularly multimodal data, even though self-supervised learning in particular has shown rapid advancement in USL (Palomares et al. 2021). Because there isn't a ton of labeled data to work with, TL, SSL, and FSL may also help address issues brought on by the emergence of novel classes, the discovery of unusual edge cases, and the gradual change in a device's state that characterizes AIoT. Some other challenges are as follows:

- **Data Monopoly:** In the age of AI, data are a precious commodity for developing innovative goods and enhancing existing ones. Companies acquire and use a lot of data, which opens up new avenues for data mining. This virtuous cycle has the potential to create a data monopoly. This is when large amounts of confidential information are held inaccessible by a few powerful organizations. As a result, there is a hurdle for new entrants to get the piece of information.

- **Privacy and Data Protection:** As devices become more commonplace in places like smart homes, hospitals, and cities, massive amounts of biometric data (such as a person's facial image, voice, activity, pulse, imaging data, etc.) may be captured from both educated and ignorant individuals via AIoT. This brings up serious issues with the confidentiality and integrity of personal information.

- **Growing Energy Consumption in Data Centers:** It is estimated that data centers use more than a third of communication technologies' power worldwide. Therefore, for future sustainability, it is essential to improve data center energy efficiency. Some data centers, for instance, set up shops in chilly regions to use the weather as air conditioning. Servers may also be submerged in a bath of non-conductive oil or minerals, or cooled with water. Analysis of workload, planning of tasks, and consolidation of virtual machines are three further areas of research into making data centers more power efficient. Like the proliferation of AIoT use cases, cloud data centers are expanding quickly. As a result, we need to keep up our efforts to reduce data center energy use.

- **Capability for Neural Processing at the Edge:** In many edge devices, the calculation of neural networks is boosted by specialized processors (such as the graphics processing units in smartphones and intelligent cameras). Therefore, it is very beneficial for AIoT applications to include neural processing capabilities in edge devices. For one, it lessens wait times and saves bandwidth on the back end. With on-site processing of sensing data, just a minimal quantity of managed data has to be transferred. Second, it can keep your information safe and private. The danger of data leakage may be reduced, for instance, if the biometric data of registered users is encrypted and kept on local hardware, with just the built-in verification capability on the edge devices accessible to the apps. Third, it allows for asymmetric and dispersed model training. Models may be trained across edge devices using their local sensor data and an FL framework. Furthermore, distinct groups of strategies may choose various model update procedures based on their respective use conditions.

- **Neuromorphic Computing with Event-based Sensors:** Once activated, deep CNNs receive a constant stream of data from traditional camera sensors, which is then processed by GPUs. Since every one of those pixels goes towards the final tally, costs are usually high. The use of neuromorphic computers and event-based sensors has been proposed in recent suggestions. For instance, event-based cameras only save images with a pixel-level brightness change, reducing the amount of data that is sent and created. Event-based neuromorphic computers, unlike GPUs, can avoid performing dense and redundant computations on traditional sensory input by functioning directly on sparse and asynchronous event streams. These may be used in many different areas of AIoT because of their low latency and low power consumption.

- **Taking Deep Learning into the Real World:** Embodied AI is useful in contexts where regular AI would be impractical. Voyage Deepdrive13, Open-air gym14, and Habitat15 are only a few examples of 3D virtual platforms made specifically for deep RL model training. Before using the trained model, the domain shift between digital and physical domains must be resolved. There is a lot of interest in utilizing TL and Data Analytics (DA) to solve this problem in USL and RL.

- **Data and Knowledge Integration for Perceiving:** DL models' ability to learn, reason, and behave depends heavily on the quantity and quality of their training data. However, people acquire new ideas by combining facts and their own stored information. In a similar vein, past knowledge may be quite helpful when training deep learning models with less data. For instance, Zero-Shot Learning (ZSL) for novel ideas is made possible via attribute transfer thanks to the attribute-based class description. Knowledge Graphs (KGs) are another example since they depict the structural connections between things. KGs, knowledge-embedding representation learning, and reasoning all benefit from knowledge extraction from unstructured data. When combined, this is a possible method for achieving human-level cognitive ability using question-and-answer DL (such as graph neural networks) which has a wide variety of applications, including but not limited to system and fault/disease diagnostics.

9.7 CONCLUSION

In this chapter, we examined the history of Big Data analytics for AIoT, the computational architectures that power it, the AI technologies that give the capability to observe, learn, reason, and behave, the most promising applications of Big Data analytics in AIoT, and the difficulties and possibilities that lie ahead for this field of study. While the AIoT's three-tier computing architecture offers a variety of computational resources for DL, it also introduces additional issues, related to the creation and exploration of lightweight models, as well as computation scheduling within the three-tier architecture. Various types of perception have shown tremendous advancements because of DL, and it allows various AIoT applications. However, more work has to be done to enhance intelligence at the edge. DL has gained popularity in unverified learning, helping A-IoT systems deal with complicated and changing circumstances using predictive techniques like RL settings. Research on for KG-based reasoning and causal analysis to attain human levels of cognitive ability is challenging. AIoT acts in response to the ever-changing environment via control and interaction; DL has proven useful for increasing control precision and allowing new kinds of multimodal interactions. Many quick, smart, environmentally friendly, and secure AIoT applications are anticipated to profoundly transform our society in the future, enabled by rapidly developing AI technologies.

REFERENCES

Abiodun, O. I., Abiodun, E. O., Alawida, M., Alkhawaldeh, R. S. & Arshad, H. "A review on the security of the internet of things: Challenges and solutions. Wireless Personal Communications", 119, (2021): 2603–637.

Ashfaq, Ahmed, et al. "Role of Artificial Intelligence in Renewable Energy and Its Scope in Future." 2022 5th International Conference on Energy Conservation and Efficiency (ICECE). IEEE, 2022.

Aslam, Sheraz, Michalis P. Michaelides, and Herodotos Herodotou. "Internet of Ships: A Survey on Architectures, Emerging Applications, and Challenges." *IEEE Internet of Things Journal* 7.10 (2020): 9714–27.

Ballin, Ben. "The World in Numbers Primary Geography." *Interaction* 44.2 (2016): 38–39.

Bonomi, Flavio. "Connected Vehicles, the Internet of Things, and Fog Computing." *The Eighth ACM International Workshop on Vehicular Inter-Networking (VANET)*, Las Vegas. 2011.

Catarinucci, Luca, et al. "An IoT-Aware Architecture for Smart Healthcare Systems." *IEEE Internet of Things Journal* 2.6 (2015): 515–26.

Che, Dunren, Mejdl Safran, and Zhiyong Peng. "From Big Data to Big Data Mining: Challenges, Issues, and Opportunities." *Database Systems for Advanced Applications: 18th International Conference, DASFAA 2013*, International Workshops: BDMA, SNSM, SeCoP, Wuhan, China, April 22–25, 2013. Proceedings 18. Springer, 2013.

Chiang, Mung, and Tao Zhang. "Fog and IoT: An Overview of Research Opportunities." *IEEE Internet of Things Journal* 3.6 (2016): 854–64.

Contreras-Castillo, Juan, Sherali Zeadally, and Juan Antonio Guerrero Ibáñez. "A Seven-Layered Model Architecture for Internet of Vehicles." *Journal of Information Telecommunication* 1.1 (2017): 4–22.

Di Pierro, Massimo. "What Is the Blockchain?" *Computing in Science & Engineering* 19.5 (2017): 92–95.

Floridi, L., et al. "IDC (2019). The Growth in Connected IoT Devices Is Expected to Generate 79.4 ZB of Data in 2025." *International Data Corporation*.

Guan, Zhitao, et al. "Achieving Efficient and Secure Data Acquisition for Cloud-Supported Internet of Things in Smart Grid." *IEEE Internet of Things Journal* 4.6 (2017): 1934–44.

Iorga, Michaela, et al. "Fog Computing Conceptual Model." (2018).

Jin, Xiaofeng, et al. "Artificial Intelligence Biosensors: Challenges and Prospects." *Biosensors and Bioelectronics* 165 (2020): 112412–12.

Khan, Tariq, et al. "Multipath Transport Control Protocol for 5G Mobile Augmented Reality Networks." *International Journal of Communication Systems* 35.5 (2022): e4778.

Lamarre, Eric, and Brett May. "Ten Trends Shaping the Internet of Things Business Landscape." *McKinsey Digital* (2019).

Li, Xu, et al. "Smart Community: An Internet of Things Application." *IEEE Communications magazine* 49.11 (2011): 68–75.

Macaulay, James, Lauren Buckalew, and Gina Chung. "Internet of Things in Logistics: A Collaborative Report by DHL and Cisco on Implications and Use Cases for the Logistics Industry." *DHL Trend Research and Cisco Consulting Services* (2015): 439–49.

Palomares, Iván, et al. "A Panoramic View and SWOT Analysis of Artificial Intelligence for Achieving the Sustainable Development Goals by 2030: Progress and Prospects." *Applied Intelligence* 51 (2021): 6497–527.

Qureshi, Kashif Naseer, Abdul Hanan Abdullah, and Raja Waseem Anwar. "Vehicular Road Side Backbone Network with Multiprotocol Label Switching." *1st International Conference of Recent Trends in Information and Communication Technologies*, UTM, 2014.

Qureshi, Kashif Naseer, et al. "Trust Aware Energy Management System for Smart Homes Appliances." *Computers & Electrical Engineering* 97 (2021): 107641.

Qureshi, Kashif Naseer, et al. "Trust Management and Evaluation for Edge Intelligence in the Internet of Things." *Engineering Applications of Artificial Intelligence* 94 (2020): 103756.

Rehman, Faisal, et al. "Human Identification Using Dental Biometric Analysis." *2015 Fifth International Conference on Digital Information and Communication Technology and its Applications (DICTAP)*. IEEE, 2015.

Riaz, Naveed, et al. "Fault Signal Detection of Linear Actuators Based on Intelligent Remnant Filter." 2019 8th International Conference on Information and Communication Technologies (ICICT). IEEE, 2019.

Riaz, Naveed, et al. "An Approach to Measure Functional Parameters for Ball-Screw Drives." *Intelligent Technologies and Applications: Second International Conference, INTAP 2019*, Bahawalpur, Pakistan, November 6–8, 2019, Revised Selected Papers 2. Springer, 2020.

Riaz, Naveed, et al. "An Intelligent Approach to Detect Actuator Signal Errors Based on Remnant Filter." *Intelligent Technologies and Applications: Second International Conference*, INTAP 2019, Bahawalpur, Pakistan, November 6–8, 2019, Revised Selected Papers 2. Springer Singapore, 2020.

Shi, Wenzhong, et al. "Change Detection Based on Artificial Intelligence: State-of-the-Art and Challenges." *Remote Sensing* 12.10 (2020): 1688–88.

Silverio-Fernández, Manuel, Suresh Renukappa, and Subashini Suresh. "What Is a Smart Device? - A Conceptualisation within the Paradigm of the Internet of Things." *Visualization in Engineering* 6.1 (2018): 1–10.

Tordera, Eva Marín, et al. "What Is a Fog Node a Tutorial on Current Concepts Towards a Common Definition." *arXiv preprint arXiv:1611.09193* (2016).

Un Nisa, Khaleeq, et al. "Security Provision for Protecting Intelligent Sensors and Zero Touch Devices by Using Blockchain Method for the Smart Cities." *Microprocessors and Microsystems* 90 (2022): 104503.

Wang, Xiang, et al. "Explainable Reasoning Over Knowledge Graphs for Recommendation." *Proceedings of the AAAI Conference on Artificial Intelligence* 33.1 (2019).

Yang, Jiachen, et al. "Visual Perception Enabled Industry Intelligence: State of the Art, Challenges and Prospects." *IEEE Transactions on Industrial Informatics* 17.3 (2020): 2204–19.

Zhang, Caiming, and Yang Lu. "Study on Artificial Intelligence: The State of the Art and Future Prospects." *Journal of Industrial Information Integration* 23 (2021): 100224–24.

Zhang, Yingying, et al. "Multi-Modal Knowledge-Aware Hierarchical Attention Network for Explainable Medical Question Answering." *Proceedings of the 27th ACM International Conference on Multimedia*. Nice France, 2019.

CHAPTER 10

Green Communication Systems for AIoT Networks

Aizaz Raziq

SZABIST University Islamabad

Kashif Naseer Qureshi, Muzaffar Rao

Department of Electronic & Computer Engineering, University of Limerick, V94 T9PX Limerick, Ireland

10.1 OVERVIEW

The Internet of Things (IoT) technology is based on different network technologies and a variety of electronic devices to perform signal sensing, signal processing, and data transmission over the network. Artificial Intelligence (AI) based communication systems are utilized to meet the different requirements of the communication systems as well as to assist in resource management and high efficiency in performance. The AI methods are used in IoT networks to minimize environmental impact and provide green communication methods. This chapter examines green communication systems designed for AIoT networks to address energy effectiveness and environmental compatibility.

10.2 ARTIFICIAL INTERNET OF THINGS

The Internet of Things (IoT) plays a significant part in connecting cyber and physical space, for creating new services. IoT development has led to the digitization of the real world, resulting in a high demand for the creation of novel applications and services. These new inventions include Radio Frequency Identification (RFID) tags, ZigBee, and Wi-Fi standards for data communication. There is a wide variety of applications, including businesses, homes, logistics, energy systems, cities, healthcare, and agriculture. The IoT can enable physical objects to interact with one another and carry out tasks without human intervention. It is predicted that in 2024 around 45% of internet traffic will be Machine-to-Machine (M2M) traffic (Al-Fuqaha et al. 2015). Figure 10.1 shows the advantages of IoT devices.

The goal of Artificial Intelligence (AI) is to create computers that are intelligent as people. AI has long been used to optimize communication networks in a variety of configurations. Machines can offer multiple, pre-defined choices and react to the environment in a variety of different, yet deterministic ways, which is the first and most fundamental level

DOI: 10.1201/9781003430018-12

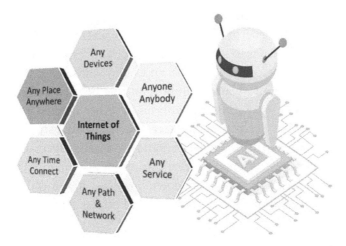

FIGURE 10.1 Advantages of IoT devices.

of AI. One machine has the entire capability to interact with the environment, which is the second complete level of AI (Li et al. 2017). AI usually has two places to fit into an IoT system: the center and the edge. Implementing AI in IoT networks' core components, such as the cloud, may use the vast volumes of data from the entire network to produce more precise predictive analytics or models. AI can be implemented locally or on edge servers in IoT networks to improve security and privacy while reducing bandwidth and latency. The edge intelligence framework is created by combining local and global intelligence by using AI techniques to coordinate heterogeneous resources across different domains for network energy savings, but it can also add a variety of new functions to IoT devices with minimal energy consumption (W. Mao et al. 2021). Big data, deep learning, and Machine Learning (ML) are adopted for modern networks. Many famous leading corporations, including Microsoft, IBM, Google, and Amazon, are concentrating on AI to create their remarkable products such as ChatGPT, Bing, and Dall-E, and give their customers a better overall experience. Many research projects have used AI algorithms, particularly ML algorithms, to determine the precise location of AIoT devices, to allocate resources quickly, to optimize reliable resources, and to transmit data securely.

Huge quantities of data traffic are expected to be generated by new applications like high-resolution video streaming, tactile Internet, remote monitoring, and real-time control systems. Due to the large size of the technological environment, the number of users, and the number of devices, energy consumption levels have been alarming. Scientists predict extraordinarily high data rates and enormous content sizes, 10,000 times greater than in 2010, at the cost of extremely high environmental carbon emissions (Mahmoud AM Albreem et al. 2017). The number of power transmitters grows as the number of connected electronic devices rises. As a result of the impact, a large amount of energy will be consumed. Approximately 75.44 billion connected gadgets will be present worldwide by 2025 (Alam and Tanweer. 2018).

Rapid increases in battery consumption on AIoT applications have a significant impact on security performance. Secure transmission in AIoT networks requires energy efficiency. Security, data storage from devices, energy consumption, data integration, and privacy are some of the existing issues with IoT network deployment. The battery of sensor nodes runs out faster if there are no energy control systems in place. Therefore, the objective of energy supply and management is to increase the network's lifespan. The full adoption and rising demand for smart services need power and bandwidth management rather than more resources. Energy efficiency plays an important role because IoT devices constantly gather and share data while operating on batteries or other limited power sources. IoT devices' energy consumption needs to be reduced because their batteries deplete quickly (Maddikunta et al. 2020). By utilizing on-demand protocols, specialized optimization algorithms, and AI techniques, the green AIoT paradigm has emerged as an energy-saving and environmentally friendly way to cut down on power usage and carbon emissions. The green planning, manufacturing, use, and disposal phases AIoT lifecycle are included (Halabi, Bellaiche, and Fung. 2022).

An intelligent transmission process that improves energy efficiency and extends the life of smart gadgets is required. IoT resource management and energy efficiency have drawn a lot of research attention. To prevent resource waste or lessen the impact of the green procedure itself, new energy-efficient procedures (whether involving hardware or software) should be implemented during the design of AIoT services.

10.3 APPLICATION AND TECHNOLOGIES

AI is being used in many ways, from data collection to output optimization. The goal of applying AI to the mobile sector is to provide seamless network operation and increase the wireless network's energy efficiency using real-time data from many modes of transportation, such as trains, buses, and vehicles, AI is utilized in road traffic management to assist in data analysis. AI examines this data for trends that might point to security vulnerabilities. This knowledge is then applied to identify solutions to lessen risks and the likelihood of accidents. Long-term and short-term traffic trends are the two types of tendencies used in AI-driven traffic prediction.

The most challenging procedure in networks is maintenance and monitoring. Maintaining the network to keep up with consumer demand is a challenging operation since it is highly challenging to analyze client requirements because they change dynamically. AI has a lot to offer in network monitoring. The most typical application of AI in networks is anomaly detection. The practice of analyzing network behavior and separating genuine activities from cyberattacks is known as anomaly detection. Troubleshooting is enhanced with AI/ML, which also accelerates problem resolution and offers remediation advice. It provides important insights to enhance the user and application experience. AI technology is used to accurately analyze and forecast the network behavior of 5G/6G to prevent energy waste. These analyses and forecasts include network overhead and collision predictions (Anwar et al. 2018).

The use of AI in service monitoring can quickly analyze massive amounts of real-time data to find anomalies and patterns that could affect service quality or user experience. AI can anticipate potential problems before they become more serious by utilizing ML algorithms, enabling proactive efforts to maintain the highest possible service levels. This cutting-edge method improves monitoring accuracy while simultaneously lowering downtime and minimizing service interruptions. There are many uses for green AI-based communication in 5G/6G wireless communication. These involve massive antenna arrays and coordinating the transmission and receiving of signals from various sites (Qureshi, Abdullah, et al. 2016).

Green AIoT enables remote control of household appliances, including lighting, electronic devices, and heating, from a computer, smartphone, or laptop. A smart home gadget may include a phone, television, computer, or other smart devices. There are a few new factors for green AIoT to consider, such as green operation, green design, green reuse, and green manufacturing, which will lessen environmental harm.

10.3.1 Mobile Edge Computing in M2M Communications

Mobile Edge Computing (MEC) is a developing technology which is essential for current systems and servers running cloud computing and Information Technology (IT). It is very important for new network technology of the next generation. MEC is capable of handling critical computations in large networks, including content caching, scheduling, collaborative processing, and several other activities. MEC relies heavily on Network Functions Virtualization (NFV), Software Defined Networks (SDN), and cloud computing (Iqbal et al. 2020). Using MEC increases the responsiveness of the edge and the speed of services, applications, and contents. This technology is more user-friendly than previous technologies and can analyze data from multiple IoT devices at once for the creation of new enterprises. The capabilities of MEC technology are very successful at advancing the idea of smart cities and making it easier to analyze massive data, which helps cities become more intelligent entities (Lv et al. 2021).

- **On-grounds:** MEC technology can operate only local sources and can be used independently of other system components. It may be necessary for some allocations, such as security and flexibility.

- **Closeness:** MEC has the potential to do computer tasks directly, which may be appealing to some specialized applications. This occurs as a result of proximity to data sources.

- **Lesser Computing:** MEC servers are located close to constrained clients, which might aid in reducing computation time and provide other benefits including quick processing, a positive customer experience, and less congestion.

- **Network Framework Information:** Network framework information is information from the network that is used by many services and applications. Utilizing MEC mobile service.

- **Locality Understanding:** MEC servers assist in supplying local information that influences low-level signaling data to determine the positions of each linked device.

10.3.2 Wireless Network Virtualization and e-SIM in M2M Communications

For IoT services, scalability and flexibility features are primarily provided by virtualization. Network virtualization is taking place at the same time as SDN and NFV. Cloud computing, SND, and NFV are expected to operate together as a crucial enabling technology to fundamentally alter how network operators design and benefit from their infrastructure. The procedure comprises combining physical network hardware resources with embedded software's operational capabilities and merging them into a single logical structure known as a virtual network. Wireless Network Virtualization (WNV) is regarded as an effective and dependable technique for managing network infrastructure and making use of network resources. The hypervisor is a crucial part of WNV, which is maintained by the primary operating method, which analyses the network and links sources in terms of Quality of Services (QoS) and applications or network requirements (Qureshi and Abdullah. 2013). MNV may aid in the improvement of new technologies and demonstrates greater flexibility in the design of communication technologies like M2M technology. M2M communications technology is now employed in a variety of ways. The IoT's virtualization mechanisms enhance the system's performance. This can also ensure the network's adaptability, scalability, dependability, and data throughput. Additionally, these methods are also helpful for low energy consumption, great throughput, and minimal overhead (Ramakrishnan et al. 2020).

The Embedded Subscriber Identity Module (eSIM) has several notable benefits for M2M communications in two areas. The first area is disconnecting the SIM module from a Machine-Type Communication Device (MTCD). This process is difficult because the SIM module is typically placed in remote areas. As a result, it is impossible to make the MTCD move to a different virtual network using a SIM. The second area is the difficulty in ensuring service continuity between networks due to an increase in MTCDs; conventional SIMs may need to be changed in each separate location.

10.3.3 AI-Based Wireless Communication

As the demands for user data and data traffic rates increase, AI-based wireless communication systems have become a novel option. The addition of AI-driven technologies is necessary for the traditional wireless communication techniques which are proving insufficient to handle this sudden increase in traffic. It's important to recognize that wireless communication systems currently make a major contribution to the overall energy consumption of the information and communication technology industry, notwithstanding any potential benefits they may have in the future. Numerous access technologies, including Narrow-Band IoT (NB-IoT), IEEE 802.15.4, Wi-Fi, cellular communications, backscatter communications, and others, have been developed for various Machine Type Communication (MTC) scenarios. Unmanned Aerial Vehicles (UAVs) and satellites are new platforms for connecting things to the Internet (Qureshi, Alhudhaif, et al. 2022; B. Mao et al. 2021).

A significant portion of the total energy used in the field of information and communication technology is consumed by wireless communication systems. This shows how urgent it is to create systems for communication that utilize green AI rules, ensuring the best possible use of energy resources. The development of green AI-based communication systems is urgently needed given the requirement for environmentally responsible behaviour. These cutting-edge systems not only use AI to improve performance but also place a strong emphasis on energy saving. Green AI-based communication systems reduce the demand for energy resources by intelligently optimizing network operations and signal transmission and maintaining a sustainable balance between advancements in technology.

10.4 CHALLENGES

The everyday lives of consumers have benefited from the IoT, and manufacturers have been motivated to release new devices with more features and better designs due to consumers' excitement and accessibility. The green AIoT is still in its infancy. The theory behind green communication is that it uses very little energy and gives high performance. Numerous issues need to be resolved as well as hurdles. Spectral efficiency, cost, energy consumption, environment friendly hardware and battery, and bandwidth are just some of the challenges. Heterogeneous Networks (HetNets) integration can be expensive, and upgrading the infrastructure to handle this technology would be very expensive. Similar to this, expenses may increase with the use of large-scale Multiple-Input Multiple-Output (MIMO) systems. For some businesses, these costs can be an obstacle to implementation. For others, the expenditure may be justified by the prospective advantages of these technologies, such as increased network capacity and coverage. Energy-efficient technology is also expensive to produce. Cost is also a major obstacle to green communication (Jamil et al. 2020). Figure 10.2 shows the challenges in AIoT networks.

In green communication networks, attaining high data throughput while preserving energy efficiency is one of the problems. When developing and accessing communication systems, it is essential to take into account data throughput, commonly referred to as Spectral Efficiency (SE). According to Shannon's equation, the speed and amount of transferred power have a direct impact on the transmission rate. However, increasing speed and strength might also result in higher energy usage. A major difficulty in developing green communication networks is balancing these variables to maximize throughput while minimizing energy use (Jamil et al. 2020).

Utilizing the millimeter wave (mmWave) band for 5G/6G communication poses a problem for green communication networks. While this band offers high data rates and capacity, current antennas are inefficient at these frequencies. Phased-array antennas are necessary for communication on the mm-wave frequency. However, designing and deploying phased-array antennas is a challenging task that needs a lot of resources and knowledge. A significant difficulty for green communication networks is ensuring that these antennas are energy-efficient while still offering good performance (Jamil et al. 2020).

Large volumes of data that are sensitive to privacy and security are generated, processed, and exchanged by these systems, making them appealing targets for attacks. AIoT devices are frequently poorly secured and vulnerable to cyberattacks such as distributed denial

FIGURE 10.2   Challenges in AIoT networks.

of service or sabotage attempts. The overhead associated with cryptography techniques is frequently too high. AIoT system overhead is further increased by the heterogeneity of networks. Therefore, it is crucial to develop simple algorithms that ensure the security and privacy of devices while using less energy (W. Mao et al. 2021).

For green communication networks, IoT and AI integration opens new challenges for researchers. The complexity of this integration is boosting the existing issues such as processing power, memory, and delay in real-time applications. Additionally, ensuring compatibility and standardization may be challenging due to the heterogeneity of AIoT devices and networks (Mahmoud A Albreem et al. 2021). In a wireless setting, security and privacy problems must also be addressed. It is crucial for the merging of IoT and AI in green communication networks to successfully handle these issues. The difficulty with huge data accumulation is predicting and estimating the amount of energy needed for data analysis. Big data analysis performed quickly might be considered, but the cost and resources needed for the analysis will increase exponentially as the volume of big data rises. Consequently, big data analytics could be viewed as enhancing the prediction of energy efficiency as opposed to the enhancement of the quality of life from the integration of IoT devices with AI technology.

Hardware-related issues are raised by the integration of AI and IoT in green communication networks. The processing and memory capabilities of IoT devices are frequently constrained, which can make it challenging to deploy advanced AI algorithms on the devices. Furthermore, for these devices to function well, their energy consumption needs to be properly controlled. It might be difficult to guarantee the dependability and endurance of IoT devices in challenging conditions. The system's overall sustainability may be compromised by the need for periodic hardware maintenance and replacement. The successful integration of AIoT in green communication networks depends on the development of hardware solutions that are dependable, long-lasting, and energy efficient.

10.5 GREEN COMMUNICATION SMART GRID SYSTEMS

Information and Communication Technologies (ICTs) are playing a crucial role in the modernization of the electrical grid as a result of rising electricity prices, the depletion of fossil fuels, and growing worries about Greenhouse Gas (GHG) emissions. Traditional power management services have been altered by smart grids, which also provided cutting-edge solutions. By regulating utility costs, these innovative integrated systems make it more convenient to meet energy demand. By employing cellular and other data communication networks, users of smart systems can share data about their energy use, energy supply, and utility use. Energy distribution is always given top attention in smart cities, and more advanced metering infrastructure is required for power generation to customers. The smart grid is built on decentralized generation methods, as opposed to the conventional grid's centralized generation techniques. Additionally, human monitoring is used in typical grids, and only limited, passive control is used.

Smart grids, on the other hand, use active control techniques and a self-monitoring system. One aspect of manual and locally-based traditional grids and restoration systems is the power flow. They differ from the smart grid which manages electricity flow in two directions and features a self-restoration mechanism (Qureshi and Jeon. 2021). Real-time monitoring of energy consumption can be made possible via smart meters and communication networks, enabling consumers to make educated choices about their energy use. Programs called "demand response" can be used to encourage energy efficiency by allowing consumers to alter their energy usage during periods of high demand. Based on several operations like electric generation, transmission, and distribution, the smart grid is an important field. All of these processes use wireless technologies and more modern, integrated communication standards.

To make the grid more flexible, strong, and decentralized, AI is a major contributor to this revolution. The development of smart grids that can control far more complex power generation and distribution is being fuelled by the application of AI technologies like IoT, machine learning, and data analytics. These technologies are assisting in the resolution of serious issues such as power outages and financial setbacks brought on by extreme weather events. At the same time, they are offering crucial support to make it possible for renewable energy sources to be seamlessly integrated into the grid infrastructure.

10.5.1 Smart Grid Architecture

The smart grid infrastructure is designed to offer a data communication medium for the transmission of various signals for monitoring, measurement, control, and management. The utility grid is integrated with the smart grid interface at any point, including microgrid installations, transmission, distribution, consumption, and bulk generating. The communication medium and interface must offer transmission that is secure, effective, and reliable. The smart grid is divided into three main categories: management systems, information, and communication technologies, and commercial and residential modules. Within the management systems category, there are three subcategories: monitoring management, transmission and generation, and consumer-side management. Figure 10.3 shows the smart energy management system's architecture.

Monitoring and management of a smart grid refers to the procedures and tools used to keep an eye on and regulate the many functions and elements of a smart grid system. This is essential to guarantee the grid's effective, dependable, and secure operation. Smart grid monitoring delivers in-the-moment insights into equipment health, voltage levels, and energy consumption patterns by continually collecting and analyzing data from various grid elements. These data enable grid operators to make well-informed judgments, act quickly in response to demand changes, and avert any disruptions. A key component of a smart grid system that focuses on streamlining the transfer of electricity from power production sources to consumers is transmission and generation management. The use of smart grid technology includes several methods and tools designed to increase the effectiveness, dependability, and environmentally friendly nature of energy generation and transmission. Consumer-side management refers to a variety of tactics, tools, and programs created to empower and include customers in managing their electricity usage. Consumers are given priority in this aspect of smart grid technology, giving them more control, awareness, and engagement in the energy ecosystem.

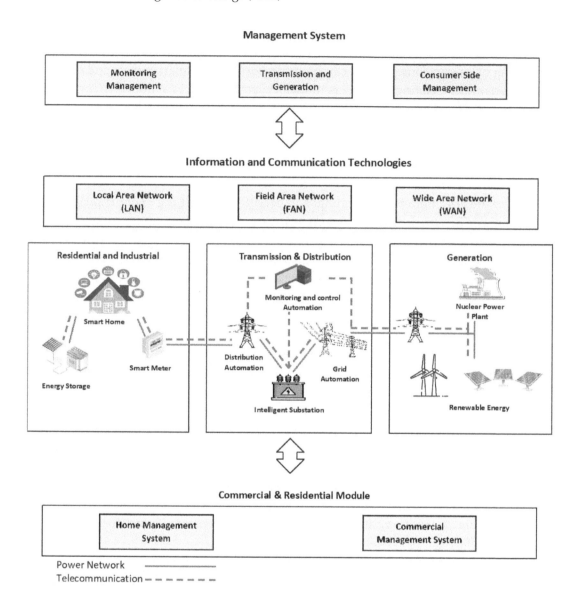

FIGURE 10.3 Smart grid architecture.

The ICT sublayer connects the management systems to the electricity network. It is divided into three categories: Local Area Network (LAN), Field Area Network (FAN), and Wide Area Network (WAN). In addition to metering, field-based equipment requires monitoring and management from the utility's point of view. The construction of a specialized network becomes necessary when the grid infrastructure deepens its coverage by including a variety of important parts, from transformers and sensors to distribution automation systems. The critical task of effectively controlling and integrating these complex components within the larger operational framework is taken on by this specialized network. Therefore, a separate network known as the FAN is used to handle the equipment in the field. The majority of the data transfer can be done using wireless communication techniques such as Wi-Fi, Global System for Mobile Communications (GSM), IEEE 802.15.4-based technologies, or 5G/6G communication technologies.

Electricity generation, transmission, and distribution are the three phases that make up a smart grid, which is a system for distributing electricity. During the generation phase, energy is produced utilizing massive, centralized power plants that are powered by a variety of natural resources, including coal, gas, or nuclear or hydroelectric systems (Qureshi and Jeon. 2021). Modern hydrogenated generation systems combine heat and power systems. Electricity transmission, which occurs after electricity generation, involves moving the energy from power plants to substations and end customers. The electricity is divided between residential and industrial zones during the distribution phase. Smart meters play an important part in the advancement of the smart grid. Smart meters are made to measure power flowing in both directions, including into and out of the meter. In a process known as net metering, users can import electricity from the grid as needed and also export any excess renewable energy production to the main grid. One of the main goals of utilizing smart meters is to give clients a real-time monitoring system, dynamic pricing, and the ability to monitor energy consumption more effectively (Qureshi and Jeon. 2022).

Home Management Systems (HMSs), which are supported by service providers, can be used to control residential loads in the context of smart grid applications. Many typical sensors, including, anemometers, current transducers, phase and flux sensors, voltage transducers, frequency sensors, pressure transducers, and power quality transducers, are dispersed across the power network's generation and transmission systems, and smart meters are also used in systems for managing smart homes, which aims to give customers more secure and comfortable living conditions. The Commercial Management System refers to a broad range of tactics, procedures, and tools used to streamline and improve financial and commercial activities within the context of the energy distribution ecosystem. The smart grid architecture includes a variety of elements such as digital systems to increase real-time communication, supply management, distribution automation, renewable resources, demand-side resources, dynamic optimization, grid security, and smart metering,

10.6 RELATED WORKS

Industrial AIoT places a high value on reliable, green communication. Unfortunately, it is difficult to provide reliable transmission due to complex industrial environment. The authors (Liu et al. 2017), proposed the Hybrid Transmission Protocol (HTP) to increase longevity while preserving reliability. To reduce energy usage, the protocol uses the Network-Coding-based Redundant Transmission (NCRT) technique with an adaptive redundancy level in non-hotspot areas and the Send-Wait Automated Repeat-Request protocol (SW-ARQ) in hotspot areas. They used the Omnet++ network simulator for modeling and theoretical research to evaluate the effectiveness of the suggested approach. The results of their algorithm showed that the SW-ARQ protocol can increase longevity by 15% to 30% and dependability by 12% to 45% while maintaining the same reliability.

When it comes to Smart Sustainable Agriculture (SSA), there is a lack of progress along with complicated challenges brought on by the division of agricultural techniques, including the management and control of data, interoperability, data storage, and large data analysis. To overcome this issue, the author Alreshidi discussed analyses of current IoT/AI technologies used for SSA in the first place and then establishes an IoT/AI technological architecture to support SSA platforms. The framework for AI and IoT includes the following levels: SSA domain, IoT sensing, network, application, security, governance, AI and data Management, physical hardware, and storage. Future studies will look into how AI and IoT technologies are implemented for SSA by developing a prototype for the proposed AI and IoT technological architecture to use in actual test cases.

By maximizing intra-cluster distance, methodically utilizing node energy, and lowering hop count, a Genetic Algorithm (GA) based sustainable and safe green data collecting and transmission technique for IoT-enabled Wireless Sensor Network (WSN) in healthcare has been proposed by the authors Singh et al. 2021 Data communication is encrypted utilizing a pseudo-randomly generated security key and stream ciphers for secure data transmission. Additionally, the hotspot issue is lessened by the suggested moveable sink and data collection and transmission procedures since they reduce the communication distance between the sink and Cluster Head (CH). When the sink nodes are physically closer to the sensor nodes than they are to the CH, the direct data collection method facilitates the direct transfer of data to the sink. Additionally, the integrated dynamic sensing range reduces the sensing range's overlap while significantly reducing transmission energy.

The majority of AI-driven applications require powerful servers to do difficult AI tasks, which increases energy usage in Industrial Internet of Things (IIoT) systems. To develop energy-efficient AI computing for IIoT applications, the authors Zhu, Ota, and Dong 2021 proposed intelligent edge computing as a cutting-edge technology. First, they proposed that AI computing for IIoT applications should perform better overall and use less energy as compared to traditional applications. The intelligent edge computing framework decreases the load on servers and speeds up reaction times by shifting AI workloads from servers to the network's edge. By maximizing the utilization of computational resources, the suggested method for scheduling AI activities improves energy efficiency even more. As a result, the system used for AI computing in IIoT applications becomes more effective and sustainable.

The security of mobile IoT networks has numerous difficulties due to the complexity of the wireless channels. In mobile IoT networks, energy efficiency is essential for secure connectivity. The authors Xu et al. 2022 proposed a transmit antenna selection-based secrecy scheme employing amplify and forward relaying. They begin by obtaining exact expressions and evaluating the effectiveness of the physical layer of security. After that, they then formulate the power allocation issue, which is a non-convex, challenging problem, to further increase energy efficiency. They provide a novel intelligent power allocation optimization technique. The allocation parameter is calculated using an Improved Grey Wolf Optimization (IGWO) algorithm based on the defined power allocation function. The proposed IGWO algorithm outperforms conventional swarm intelligence algorithms in terms of convergence precision and convergence speed. When compared to other algorithms, IGWO reduces running time by 24% while keeping the same optimization accuracy.

The authors Chavhan et al. 2022 discussed the use of AI and IoT in the transportation sector which has been made on a large scale to lower GHG emissions, enhance energy efficiency, and improve service quality. They proposed a unique, energy-efficient, intelligent transport system for smart cities based on a distributed multi-agent system and edge-based AI-IoT integration. This has been accomplished by combining the DSRC-IEEE 802.11p communication standard protocol for Vehicle-to-Everything (V2X) with Radial Basis Function Neural Network (RBF-NN), IoT, and Multi-Agent System (MAS) based real-time data collecting, analysis, prediction, and sharing. Along with the edge computing units, an ideal number of Roadside Units (RSUs) are installed at each zone. MAS installed at each RSU gathers a considerable amount of data from numerous infrastructures, devices, and sensors. The edge computing device processes, analyses, and predicts using the raw data from the MAS that has been acquired.

The environment in which green IoT devices operate is resource constrained. It is challenging to monitor, identify, and react to events in a partially or fully distributed ecosystem that requires constant access to timely information. To overcome this issue, the authors Chithaluru et al. 2023 proposed a neuro-fuzzy method used in an energy-efficient Dynamic Clustering Routing (DCR) protocol to limit the resources of IoT devices. It builds dynamic clusters in a network using a dynamically self-organizing neural network. One method for extending network lifetime in a sustainable IoT is clustering. In terms of clustering techniques, IoT is also employed for green applications to demonstrate a huge improvement in each QoS. In each cluster, there will be a CH, which will receive data from the group nodes and transmit it to a distant sink using high-energy transmission while also capturing important data packets and sending them to the sink. By preventing all nodes from processing, it lowers energy consumption and increases the network's longevity.

Cloud-based IoT technologies enable remote patient monitoring and support. Making healthcare systems environmentally friendly hasn't gotten much attention in the current environment. The authors Islam and Bhuiyan discussed cutting-edge technology to build an interactive user experience while providing an integrated framework for green healthcare. A three-layered architecture for a healthcare system is proposed. The first layer is a data-collecting layer based on IoT that collects data from patients and hospitals. The second layer is an advanced cloud system that allows for enormous data analysis from individual patients and facilities. This technique can be used to forecast potential diseases and uncover patterns. Mobile application technology, the third and final layer, will boost real-time data interchange and treatment efficiency. This is accomplished by analyzing data collected through interactive patient monitoring systems. Overall, the suggested design intends to improve healthcare by combining technology and data analysis.

The authors, Riskiawan et al. 2023, discussed a contemporary strategy for effectively enhancing greenhouse control technology through automated environmental control. The IoT and AI can be combined to create IoT devices that can forecast and be controlled on their own. The system, which acts as the central processing hub for sensors and actuators, is managed by a microcontroller. The microcontroller interprets the sensor data using a Long Short-Term Memory (LSTM) technique to predict the output parameters for regulating actuators, such as misting, fan exhaust, and motor control. The outcomes of knowledge acquired through the LSTM method are used to place intelligent control on a framework

TABLE 10.1   Existing Protocols for Energy Efficiency

S.No	Protocols	IoT Domains	Objectives/Achievements
1	SW-ARQ & NCRT (Liu et al. 2017)	WSNs	Ensuring reliability, extending the lifetime, and decreasing the delay.
2	Optimized GA (Singh et al. 2021)	Health Care	To optimize intra-cluster distance, efficiency in nodes' energy, and reduce the hop count
3	AI-driven IIoT framework (Zhu, Ota and Dong. 2021)	Industrial IoT	to improve various computing resources' energy efficiency and offload the majority of AI activities from servers.
4	IGWO (Xu et al. 2022)	Mobile IoT	Increasing the energy efficiency
5	RBF-NN, IoT, and MAS (Chavhan et al. 2022)	Transport System for Smart Cities	Increase energy efficiency in the transport system and reduce greenhouse gas emissions
6	Neuro-fuzzy logic (Chithaluru et al. 2023)	Clustering Selection for IoT-based Smart Cities	During the network planning stage, reduce consumption of energy and increase network lifetime.
7	Hierarchical Clustering Algorithms, Bluetooth Low Energy (BLE) & cutting-edge technology (Islam and Bhuiyan. 2023)	IoT health Care system	surpass current systems regarding, energy efficiency treatment planning, data accessibility, and system architecture
8	modified LSTM (Riskiawan et al. 2023)	AI base IoT-Green House	Manage an existing agricultural system in a smart greenhouse using AI and IoT technologies while also creating a unique IoT sensor.

called Laravel rather than the embedded system directly. Table 10.1 shows the protocols designed for different domains to manage energy issues.

10.7 CONCLUSION

An essential step toward developing sustainable IoT systems is the use of green communication technologies in AIoT networks. The development of conventional industries including transportation, electricity, education, agriculture, and healthcare has benefited from IoT devices. Energy-efficient data acquisition and communication are the goals of green communication techniques. The design of reliable communication systems and centralized as well as decentralized deployment of IoT systems have all attracted substantial research interest. Scalability and latency problems are addressed via cloud computing, fog computing, and edge computing. Due to its capacity to increase response time and lower energy consumption, methods like MEC have become more well-liked. There is great potential to increase the energy efficiency of IoT systems by developing green communication methods for AIoT networks, which is an active field of research. Some research areas include green network management, green network monitoring, green intelligent transportation systems, green optical communications, switching, and networking, green software, hardware, devices, and equipment, green scheduling for communications and computing, and green storage, as well as fog and cloud computing.

REFERENCES

Al-Fuqaha, Ala, et al. "Internet of Things: A Survey on Enabling Technologies, Protocols, and Applications." *IEEE Communications Surveys Tutorials* 17.4 (2015): 2347–76.

Alam, Tanweer. "A Reliable Communication Framework and Its Use in the Internet of Things (IoT)." *SSRN, CSEIT1835111* 10 (2018): 450–56.

Albreem, Mahmoud A, et al. "Green Internet of Things (GIoT): Applications, Practices, Awareness, and Challenges." *IEEE Access* 9 (2021): 38833–58.

Albreem, Mahmoud AM, et al. "Green Internet of Things (IoT): An Overview." *2017 IEEE 4th International Conference on Smart Instrumentation, Measurement and Application (ICSIMA)*. 2017. IEEE.

Alreshidi, Eissa. "Smart Sustainable Agriculture (SSA) Solution Underpinned by Internet of Things (IoT) and Artificial Intelligence (AI)." *arXiv preprint arXiv:.03106* (2019).

Anwar, Muhammad, et al. "Green Communication for Wireless Body Area Networks: Energy Aware Link Efficient Routing Approach." *Sensors* 18.10 (2018): 3237.

Chavhan, Suresh, et al. "Edge Computing AI-IoT Integrated Energy-Efficient Intelligent Transportation System for Smart Cities." *ACM Transactions on Internet Technology* 22.4 (2022): 1–18.

Chithaluru, Premkumar, et al. "Energy-Balanced Neuro-Fuzzy Dynamic Clustering Scheme for Green & Sustainable IoT Based Smart Cities." *Sustainable Cities Society* 90 (2023): 104366.

Halabi, Talal, Martine Bellaiche, and Benjamin CM Fung. "Towards Adaptive Cybersecurity for Green IoT." *2022 IEEE International Conference on Internet of Things and Intelligence Systems (IoTaIS)*. 2022. IEEE.

Iqbal, Saleem, et al. "Collaborative Energy Efficient Zone-Based Routing Protocol for Multihop Internet of Things." *Transactions on Emerging Telecommunications Technologies* 33.2 (2020): e3885.

Islam, Md Motaharul, and Zaheed Ahmed Bhuiyan. "An Integrated Scalable Framework for Cloud and IoT Based Green Healthcare System." *IEEE Access* 11 (2023): 22266–82.

Jamil, Sonain, et al. "A Review of Techniques and Challenges in Green Communication." *2020 International Conference on Information Science and Communication Technology (ICISCT)*. 2020. IEEE.

Li, Rongpeng, et al. "Intelligent 5G: When Cellular Networks Meet Artificial Intelligence." *IEEE Wireless Communications* 24.5 (2017): 175–83.

Liu, Anfeng, et al. "A Green and Reliable Communication Modeling for Industrial Internet of Things." *Computers Electrical Engineering* 58 (2017): 364–81.

Lv, Zhihan, et al. "Intelligent Edge Computing Based on Machine Learning for Smart City." *Future Generation Computer Systems* 115 (2021): 90–99.

Maddikunta, Praveen Kumar Reddy, et al. "Green Communication in IoT Networks Using a Hybrid Optimization Algorithm." *Computer Communications* 159 (2020): 97–107.

Mao, Bomin, et al. "Ai Models for Green Communications Towards 6G." *IEEE Communications Surveys Tutorials* 24.1 (2021): 210–47.

Mao, Wenliang, et al. "Energy-Efficient Industrial Internet of Things: Overview and Open Issues." *IEEE Transactions on Industrial Informatics* 17.11 (2021): 7225–37.

Qureshi, K. N., and A. H. Abdullah. "Industrial Wireless Sensor Network Architecture Standards, Applications." *AsiaSense, The Sixth International Conference 2013*, Melaka, Malaysia. 2013. AaiaSense.

Qureshi, Kashif Naseer, et al. "Weighted Link Quality and Forward Progress Coupled with Modified RTS/CTS for Beaconless Packet Forwarding Protocol (B-PFP) in Vanets." *Telecommunication Systems* 75 (2016): 1–16.

Qureshi, Kashif Naseer, et al. "Secure Data Communication for Wireless Mobile Nodes in Intelligent Transportation Systems." *Microprocessors and Microsystems* 90 (2022): 104501.

Qureshi, Kashif Naseer, and Gwanggil Jeon. "A Trust Evaluation Model for Secure Data Aggregation in Smart Grids Infrastructures for Smart Cities." *Journal of Ambient Intelligence Smart Environments* 13.3 (2021): 235–52.

Ramakrishnan, Jayabrabu, et al. "A Comprehensive and Systematic Review of the Network Virtualization Techniques in the IoT." *International Journal of Communication Systems* 33.7 (2020): e4331.

Riskiawan, Hendra Yufit, et al. "Artificial Intelligence Enabled Smart Monitoring and Controlling of IoT-Green House." *Arabian Journal for Science Engineering* (2023): 1–19.

Singh, Samayveer, et al. "A Ga-Based Sustainable and Secure Green Data Communication Method Using IoT-Enabled WSN in Healthcare." *IEEE Internet of Things Journal* 9.10 (2021): 7481–90.

Xu, Lingwei, et al. "Intelligent Power Allocation Algorithm for Energy-Efficient Mobile Internet of Things (IoT) Networks." *IEEE Transactions on Green Communications Networking* 6.2 (2022): 766–75.

Zhu, Sha, Kaoru Ota, and Mianxiong Dong. "Green Ai for IIoT: Energy Efficient Intelligent Edge Computing for Industrial Internet of Things." *IEEE Transactions on Green Communications Networking* 6.1 (2021): 79–88.

CHAPTER 11

Cybersecurity Standards for AIoT Networks

Usman Ahmad

Bath Spa University Academic Centre RAK, UAE

Hassan Zaib

Computer Science Department, Air University, Islamabad, Pakistan

Kashif Naseer Qureshi

Department of Electronic & Computer Engineering, University of Limerick, V94 T9PX Limerick, Ireland

11.1 OVERVIEW

This chapter provides an overview of Artificial Intelligence of Things (AIoT) networks and their associated security challenges. It emphasizes the importance of implementing cybersecurity standards to safeguard these networks from cyberattacks. This chapter covers various topics such as the introduction of AIoT, identification and authentication protocols, data encryption, and integrity protection. It also discusses the challenges faced in implementing cybersecurity standards for AIoT networks, including the complexities introduced by interconnected devices and emerging technologies. By addressing these challenges and staying informed about emerging technologies, organizations can enhance the security of AIoT networks and protect sensitive data from unauthorized access or manipulation.

11.2 AIoT

AIoT is a paradigm that combines the power of Artificial Intelligence (AI) with the vast connectivity and data-sharing capabilities of the Internet of Things (IoT). In AIoT systems, AI algorithms and machine learning techniques are integrated into IoT devices and networks, enabling them to collect, analyze, and interpret data in real-time. This integration empowers AIoT systems to make intelligent decisions, adapt to changing environments, and automate processes, leading to improved efficiency, accuracy, and responsiveness (Hasan and Qureshi. 2018). AIoT finds applications across various industries and sectors. In manufacturing, AIoT enables smart factories where IoT devices equipped with AI algorithms can monitor and optimize production lines, detect faults, and predict maintenance

DOI: 10.1201/9781003430018-13

needs (Iqbal et al. 2021). In healthcare, AIoT systems can enhance patient monitoring, assist in remote diagnostics, and enable personalized treatment plans. Smart cities leverage AIoT to optimize traffic management, enhance energy efficiency, and improve public safety through intelligent surveillance and monitoring systems. Additionally, AIoT has applications in agriculture, retail, transportation, and many other domains, revolutionizing processes and creating new opportunities for innovation.

Several technologies enable the realization of AIoT systems. IoT devices, such as sensors, actuators, and wearables, serve as the foundational components that collect and transmit data. Cloud computing infrastructure provides the storage, processing, and scalability required to handle the massive amount of data generated by IoT devices. Edge computing complements cloud computing by bringing AI capabilities closer to the data source, reducing latency, and enabling real-time decision-making. Machine learning algorithms, including deep learning and reinforcement learning, are employed to extract insights, detect patterns, and make predictions based on the collected data. These technologies work together to create a powerful AIoT ecosystem that drives intelligent automation and decision-making.

In conclusion, AIoT combines AI and IoT technologies to create intelligent systems that leverage data analysis and machine learning to make informed decisions and automate processes. With its diverse applications across industries, AIoT has the potential to transform various sectors and drive innovation. The integration of IoT devices, cloud computing, edge computing, and machine learning algorithms form the foundation of AIoT systems, enabling them to collect, process, and interpret data in real-time. As the capabilities of AI and IoT continue to advance, the AIoT paradigm holds great promise for enhancing efficiency, accuracy, and responsiveness in a wide range of domains.

11.3 SECURITY CHALLENGES IN AIOT

AIoT networks face numerous security challenges that need to be addressed to ensure the integrity, confidentiality, and availability of the network and its data. These challenges include vulnerability to cyberattacks, such as data breaches and unauthorized access due to the interconnected nature of devices and the large volume of data they generate. Privacy concerns arise from the collection and analysis of sensitive data, requiring robust security measures and compliance with data protection regulations. The complexity and scalability of AIoT networks pose difficulties in managing and securing numerous devices and data sources effectively. The lack of standardization hinders the implementation of consistent security measures, while resource constraints in IoT devices make it challenging to implement robust security without compromising performance. Zero-day attacks and emerging threats add to the risks, necessitating adaptive and proactive security measures (Kiyani et al. 2023). Addressing these challenges is crucial to ensure the trust, reliability, and resilience of AIoT networks.

11.3.1 Vulnerability to Cyberattacks

AIoT networks are highly susceptible to various cyberattacks due to their interconnected nature and the vast amount of data they generate and transmit. They face risks such as data breaches, unauthorized access, and malicious manipulation. The distributed and diverse nature of AIoT devices makes it challenging to ensure the security of each device and the overall network.

11.3.2 Privacy Concerns

AIoT networks involve the collection, analysis, and storage of large amounts of personal and sensitive data. This raises significant privacy concerns as the potential misuse or unauthorized access to this data can lead to severe consequences for individuals. Safeguarding privacy in AIoT networks requires robust security measures, encryption techniques, and compliance with data protection regulations.

11.3.3 Complexity and Scalability

AIoT networks are complex systems that consist of a multitude of devices, sensors, and data sources. Managing and securing these networks at scale can be challenging. Each device must be individually secured, and data transmission and storage points need to be protected. The dynamic nature of AIoT networks, with devices joining and leaving the network frequently, further adds to the complexity of security management.

11.3.4 Lack of Standardization

The lack of standardized security protocols and frameworks for AIoT networks poses challenges in implementing consistent and comprehensive security measures. Different devices and platforms may have varying security capabilities and vulnerabilities, making it difficult to ensure a uniform security posture across the network. The absence of standards also hinders interoperability and collaboration between different AIoT systems.

11.3.5 Resource Constraints

Many IoT devices in AIoT networks have limited computational power, memory, and energy resources. Implementing robust security measures while considering these constraints can be challenging. Resource-efficient security solutions that provide adequate protection without significantly impacting device performance are required. This necessitates the development of lightweight cryptographic algorithms, optimized protocols, and efficient authentication mechanisms.

11.3.6 Zero-day Attacks and Emerging Threats

AIoT networks face the risk of zero-day attacks, where new vulnerabilities are exploited before security measures can be put in place. The rapid evolution of threats and emerging attack techniques make it crucial to have adaptive and proactive security measures. Constant monitoring, threat intelligence, and timely updates to security systems are necessary to detect and mitigate emerging risks effectively. Addressing these challenges requires a comprehensive approach to security in AIoT networks. The following measures should be considered.

11.3.7 Strong Authentication and Access Control

Implementing robust authentication mechanisms, including two-factor authentication and secure access control, ensures that only authorized devices and users can access the network and its resources.

11.3.8 Data Encryption and Integrity Protection

Employing encryption techniques, both for data transmission and storage, safeguards sensitive information from unauthorized access. Additionally, integrity checks and measures to detect and prevent data tampering are essential to maintain data integrity.

11.3.9 Intrusion Detection and Prevention Systems

Deploying intrusion detection and prevention systems helps identify and respond to potential threats in real-time. These systems can monitor network traffic, identify anomalies, and take proactive measures to mitigate risks (Hussain et al. 2023).

11.3.10 Security Audits and Penetration Testing

Regular security audits and penetration testing help identify vulnerabilities and weaknesses in AIoT networks. Conducting these assessments allows organizations to take remedial actions and strengthen security measures accordingly.

11.3.11 Collaboration and Standardization

Collaboration among industry stakeholders, regulators, and security experts is crucial to develop standardized security frameworks, protocols, and best practices for AIoT networks. This collaboration ensures consistent security implementation across different systems and promotes interoperability.

11.3.12 Security Awareness and Education

Promoting security awareness and education among users, employees, and stakeholders is vital. Regular training programs and guidelines on cybersecurity practices help mitigate human errors and improve overall security posture.

11.4 CYBERSECURITY STANDARDS FOR AIoT NETWORKS

The capabilities of AI and the IoT are combined in AIoT networks to produce intelligent systems that can learn and adapt to their environments. The protection of these networks is of the utmost importance because they are susceptible to a wide variety of cyberattacks. Cybersecurity has gained a lot of popularity over the past decade because the complexity introduced by the proliferation of networked devices makes it exceedingly difficult to monitor a big volume of data and maintain diversity. The term "cybersecurity" refers to the overall framework of measures put in place to safeguard information systems, networks, applications, and data from malicious intrusion (Rehman et al. 2022). At the application, network, host, and data levels, one can find cyber-defensive techniques. Developing barriers to prevent unauthorized access, alteration, or destruction of computing infrastructures, networks, applications, and data is a primary focus of cybersecurity. The tremendous rise of data using interconnected networks and technologies like big data, IoT, cloud computing, and fog/edge computing has led to the rapid development of cyberspace, which in return had impacted changes in cyber-infrastructure.

In recent years, layered security architecture has acquired global popularity, with intrusion detection systems playing a crucial part in network state monitoring. The architecture of layered security demonstrates that there is no single active/passive security solution that can defend against a wide variety of threats. Active security solutions, such as firewalls, intrusion prevention systems, antivirus software, and access control lists, are commonly deployed to address vulnerabilities and attacks at various Open Systems Interconnection (OSI) model layers. Their ability to defend against innovative and zero-day threats is, however, severely constrained. Thus, passive monitoring plays a crucial role, and intrusion detection systems at both the network and host level offer security professionals considerable insight. Passive monitoring gives the Cyber Incident Response Team (CIRT) network insight and directs them to upgrade their active security solutions by writing new Intrusion Prevention System (IPS) rules, installing updated software patches, and adopting new active solutions.

Today's ever-evolving technological landscape presents an ever-present risk of security being breached in service of malicious ends. People have experienced both the benefits and drawbacks of technology over the years. Negative measures include data theft, data manipulation, and making breaches in security that could in return harm possible aspects in the concerned domain, while positive measures include setting trends and bringing huge changes to fields like Machine Learning (Angelov et al. 2019), the IoT (Gubbi et al. 2013), cybersecurity, and wireless sensor networks (Wang and Balasingham. 2010).

Digital technologies demand new frameworks. All economically advanced nations view AI development as essential to worldwide competitiveness and national security. AI is used in education, personalized treatment, environmental preservation, and more. AI is now crucial to any nation's digital economy. Yet, the risks of AI technologies require legislative safeguards for AI system security (Kseniia and Minbaleev. 2020). Table 11.1 illustrates the existing standards and their description.

11.5 IMPORTANCE OF SECURITY FOR AIoT

Integrating AI into IoT devices can bring many benefits, such as improved efficiency, enhanced decision-making capabilities, and increased automation. However, it also introduces new security concerns that must be addressed. Incorporating AI into IoT devices enhances the attack surface, as more devices and data kinds are communicated when AI is incorporated. This can make it easier for attackers to identify system weaknesses.

1. **Complex Algorithms:** It can be hard to protect AI's complex algorithms from attacks like adversarial attacks, in which an attacker changes the input data to trick the system into making bad decisions.

2. **Increased Attack Surface:** Integrating AI in IoT devices increases the attack surface, as there are more devices and more types of data being transmitted. This can make it easier for attackers to find vulnerabilities in the system.

TABLE 11.1   Existing Standards and Description

Standard/Regulation	Description	Focus Areas
ISO/IEC 27001	Information Security Management System (ISMS)	General cybersecurity management
ISO/IEC 27019	Information security for energy/utility sectors	Critical infrastructure protection
NIST SP 800-183	Network of Things (NoT) – Cybersecurity Framework	IoT device lifecycle
NIST SP 800-183A	Security Capabilities of IoT Devices	Device security features
NIST SP 800-183B	IoT Non-Technical Supporting Capability Baseline	Non-technical considerations
IEC 62443	Industrial Communication Networks	Industrial IoT cybersecurity
EN 303 645	Cybersecurity for Consumer IoT	Consumer IoT device security
EN 303 645-1	Requirements for Consumer IoT	Baseline security requirements
EN 303 645-2	Guidelines for implementation	Implementation guidelines
UL 2900	Software Cybersecurity for Network-Connectable Products	Software security for connected devices
CIS Controls	Center for Internet Security (CIS) Controls	General cybersecurity best practices
CSA IoT Controls Framework	Cloud Security Alliance (CSA) IoT Controls Framework	IoT security controls and guidelines
HIPAA	Health Insurance Portability and Accountability Act	Healthcare IoT data security
GDPR	General Data Protection Regulation	Data protection and privacy
CCPA	California Consumer Privacy Act	Consumer data privacy (California)

3. **Data Privacy:** To learn and make choices, AI relies on vast volumes of data, which may include sensitive information. This raises issues regarding the privacy of the data as well as the possibility of data breaches.

4. **System Failure:** Failure of a system can have severe repercussions, particularly when it occurs in systems that are employed in essential infrastructure, such as those used in the healthcare industry, the transportation industry, or the energy industry. It is therefore of the utmost importance to make certain that AI systems are built to be resilient and can continue to function if they are targeted by an attack.

5. **Human Error:** Incorporating AI into IoT devices can also raise the danger of error caused by humans, particularly if users are not adequately taught or do not comprehend how the system operates. This can result in the accidental disclosure of sensitive information as well as various types of security flaws.

It is crucial to make certain that security is incorporated into the AIoT system from the very beginning to help alleviate these security problems. This includes putting into practice the concepts of security by design, carrying out regular security assessments, and making certain that all devices are kept up to date with the latest security patches. In addition, it is essential to give users with the appropriate training and knowledge, as well as to have response strategies in place, so that any security incidents may be rapidly contained and mitigated.

There are not enough precise standards for the security of AIoT yet. Although numerous broad cybersecurity standards can be applied to AIoT systems, there is a need for more specific standards that meet the unique security issues that are presented by AIoT. The necessity for decisions to be made in real-time is one of these problems, along with the utilization of machine learning algorithms and the integration of AI with legacy systems. Existing cybersecurity guidelines for AIoT tend to place more emphasis on security and preliminary risk evaluations than they do on privacy issues and do not offer any recommendations regarding continuous monitoring and enhancement. There is a need for standards that address privacy problems such as the reduction of data, user consent, and the retention of data, because of the vast amounts of personal and sensitive data that can be acquired by AIoT devices.

Moreover, cybersecurity requirements and laws for AIoT vary greatly among nations and regions, causing confusion and compliance issues for firms that operate in several jurisdictions. Further international collaboration and harmonization are required to produce consistent and interoperable AIoT security standards.

11.6 CYBERSECURITY STANDARDS FOR AIoT NETWORKS

AIoT networks combine the power of AI with the devices connected to the IoT, resulting in a complex system with its own set of unique security concerns. Several different cybersecurity standards have been developed to guarantee the safety of IoT networks. As is common knowledge, several Standard Development Organizations (SDOs) including the International Organization for Standardization (ISO), the International Electrotechnical Commission (IEC), the European Committee for Standardization (CEN), the European Committee for Electrotechnical Standardization (CENELEC), and the European Telecommunications Standards Institute (ETSI) are developing AI-related manuals and standardization deliverables. Such investigations may aid in appreciating the nature of the new and assessing if it is sufficiently distinct from what has come before to warrant or necessitate the development and implementation of new methods. In addition, they could guide the application of existing methods to new ones or describe new procedures to fill in the gaps.

The following is a list of some of the most essential standards for the cybersecurity of IoT networks:

11.6.1 NISTIR 8259A IoT Device Cybersecurity Capability Core Baseline

The National Institute of Standards and Technology (NIST) report NISTIR 8259A provides advice for controlling cybersecurity and privacy concerns in IoT devices. The research addresses critical design and development considerations for IoT devices, including security capabilities, data protection, and interoperability. In addition, it defines a risk management methodology for IoT devices, including methods for identifying, assessing, and mitigating cybersecurity and privacy threats throughout the device lifecycle. The purpose of this paper is to assist enterprises in formulating and implementing appropriate security and privacy strategies for IoT devices (Michael Fagan (NIST). 2020).

11.6.2 ESTI EN 303 645 Cybersecurity Standard for IoT

The ETSI EN 303 645 standard specifies the minimum requirements for information security in IoT devices. It outlines thirteen requirements that makers of IoT devices need to follow to make their products resistant to hacking attempts. These rules include requirements for unique default passwords, protection against known vulnerabilities, secure software, firmware updates, and transparency in reporting security concerns to end users. The purpose of the standard is to address concerns about the potential for cybercriminals to exploit IoT devices and to improve the privacy and security of IoT devices. The standard will also increase the privacy of IoT devices. It is relevant to all varieties of IoT devices, including those for the smart home, those that may be worn, and those used in industry (ETSI).

11.6.3 ISO 30141 IoT Reference Architecture

ISO/IEC 30141:2018 is an international standard that defines an IoT reference architecture (IoT). It lays out the fundamental components of an IoT system and offers recommendations for implementing established standards and cutting-edge technologies. Concerns for privacy and security have been incorporated into the standard, making it useful for ensuring the interoperability, stability, and security of IoT devices. Stakeholders including designers, implementers, and regulators can use it to guarantee the interoperability, dependability, and security of IoT systems as it provides a standard language and structure for understanding and developing such systems. Privacy and security in IoT systems are also addressed, as well as the utilization of existing IoT standards and future technologies (ISO "Iso/Iec 30141:2018 Internet of Things (Iot)—Reference Architecture").

11.6.4 ISO 27400 IoT Security and Privacy

The international standard ISO/IEC 27400 is a comprehensive document that offers recommendations for the management of cybersecurity risks in the context of the IoT. It contains guidelines, protocols, and procedures for detecting, evaluating, treating, and monitoring cybersecurity threats that are unique to IoT devices and systems. The objective of the standard is to provide businesses with guidance that will assist them in establishing and maintaining efficient cybersecurity risk management frameworks for their respective IoT environments. Additionally, it offers direction on how to address the privacy threats that are linked with the devices and systems of the IoT (ISO "Iso/Iec 27400:2022 Cybersecurity—Iot Security and Privacy—Guidelines").

11.6.5 ISO 27000 Information Security Management Systems

ISO/IEC 27000 for Information Security Management provides an overview and framework for enterprises implementing the ISO/IEC 27000 set of standards. The standards include different elements of information security, such as risk management, security controls, and legal and regulatory compliance. These standards outline the requirements for an ISMS and provide a framework for managing and protecting sensitive data through risk management processes. This framework comprises requirements for building and maintaining an information security management system, assessing and treating information security risks, and applying security controls. This set of standards is widely recognized and accepted as a recommended practice for managing information security by enterprises worldwide (ISO "Iso/Iec 27000:2018 Information Technology—Security Techniques—Information Security Management Systems—Overview and Vocabulary").

11.6.6 ISO 27001 & 27002

ISO/IEC 27701 standard is an extension of the ISO/IEC 27001 information security management standard. ISO/IEC 27701 provides a framework for implementing a privacy information management system (PIMS) in organizations, with a focus on protecting personal data. It specifies requirements and guidelines for managing privacy risks, ensuring regulatory compliance, and demonstrating accountability to stakeholders. The standard is designed to be integrated with the ISO/IEC 27001 management system and can help organizations achieve compliance with privacy regulations such as the EU's General Data Protection Regulation (GDPR) (ISO "Iso/Iec 27001:2022 Information Security, Cybersecurity and Privacy Protection—Information Security Management Systems—Requirements"). The standards cover aspects such as risk management, security controls, and legal compliance. ISO/IEC 27001 specifies requirements for an information security management system, while ISO/IEC 27002 provides a code of practice for information security management. These standards are widely adopted as best practices for managing information security (Disterer. 2013).

11.6.7 ISO 27032 Guidelines for Cybersecurity

The ISO/IEC 27001 standard stipulates the standards for establishing, implementing, maintaining, and continuously improving an organization's ISMS. The standard is intended to assist organizations in managing and protecting their information assets, including customer data, financial data, and intellectual property, by recognizing risks and adopting controls to mitigate them. The standard is widely recognized and accepted as a best practice for managing information security by enterprises around the world (ISO "Iso/Iec 27032:2012 Information Technology—Security Techniques—Guidelines for Cybersecurity").

11.6.8 ISO 27033 Network Security

ISO 27033 is a series of network security standards from ISO. It guides network infrastructure security and data confidentiality, integrity, and availability. The three-part series ISO 27033-1 gives an introduction to network security and defines important ideas, models, and architectures; ISO 27033-2 provides guidelines for the design, implementation, and management of network security measures; and ISO 27033-3 addresses cloud computing network security.

The ISO 27033 series can be used with ISO 27001 for information security management and ISO 27002 for information security controls in enterprises of all sizes. The series helps organizations build a comprehensive network security strategy that protects important assets and information from internal and external threats (ISO "Iso/Iec 27033-1:2015

Information Technology—Security Techniques—Network Security—Part 1: Overview and Concepts").

11.6.9 ISO 27034 Application Security

ISO 27034 sets application security requirements. It helps enterprises manage and improve application security from design to testing and maintenance. ISO 27034-1 gives an overview of application security and describes the ideas, principles, and processes essential to protecting applications; ISO 27034-2 provides guidelines for implementing application security controls; and ISO 27034-3 guides managing application security risks.

The ISO 27034 series can be used with ISO 27001 for information security management and ISO 27002 for information security controls in enterprises of all sizes. The series helps organizations develop a comprehensive application security strategy that protects vital assets and information by addressing technical and non-technical elements (ISO "Iso/Iec 27034-1:2011/Cor 1:2014 Information Technology—Security Techniques—Application Security—Part 1: Overview and Concepts—Technical Corrigendum 1").

11.6.10 CEN CENELEC Joint Technical Committee JTC's

JTC 13 and JTC 21 are the names of the two Joint Technical Committees (JTCs) that are primarily responsible for AI and cybersecurity work at European Committee for Standardization-European Committee for Electrotechnical Standardization (CEN-CENELEC) (P. Bezombes. 2023). The topic of discussion in JTC 13 is something that has been called the "limited scope" of cybersecurity. A list of standards from ISO-IEC that are of interest for AI cybersecurity are selected and then CEN-CENELEC may adopt or adapt these standards based on their agreement to technically cooperate. The most prominent standards that have been identified are those that are part of the ISO 27000 series, which focuses on information security management systems. These standards may be supplemented by the ISO 15408 series, which focuses on the development, evaluation, and/or procurement of information technology products that have security functionality. Additionally, sector-specific guidance may be utilized. ISO 27001–27008, ISO 27010–11, ISO 27013–14, ISO 27016–17, ISO 27021–23, ISO 27031–32, and ISO 27035 are some of the standards that are covered. These standards were identified by CEN-CENELEC followed by ISO/IEC AWI 27090 Cybersecurity-Artificial Intelligence, which addresses the loop holes and criteria in AI and ISO/IEC CD TR 27563. Cybersecurity-Artificial Intelligence addresses the partial impact of AI in security at initial stages to test systems impacts.

Trustworthiness features, data quality, artificial intelligence governance, artificial intelligence management systems, etc. are all part of the broader cybersecurity topic that JTC 21 is tackling. Considering this: ISO/IEC 22989, ISO/IEC 23053, ISO/IEC TS 4213, ISO/IEC DIS 42001 for AI management system, the ISO/IEC 23894 is for Guidance on AI risk management, the ISO/IEC FDIS 24029-2 is for methodology for the use of formal methods, and ISO/IEC CD 5259 series are for data quality and for data analytics in Machine Learning (ML) should be consider.

11.7 IDENTIFICATION AND AUTHENTICATION PROTOCOLS

Due to the increase in the number of IoT devices, the security of these devices is very important. IoT technology is a network of small, lightweight devices that is growing at a very fast speed. Security concerns must be addressed for IoT deployment so that it is effective for daily life. Security concerns related to commercial and personal purposes must be kept in mind while deploying these devices (Eijndhoven. 2020). To address these security problems, authorization and identification protocols are applied. Ensuring the integrity of the IoT network's authorization control is an effective method as it prevents unauthorized people from accessing these devices. To enhance the quality and to add automation in this process, AIoT networks are gaining popularity. Due to the increased number of devices and complex networks, it is crucial to take help from the latest technologies of Artificial Intelligence.

For this purpose, multiple protocols can be employed to enhance the security of AIoT networks. Some of these protocols are traditional like passwords and digital certificates. Modern methods like biometric authentication and OAuth2 can add additional layers to the security of the networks. Let's examine each protocol more deeply.

11.7.1 Passwords

Passwords are one of the traditional methods of authentication to prevent unauthorized activity in IoT networks. To gain access to the network, the user must put in a valid password. Although this prevalent method is effective to some extent, due to the presence of brute-force attacks, this technique is susceptible. Once the user finds the right combination of the characters as a valid password, the network will be compromised, and it can lead to data and security breaches. Now this encourages us to find alternatives and more secure authentication protocols.

11.7.2 Digital Certificates

Digital certificates are also used to detect the validity of the users. These certificates are issued by a well-known third-party certification authority, and the certificates have critical information related to devices like devices name, public key, and expiry date. The certificates are widely used in web applications and IoT devices such as Secure Sockets Layer, and Transport Layer Security (SSL/TLS) to enhance security. Digital certificates are also vulnerable to cyber-attacks as intruders may hack third-party systems and tamper with the information on the certificate (Lal, Prasad and Farik. 2016). Figure 11.1 shows the identification and authentication protocols.

11.7.3 Biometric Authentication

Biometric authentication involves the physical verification of the user. The user must provide fingerprints, facial recognition, or voice recognition to log into IoT networks. This seems a more secure method as it involves the physical characteristics of the users, and it is very difficult to change these features (Lal, Prasad and Farik. 2016). Although biometrics is considered one of the safest methods to enhance the security of IoT devices, there are some limitations to the effectiveness of this methodology.

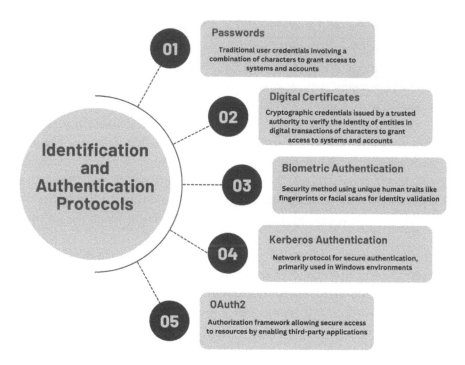

FIGURE 11.1   Identification and authentication protocols.

11.7.4 Kerberos Authentication

Kerberos Authentication is a third-party authentication system developed by MIT and is considered very safe due to its complexity. It is mostly used in distributed networks where users need access to different stations. Kerberos uses symmetric key encryption techniques and a key distribution center (Baiello, Basso and Giusto. 2002).

11.7.5 OAuth2

OAuth2 is an authentication protocol that is widely used due to its easiness. It enables users to log into different online applications and networks using third-party software that has the information of the user. This protocol is a kind of permission for the application to use the data of the user on his behalf to log in to a new system (Richer and Sanso. 2017). This methodology is frequently used in social media and cloud-based applications. In addition to these protocols for authentication, AIoT networks may use some other methods like encryption, firewall, and intrusion detection systems. The range of these protocols indicates that organizations should use different combinations for the authentication and identification of the users. Figure 11.2 shows the general digital signature system.

11.8 DATA ENCRYPTION AND INTEGRITY PROTECTION

11.8.1 Data Encryption

IoT devices are producing large amounts of data in real-time. With the implementation of cloud computing devices, this data is stored in cloud servers. Cloud computing is an

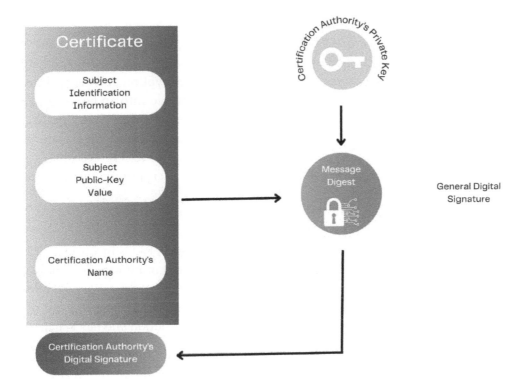

FIGURE 11.2   General digital signature system.

emerging field that involves the storage and processing of the data produced by IoT devices in complex networks. However, the data on the internet is at risk as intruders may attack and steal the data. The resources needed for IoT devices are less compared to normal computers as IoT devices consume less power and network bandwidth. To secure the data of these devices, traditional encryption algorithms can be used like Advanced Encryption Standard (AES), Data Encryption Standard (DES), and Triple Advanced Encryption Standard (3AES). But, because these particular algorithms are very complex and need high computation resources, these methods are not suitable especially for limited resources enabled IoT devices (Mehmood et al. 2019).

Encryption is the process of converting normal text into encrypted text. This is helpful to prevent unauthorized access to the data being transformed. For each data transfer, an encryption key is generated to protect the data. Mathematical functions are used to transform the normal data into an unrecognizable form so it will not be understandable to intruders. Once the data are reached, the destination decryption key is used to convert the encrypted data back into its original form. In IoT devices, large amounts of data are being transferred, so encryption methodologies are applied to protect the data. The unauthorized persons will not be able to understand or decode the data being transferred. Different combinations of symmetric and asymmetric algorithms are used to further protect the systems. The following are some of the algorithms used for the data encryption of AIoT devices.

11.8.2 Cryptography

Cryptography is considered one of the most powerful techniques to secure the data transmitted over a network. The integrity of data can be protected with the help of cryptography as no one can access and modify the data. Encryption and decryption are the processes applied in cryptography. The data is transformed into an unrecognizable form so the third party will not be able to understand the data even if they get access. The data is then converted back to its original form with a decryption key. Symmetric cryptography uses the same keys for encryption and decryption. On the other hand, asymmetric cryptography uses different keys for the encryption and decryption of the data.

11.8.3 Blockchain Based Encryption

In blockchain-based encryption, a Third-Party Authenticator (TPA) is involved to protect the security of the data. It uses multiple blockchain groupings of information and signature keys of IoT networks. The data is protected with hash keys that are assigned randomly in constant-size blocks. This methodology is cost-effective as it calculates the cost of the IoT integrity from the central server to the device. Cross distribution and blockchain linkage are applied to manage multiple devices at a time at a low cost (Sim and Jeong. 2021).

11.8.4 Public Key Infrastructure (PKI)

Public Key Infrastructure is a complex system to manage the AIoT network's credentials. Due to millions of IoT devices, it is very difficult to manage a centralized system to allocate security certificates to these devices. AIoT devices have constraints like low power and computation resources. PKI is a lightweight mechanism that provides the certificate for AIoT devices. This enrolment process is very useful for devices with low battery and low Random Access Memory (RAM) (Höglund et al. 2020).

11.8.5 Message Authentication Code (MAC)

Generally, single cryptographic techniques lack security and integrity. With the growing demand for IoT devices, the mechanism of encryption should be developed with the combination of different methodologies to enhance security. Implicit message authentication code (iMAC) is an encryption technique that is based on a combination of polygraphic substitution, Exclusive OR (XoR), and simple columnar transportation to calculate MAC. It also uses real-time environmental parameters like temperature, pressure, and Received Signal Strength Indicator (RSSI) to create secret keys for data transportation (Ullah, Meratnia and Havinga. 2020).

11.8.6 Secure Boot

Secure boot technology makes the device boot-up process protective which enables security while the device is in boot state. It prevents intruders from making any changes in the firmware or hardware settings of the devices. Secure boot is essential in AIoT networks as it provides security to devices in the booting process. Once the device is booted successfully, the next process is trusted boot. It works on a digital signature that is used to verify the authenticity of the firmware and system settings. The digital signature also confirms that the system is not infected with any malware (Wang and Yan. 2022).

11.9 NETWORK SEGMENTATION AND ACCESS CONTROLS

Network segmentation and access controls are a very important part of the security of AIoT. Segmentation of the network is done by dividing the complex network into smaller networks or subnetworks. This is helpful in order to manage the network easily and improve its performance. In the context of AIoT devices, the segmentation is slightly different, as it involves the separation of different components of the devices. AIoT devices are a combination of different sensors, controllers, and actuators. By separating each component, the security and integrity of these devices can be improved. Access controls are deployed to permit access to the network settings to only authorized persons. In the AIoT network context, access control is specifically applied to limit the access of the users to the network settings of the devices.

Network segmentation is a very effective mechanism for dividing the network into subnetworks and creating different layers. Most enterprises develop their network like a fortress. Different network security techniques are deployed to secure this fortress. Network segmentation expands the idea of the fortress and creates multiple layers for the defence of this fortress. The intruders and attackers will need more time to break these layers to get into the settings of the network (Simpson and Foltz. 2021).

11.10 CHALLENGES TO IMPLEMENT CYBERSECURITY STANDARDS FOR AIoT NETWORKS

As most of the AIoT devices are built on the latest technologies, it is a challenge to connect new devices to old networks. The newly built devices connected to traditional networks are working on legacy protocols. Most of the old networks are working on protocols that were specifically designed for computers and devices that have good computation resources. In the case of AIoT devices, the computation resources are limited, which causes the devices to have some vulnerabilities (Payne and Abegaz. 2018). Some of the reasons the attackers prefer to attack IoT devices are the usage of default passwords, lack of encryption, non-segmented networks, and lack of security updates. Most manufacturers use very weak default passwords for the devices, and then these passwords are provided in user manuals, so chances of intrusion into these devices are high. Very few users bother to change the default passwords because of the complex user interfaces provided by the manufacturers (Payne and Abegaz. 2018).

The lack of encryption of IoT networks encourages hackers to intrude on the devices and steal commands to get into the data of the devices. In one DEF CON presentation in 2016, testing revealed that almost 75% of the devices in the test were easily hackable with hardware costing only $200 (Coldewey. 2016). As most users are not aware of the network segmentation techniques, it is difficult to segment the network, and this leads to security threats. Internet Service Providers (ISPs) can provide this feature in the routers and networking devices to apply segmentation easily without any technical knowledge (Payne and Abegaz. 2018). Virtual Local Area Networks (VLANs) are mostly used in organizations and offices that employ technical people to separate different devices and networks. But it is a challenge for a non-technical user to do network segmentation to protect it (Payne and Abegaz. 2018).

11.11 EMERGING TECHNOLOGIES AND THEIR IMPACT ON CYBERSECURITY

Cybersecurity concerns are increasing day by day due to the increase in the number of network devices. IoT is being used in everyday life to automate different tasks. Protecting these devices and networks from intruders is very important. With new technologies emerging, there should be a check on the impact of these technologies on cybersecurity. While some of these technologies have the potential to improve cybersecurity, others may create new challenges and threats. Following are some of the emerging technologies impacting cybersecurity.

11.11.1 Artificial Intelligence (AI)

Artificial intelligence is being used in (IoT) devices to detect cyber threats and mitigate cyber attacks automatically. With deep learning and unsupervised learning algorithms, IoT devices can analyze big volumes of potential threats and problems. However, these AI algorithms are available to hackers as well, and they can use them for harmful purposes. Due to AI, the number of cyberattacks is growing at a very high speed, and the nature of the attacks is also very complex as hackers are using automated tools to create large volumes of malicious traffic (Patel. 2023).

The purpose of emerging technologies is to develop intelligent systems with high capabilities, like humans, to identify potential threats in IoT devices. In this digital era, AI methodologies can help organizations and individuals to be safe from cyber threats. The massive use of social media applications creates huge volumes of data. To protect and analyze this data, the traditional methods will not be effective anymore. AI rescues us in textual and graphical data analysis to extract meaningful data and then protect it (Li. 2018).

A typical Machine Learning (ML) process consists of the following steps (Xin et al. 2018).

- Extraction of the features

- Selection of the ML algorithm

- Training of the model

- Classification or prediction of the unknown using the trained model

Different ML algorithms are deployed for different situations and datasets. Common ML algorithms for classification and prediction are Support Vector Machine (SVM), k-nearest neighbour (k-NN), decision tree, and neural networks. It is important to select the right algorithm for specific industrial problems (Li. 2018).

11.11.2 Blockchain

The lack of security protocols for IoT devices brings many challenges and risks. Blockchain is distributed technology that can be deployed to secure IoT devices. A blockchain is a combination of linked blocks that are cryptographically protected, and their data is saved in a distributed and decentralized ledger. With many advantages over traditional methods, blockchain technology is considered one of the most secure to protect IoT devices (Saxena, Bhushan and Ahad. 2021). First, blockchain technology solves the problem of a single point of failure, provides fault tolerance abilities, and incorporates communication at both ends in devices. Second, the users of blockchain technology can verify the other users for communication which protects the devices and data from unauthorized access. Third, the storage capacity of blockchain servers is enough to handle and save huge amounts of data with all the security updates for IoT devices (Saxena, Bhushan and Ahad. 2021). Furthermore, blockchain technology enables the devices to secure the data in immutable ledgers which cannot be changed by any unauthorized user (Saxena, Bhushan and Ahad. 2021) (Wu et al. 2019).

Network security can be improved with access control using blockchain technology. Multiple layers are applied to handle the data and protect it from intruders. These layers are connected with a decentralized blockchain network. The data is protected in the multilayer blockchain model and the records of the blockchain links are saved in a ledger (Axon and Goldsmith. 2002).

11.12 CONCLUSION

To summarize, there are a lot of security-based standards available concerning IoT security, although ISO 27000-based information security management systems have a complete set of instructions for effective security measurement. Change in the trends for effective security solutions using AI methods creates a gap to fill due to AI applications in a cybersecurity context. AI-based cybersecurity procedures are being developed to safeguard CPSs from zero-day attacks. In cybersecurity, machine learning algorithms are used to manage large amounts of heterogeneous data from many sources to generate attack patents and accurately forecast future attacker behaviour. But this has brought to cyber experts' attention the need to analyze cybersecurity standards after the integration of AI. It is becoming increasingly critical to ensure the safety of these connected devices as the number of linked devices and reliance on IoT continues to rise. The difficulty of ensuring data privacy and integrity in the IoT is further complicated by the integration of AI.

REFERENCES

Angelov, Plamen P., et al. "Brief Introduction to Statistical Machine Learning." *Empirical Approach to Machine Learning* (2019): 17–67.

Axon, L. M., and Michael Goldsmith. "PB-PKI: A Privacy-Aware Blockchain-Based PKI." (2016).

Baiello, Carlo, Alessandro Basso, and C. D. Giusto. "Kerberos Protocol: An Overview." *Distributed Systems*, Italy, Fall (2002).

Bezombes, P., S. Brunessaux, and S. Cadzow. "Cybersecurity of AI and Standardisation." *enisa* (2023). https://www.enisa.europa.eu/publications/cybersecurity-of-ai-and-standardisation

Coldewey, Devin. "'Smart' Locks Yield to Simple Hacker Tricks." Techcrunch 2016. Web. August 9 2016.

Disterer, Georg. "ISO/IEC 27000, 27001 and 27002 for Information Security Management." *Journal of Information Security* 4.2 (2013).

Eijndhoven, D. "The Internet of (Insecure) Things: Cyber Security Goofs in IoT Devices." 2016.

ETSI. "Cyber Security for Consumer Internet of Things: Baseline Requirements." ETSI EN 2020. Web.

Gubbi, Jayavardhana, et al. "Internet of Things (IoT): A Vision, Architectural Elements, and Future Directions." *Future Generation Computer Systems* 29.7 (2013): 1645–60.

Hasan, Anum, and Kashif Naseer Qureshi. "Internet of Things Device Authentication Scheme Using Hardware Serialization." *2018 International Conference on Applied and Engineering Mathematics (ICAEM)*. 2018. IEEE.

Höglund, Joel, et al. "PKI4IoT: Towards Public Key Infrastructure for the Internet of Things." *Computers & Security* 89 (2020): 101658.

Hussain, Adil, et al. "An Enhanced Intelligent Intrusion Detection System to Secure E-Commerce Communication Systems." *Computer Systems Science and Engineering* 47.2 (2023): 2513–28.

Iqbal, Saleem, et al. "Automised Flow Rule Formation by Using Machine Learning in Software Defined Networks Based Edge Computing." *Egyptian Informatics Journal* 23.1 (2021).

ISO. "ISO/IEC 27000:2018 Information Technology—Security Techniques—Information Security Management Systems—Overview and Vocabulary." ISO 2018. Web.

———. "ISO/IEC 27001:2022 Information Security, Cybersecurity and Privacy Protection—Information Security Management Systems—Requirements." ISO 2022. Web.

———. "ISO/IEC 27032:2012 Information Technology—Security Techniques—Guidelines for Cybersecurity." ISO 2012. Web.

———. "ISO/IEC 27033-1:2015 Information Technology—Security Techniques—Network Security—Part 1: Overview and Concepts." ISO 2015. Web.

———. "ISO/IEC 27034-1:2011/Cor 1:2014 Information Technology—Security Techniques—Application Security—Part 1: Overview and Concepts—Technical Corrigendum 1." ISO 2011. Web.

———. "IISO/IEC 27400:2022 Cybersecurity—IoT Security and Privacy—Guidelines." ISO 2022. Web.

———. "ISO/IEC 30141:2018 Internet of Things (IoT) —Reference Architecture." ISO 2018. Web.

Kiyani, Faisal, et al. "ISDA-BAN: Interoperability and Security Based Data Authentication Scheme for Body Area Network." *Cluster Computing* 26.4 (2023): 2429–42.

Kseniia, Nikolskaia, and Aleksey Minbaleev. "Legal Support of Cybersecurity in the Field of Application of Artificial Intelligence Technology." *2020 International Conference Quality Management, Transport and Information Security, Information Technologies (IT&QM&IS)*. 2020. IEEE.

Lal, Nilesh A., Salendra Prasad, and Mohammed Farik. "A Review of Authentication Methods." *International Journal of Scientific & Technology Research* 5 (2016): 246–49.

Li, Jian-hua. "Cyber Security Meets Artificial Intelligence: A Survey." *Frontiers of Information Technology & Electronic Engineering* 19.12 (2018): 1462–74.

Mehmood, Muhammad Sheraz, et al. "A Comprehensive Literature Review of Data Encryption Techniques in Cloud Computing and IoT Environment." *2019 8th International Conference on Information and Communication Technologies (ICICT)*. 2019. IEEE.

Fagan, M., et al. "IoT Device Cybersecurity Capability Core Baseline." (National Institute of Standards and Technology, Gaithersburg, MD.) NIST Interagency or Internal Report (IR) 8259A. 2020.

Patel, Hrishitva. "The Future of Cybersecurity with Artificial Intelligence (Ai) and Machine Learning (Ml)." (2023).

Payne, Bryson R., and Tamirat T. Abegaz. "Securing the Internet of Things: Best Practices for Deploying IoT Devices." *Computer and Network Security Essentials* (2018): 493–506.

Peer-to-Peer Netw. Appl. 2017. https://dblp.org/db/journals/ppna/index.html.

Rehman, M., et al. "A Cyber Secure Medical Management System by Using Blockchain." *IEEE Transactions on Computational Social Systems* (2022): 1–14.

Richer, Justin, and Antonio Sanso. *OAuth 2 in Action.* Simon and Schuster, 2017.

Saxena, Shivam, Bharat Bhushan, and Mohd Abdul Ahad. "Blockchain Based Solutions to Secure IoT: Background, Integration Trends and a Way Forward." *Journal of Network and Computer Applications* 181 (2021): 103050.

Sim, Sung-Ho, and Yoon-Su Jeong. "Multi-Blockchain-Based IoT Data Processing Techniques to Ensure the Integrity of IoT Data in AIoT Edge Computing Environments." *Sensors* 21.10 (2021): 3515.

Network Segmentation and Zero Trust Architectures. Lecture Notes in Engineering and Computer Science, Proceedings of the World Congress on Engineering (WCE). 2021.

Ullah, Ikram, Nirvana Meratnia, and Paul J. M. Havinga. "Imac: Implicit Message Authentication Code for IoT Devices." *2020 IEEE 6th World Forum on Internet of Things (WF-IoT).* 2020. IEEE.

Wang, Qinghua, and Ilangko Balasingham. "Wireless Sensor Networks-an Introduction." *Wireless Sensor Networks: Application-Centric Design* (2010): 1–14.

Wang, Rui, and Yonghang Yan. "A Survey of Secure Boot Schemes for Embedded Devices." *2022 24th International Conference on Advanced Communication Technology (ICACT).* 2022. IEEE.

Wu, Mingli, et al. "A Comprehensive Survey of Blockchain: From Theory to Iot Applications and Beyond." *IEEE Internet of Things Journal* 6.5 (2019): 8114–54.

Xin, Yang, et al. "Machine Learning and Deep Learning Methods for Cybersecurity." *IEEE Access* 6 (2018): 35365–81.

CHAPTER 12

Future Privacy and Trust Challenges for AIoT Networks

Ayesha Aslam

School of Information Engineering, Chang'an University, Xi'an, China

Kashif Naseer Qureshi, Thomas Newe

Department of Electronic & Computer Engineering, University of Limerick, V94 T9PX Limerick, Ireland

12.1 INTERNET OF THINGS

The development of the Internet of Things (IoT) has been a gradual process starting with individual machines and evolving into networking and the emergence of the Internet. The Internet encompasses a variety of personal and organizational computing devices, intranets, and other related technologies. The emergence of wireless communication and the development of compact computing devices have facilitated the realization of mobile computing. The proliferation of diverse electronic devices, including sensors and actuators, has led to the assumption that each device is equipped with intelligent sensing and computing capabilities, thus heralding the advent of the IoT era. The IoT comprises three primary constituents: the "things" themselves, encompassing a wide range of technologies, devices, items, animals, and humans; the communication networks interconnecting these devices; and the computer networks responsible for transmitting data from the Internet to the respective devices.

The IoT is a network of physical objects equipped with electronics, sensors, software, and network connections, allowing them to collect and modify data. Its main benefit is its significant impact on daily life and user behavior, such as home security systems enabling remote temperature and lock status monitoring. The primary goal of the IoT is to gain better insight into nearby or distant environments, allowing users to understand, manage, and respond to the data collected to enhance human existence. The integration of objects into the IoT has led to numerous business opportunities. However, addressing security and privacy concerns, particularly about telecommunications and information technology complexities, is necessary for technology advancement and success. Despite its momentum as an evolving paradigm, IoT technology still faces security and privacy challenges that must be resolved, as these are closely linked to IoT-connected devices.

DOI: 10.1201/9781003430018-14

The impact of IoT is significant as it affects various aspects of life, such as people, processes, data, and things. People are affected as IoT allows for more control, monitoring, and enhancing of their capabilities by connecting machines to humans. Processes are also impacted as real-time communication between users and machines allows for quicker completion of complex tasks. The enhanced capacity to gather data at increased frequencies and with heightened dependability significantly influences the process of rational decision-making, so illustrating an essential aspect of data's impact. Furthermore, IoT significantly impacts many entities, such as devices, sensors, processors, and actuators, enabling them to establish communication channels and fulfill more substantial objectives. This adds value to objects like mobile devices. The IoT market offers numerous opportunities for businesses in various industries, and even minor variations can result in significant changes worth billions of dollars in multiple areas within a few years.

The IoT can be seen as a significant data source affecting IT infrastructure. To take advantage of this, improved data analysis techniques present unique and critical opportunities for generating data (Ahlgren, Hidell, and Ngai. 2016). However, collecting, preparing, and analyzing massive amounts of data are challenging. First, the volume of data can increase exponentially in just a few months. Second, this type of data is complex and has unique characteristics. It has a vast range of variability and is often pseudo-structured or unstructured. Evaluating and managing both structured and unstructured data are crucial to obtaining a complete view of the data produced by sensors. Depending entirely on a particular data template can substantially constrain the possibility of generating innovative ideas. By conducting comprehensive data analysis, managers can acquire a strategic perspective for making decisions about their business.

IoT devices, encompassing a range of technologies such as sensor data, smartphones, intelligent software, and social media platforms, have the potential to offer significant insights that can inform decision-making processes. In addition, consumer-oriented products such as smart speakers, smart TVs, toys, smart appliances, and wearable devices have the potential to provide relevant data for the examination of user behavior and the identification of fraudulent actions. Big data derived from IoT devices can create value for organizations, providing insights that help improve performance and understanding of customer needs (Qureshi, Alhudhaif, et al. 2021). By using analytical tools such as predictive modeling, clustering, and classification, organizations can unlock the full potential of generated data. The advent of IoT and its associated technologies, such as cloud computing, has facilitated the integration of data sources from various fields, resulting in the development of diverse methods. Decision-makers have the potential to enhance the performance of IoT and big data applications through the integration of AI technology, such as machine learning or deep learning algorithms (Alansari et al. 2018). The integration of AI in IoT has created a new area known as the Artificial Internet of Things (AIoT).

In the past, using intelligent computational systems was unfeasible due to the enormous amount of data and computational power required. However, the emergence of cloud computing and AIoT have enabled organizations to transform their processes and enhance productivity by identifying faults through emerging platforms like business intelligence and data analysis platforms. With the speed of technological advancement expected to accelerate even further, it is crucial to update AIoT technology, particularly regarding software, hardware, and security. One promising security technology currently being used is Physically Unclonable Functions (PUFs), which use unique keys and timestamps to authenticate AIoT objects. However, this approach has limitations, including the need for significant computing power to authenticate all objects and messages in the AIoT network and the potential for a bottleneck when using an authentication server (Alhalafi and Veeraraghavan. 2019). The AIoT field has experienced substantial growth due to data sensors, processing and connectivity, software information, and various intelligent services that collect and share data through the internet. However, this expansion has led to numerous challenges for AIoT, such as connectivity, scalability, big data, heterogeneity, security, and privacy, as indicated by various AIoT security assessments from different sources.

12.2 AIoT SECURITY CHALLENGES

The field of AIoT security encompasses the various protective measures employed to ensure the uninterrupted operation of devices, mitigate the risk of operational or handling harm, and minimize vulnerability to distant cyber intrusions. In the context of the increasing prevalence of ubiquitous computing, security and privacy issues have emerged as significant areas of concern. The proliferation of AIoT devices and the widespread adoption of cloud platforms have brought about a heightened concern regarding data security. Furthermore, the proliferation of internet-connected devices has led to a notable escalation in concerns around privacy. The escalating threat to AIoT devices emphasizes the need to identify viable solutions. There is a pressing need for a pragmatic resolution to effectively tackle the growing problem of vulnerability and significantly reduce the frequency at which cyber criminals operate. The occurrence of Distributed Denial of Service (DDoS) attacks in 2016, which targeted AIoT services and devices worldwide, functioned as a significant event that alerted the IT community to and confirmed the existence of security risks associated with the IoT rather than their being merely hypothetical. However, the implementation of personal security measures aimed at protecting equipment from both identified and unidentified cyber adversaries can offer a potential resolution.

The IoT network has experienced substantial growth due to the emergence of intelligent transportation, smart cities, smart homes, smart grids, smart healthcare, and various other applications. The system in question is not just classified as a sensor network, but rather a comprehensive framework that encompasses Wireless Sensor Networks (WSNs) as a constituent component within its broader ecosystem (Qureshi and Abdullah. 2013). The proliferation of Internet-connected devices gives rise to a multitude of worries about AIoT, particularly about its susceptibility to vulnerabilities. Concerns encompass a wide range of difficulties, including the expansion of botnets, inadequate encryption measures, the prevalence of weak passwords, connectivity challenges, financial breaches, inaccurate detection techniques, scalability limitations, the management of massive datasets, heterogeneity, as well as security and privacy concerns.

12.2.1 New Security Vulnerabilities

As businesses increasingly adopt AIoT devices, new security vulnerabilities will continue to emerge. These vulnerabilities are attributed to limitations in device/object capabilities and include the following:

1. **Rise of Botnets:** Recently, there has been a surge in the use of botnets for attacks. Botnets are groups of infected computers that malicious individuals control without the computer owners' knowledge. These internet-connected devices are remotely manipulated by hackers who exploit the acquired information for illicit purposes. Organizations such as hospitals can fall victim to botnets without the management's awareness, as their computer network devices can be hijacked and incorporated into the botnet.

2. **Large Volume of IoT Devices:** Cybersecurity professionals have mainly concentrated on safeguarding computers and mobile devices. Nonetheless, public and private entities' adoption of AIoT devices has gained significant momentum. Presently, there are approximately 7 billion gadgets; the figure could climb to 20 billion. The widespread use of AIoT devices has led to a surge in security vulnerabilities, which has complicated the work of security specialists.

3. **Lack of Encryption:** While encryption is a potent measure against unauthorized access to data by hackers, it poses a significant security challenge for AIoT devices. Unlike conventional computers, these devices may have limited processing and storage capabilities. Therefore, hackers can easily manipulate the security algorithms intended to safeguard AIoT devices more frequently.

4. **Outdated Legacy Security:** Connected legacy systems pose an extra worry as they seem outdated in an organization increasingly employing many AIoT devices. Such legacy systems, lacking updated security standards, could be vulnerable to a breach due to a compromise in a single AIoT device on the network.

5. **Weak Default Passwords:** Most AIoT devices come with easily guessable default passwords, and despite the customary practice of updating passwords, some IT managers need to pay more attention to this simple directive. As a result, an AIoT device with a weak or predictable password could be vulnerable to a brute-force attack. This grave issue is prevalent globally and requires urgent attention. For instance, California officials in the United States banned default passwords in 2018 as a proactive measure to tackle this problem.

6. **Unreliable Threat Detection Models:** Numerous companies adopt diverse techniques, such as monitoring user activity, scrutinizing indicators, and adhering to security standards, to detect data breaches. However, the proliferation of AIoT devices and their intricate nature challenge conventional threat control methods, rendering them less effective.

7. **Small-Scale Attacks:** While cybersecurity professionals focus primarily on averting large-scale cyberattacks, the security issue of AIoT lies in small-scale attacks,

which are relatively harder to detect and may take place without the organization's awareness. Hackers can potentially compromise various essential technologies, such as cameras, scanners, and printers.

8. **Phishing Attacks:** Phishing is a pervasive cybersecurity threat that targets all enterprise systems, and IoT devices could be the latest attack vector. Hackers may signal a particular AIoT device, leading to numerous problems. Even though it is one of the most common cyberattacks, it is preventable. However, most organizations need to educate their employees adequately about the current phishing risks and how to avoid or handle such incidents in a worst-case scenario.

9. **Inability to Predict Threats:** Some organizations need a versatile management system to monitor activities and offer insights into potential hazards. Security experts must adopt a more proactive approach to preempt AIoT security vulnerabilities before they arise. Without such a proactive strategy, an organization may fail to detect potential breaches promptly.

10. **Lack of Frequent Software Updates:** Workers use frequent software updates to manage security on mobile devices and laptops. But some AIoT devices get different software updates than other technologies, and certain companies need to give their AIoT devices essential security updates.

11. **IoT Financial Breaches:** When an institution, such as a bank, employs AIoT devices to facilitate electronic or e-payments, there is typically an inherent vulnerability that exposes them to the potential threat of unauthorized access by hackers. This unauthorized access poses a significant danger of compromising sensitive information and illicitly misappropriating funds. Numerous firms are taking proactive measures to include machine learning or blockchain technology to mitigate financial fraud. Nevertheless, there are still some businesses that have not embraced this method.

It vividly portrays the various hazards present in both hardware and software domains. The dangers encompass a range of attack vectors: physical, software, network, and encryption. To effectively tackle these difficulties, the solution must provide a communication method that is both adaptable and interoperable with the many devices involved.

12. **User Privacy:** Internal and external user data security is a top priority for organizations, especially given that many employees use IoT devices supplied by their employers. The enterprise's reputation may be significantly impacted if a breach leads to data compromise. Therefore, preserving privacy is a primary concern within the realm of IoT security, necessitating prompt attention and resolution.

13. **Heterogeneity of Connected Devices and Environment:** The administration of AIoT poses significant challenges, especially in terms of security management and service functions, due to the heterogeneous environment of the connected system. The heterogeneity of AIoT devices and their surroundings makes effective and efficient management challenging. Although AIoT has numerous uses and has the potential to enhance people's quality of life, it also presents various obstacles that must be addressed immediately for it to be widely adopted.

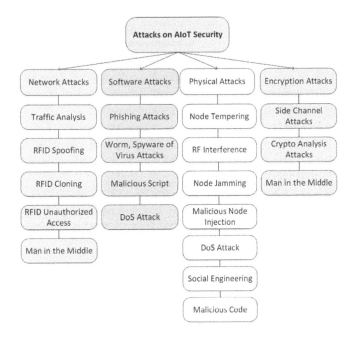

FIGURE 12.1   Classification of AIoT attacks.

Figure 12.1 provides a comprehensive depiction of the classification of security attacks in the context of the AIoT.

A flexible and interoperable communication system for AIoT devices must be developed to address these challenges. AIoT system holds promise in enhancing individuals' quality of life; nonetheless, it is imperative to confront these obstacles to facilitate widespread acceptance and implementation promptly. AIoT is often regarded as the most influential technological advancement of this era after the establishment of the Internet. The quantity of linked physical devices has risen considerably and exceeded the global human population in 2010. Recently, there has been substantial progress in creating AIoT-enabled devices. Technological developments, particularly in terms of energy-efficient and resource-constrained devices, have expanded internet access even for remote locations (Musaddiq et al. 2018; Kraijak and Tuwanut. 2015). Table 12.1 shows the AIoT attacks and countermeasures.

12.3 SECURITY REQUIREMENTS FOR AIoT

Establishing security, privacy, and authentication measures is important for standardizing any mobile communication system. The security recommendations provided by International Telecommunication Union – Telecommunication (ITU-T) encompass a range of security aspects that serve to safeguard against significant security risks. The security dimensions have several aspects, including user information, network infrastructure, and applications. Within the context of AIoT, the following dimensions are defined:

- **Access Control:** It is a fundamental and critical measure for AIoT security that ensures network resources can be accessed only by authorized devices while prohibiting unauthorized devices from accessing network elements, services, stored information, and information flows.

TABLE 12.1 Overview of AIoT Attacks and Countermeasures

Category	Attacks	Countermeasures
Network Attacks	Traffic Analysis	Secure DNP3, PKI, SSL, encryption, authentication
	RFID Spoofing	IPsec will significantly cut down on the risk of spoofing.
	RFID Cloning	Encryption, authentication, unique identifiers, jamming
	RFID unauthorized access	Device Authentication
	Man in the Middle	Secure DNP3, PKI, TLS, SSL, encryption, authentication
Software Attacks	Phishing Attacks	Antivirus, schedule signature updates
	Worm, Spyware, and Virus Attacks	MAPE, Linear SVM, Hybrid Spyware Detection
	Malicious Script	Runtime Type, Checking, Firewall Checks
	DoS Attack	SIEM, IDS, flow entropy, signal strength, sensing time measurement, transmission failure count, pushback, reconfiguration methods
Physical Attacks	Node Tempering	Physically secure design
	RF Interference	Device Authentication
	Node Jamming	JADE, anti-jamming, IPsec Security channel
	Malicious Node Injection	DLP, IDS, SIEM, Anti-virus, Diversity technique
	Social Engineering	Secure DNP3, PKI, SSL, encryption, authentication
	Malicious Code	Use FileZilla as the FTP client.
Encryption Attacks	Side Channel Attacks	Masking, EMI filtering, Noise addition
	Cryptanalysis Attack	Blowfish, RSA, ECC, DSA, AES
	Man in the Middle	Secure DNP3, PKI, TLS, SSL, encryption, authentication

- **Authentication:** It verifies the identity of AIoT devices, validates their claimed identities, and prevents masquerade or replay attacks.

- **Nonrepudiation:** It guarantees that neither the transmitter nor the receiver can deny transmitted information.

- **Data Confidentiality:** This safeguards data from unauthorized disclosure by AIoT devices and ensures that unauthorized devices cannot understand the content of the data.

- **Data Integrity:** It guarantees the accuracy and protection of data from unauthorized creation, modification, deletion, and replication, providing indications of any unauthorized device activities related to data.

- **Communication Security:** It ensures that only authorized AIoT devices exchange information and prevents unauthorized interception or diversion of information during transit.

- **Availability:** It ensures authorized AIoT devices' access to network resources, stored information, or its flow, services, and applications.

- **Privacy:** It safeguards the information of AIoT devices that may be inferred from their activities.

FIGURE 12.2   ITU-T security dimensions.

Despite significant advancements in computing power, energy capacity, and storage capabilities, potential attacks on AIoT can lead to severe negative consequences due to inadequate enforcement of security requirements. In contrast to wired communications, wireless networks possess susceptibility to external intrusions and lack the necessity of physical connections. Consequently, wireless-enabled AIoT devices are rendered more susceptible to attacks owing to the broadcast nature of wireless broadcasts. For instance, a breach of confidentiality in an intelligent factory could reveal the manufacturing process. At the same time, a lack of data integrity could result in false data injection, modifying the manufacturing process and potentially causing safety issues. If availability cannot be guaranteed, the plant could cease operating all its machinery, thereby establishing a state of safety. Furthermore, the diverse nature of AIoT systems renders conventional trust and authentication procedures potentially unsuitable. The security, privacy, and authentication of IoT devices pose essential issues in the realm of AIoT. Hence, it is imperative to understand alternative resolutions that offer a secure, privacy-conforming, and reliable authentication mechanism for AIoT to streamline the establishment of safe AIoT systems. Figure 12.2 shows the ITU-T security dimensions.

12.4 TRUSTWORTHINESS

Trustworthiness encompasses a wide range of meanings and subtleties that vary depending on the stakeholders, applications, and use cases involved. At its core, trustworthiness refers to the level of confidence a user or stakeholder has in a product or system to perform as intended. This definition applies to various technologies, systems, and domains. The attributes of trustworthiness consist of dependability, accessibility, durability, security, confidentiality, safety, answerability, clarity, soundness, genuineness, quality, ease of use, and precision. In the AI domain, trustworthiness is a fundamental concern.

The topic of digital trust, or trust in digital solutions, is a complex one. It's not always clear when users consider a digital product to be truly trustworthy. Additionally, with the addition of physical product components, such as in the case of smart, connected products, the concept of trust becomes even more complicated. Although security is essential for establishing digital trust, other factors, such as ethical considerations, data privacy, quality, and robustness (such as dependability and resiliency), also play important roles. Considering the potential direct physical influence that AIoT-enabled items can have on individuals' well-being, ensuring safety becomes an additional crucial factor to be considered. Historically, the concept of safety has been closely linked to the practices of verification and validation, as well as the notion of robustness. Hence, it is important to initially comprehend the security-related obstacles associated with AIoT requirements to effectively tackle the concerns about digital trust.

12.4.1 Security Concerns

The intentional targeting of AI-based systems can occur in various ways. The Belfer Center recently released a report that identified two main categories of AI attacks: input attacks and poisoning attacks.

1. **Input Attack:** It takes advantage of the fact that an AI model is unable to cover every possible input, relying on statistical assumptions and mathematical functions derived from training data to create a model of the real world. Adversarial attacks manipulate input data to mislead the AI model, for instance, confusing a stop sign with a small sticker to look like a green light, fooling an autonomous vehicle.

2. **Poisoning Attack:** It aims to corrupt the model during the training process. This can be accomplished by malicious training data that inserts a backdoor into the model. For example, it can be exploited to bypass a building security system or disrupt the operation of a military drone.

In the case of AIoT, security is a crucial requirement to uphold consumer trust. However, security management is often neglected due to factors such as cost, size, and power limitations. This leaves AIoT systems vulnerable to security attacks, which can result in significant financial losses and reputational damage. Investors in AIoT technology will only invest in state-of-the-art security measures as security is crucial for maintaining trust among consumers. Cybersecurity typically follows the CIA model of confidentiality, integrity, and availability. Attackers exploit vulnerabilities in communication protocols to launch attacks, which jeopardize service providers' reputations. Attacks affect all three aspects of the CIA, leading to significant concerns for service providers (Un Nisa et al. 2022). AIoT devices generate data ranging from small to large scale depending on the application, and this data can be critical, such as medical or military data. DDoS attacks pose a significant threat to the cyber world as they can bring down victims, and AIoT devices are well suited for launching these attacks. Users may not realize their devices, such as baby monitors and smart toys, are compromised because they may continue to work even when part of a botnet army. As the number of AIoT devices increases, it becomes crucial to detect botnet attacks promptly and remove compromised devices.

12.4.2 Challenges in Technology Adoption

The combination of AI and IoT shows great promise in bringing about positive transformations in society and business. However, a significant challenge that many industries currently face is using cutting-edge technology without the necessary experience and digital skills as more and more companies are connecting things. The rapid growth in the number of internet-connected "things" could result in several challenges related to technology adoption. From a cyber-physical system viewpoint, the complexity of the interconnection of IoT devices with other systems presents a significant challenge to many companies (Nozari, Szmelter-Jarosz, and Ghahremani-Nahr. 2022). When it comes to technology adoption, users have a range of problems, including limitations in budgetary resources, in acquiring the essential tools and providing comprehensive training for the total system. Insufficient knowledge and awareness present notable obstacles in the process of technology adoption.

One of the challenges that may hinder the adoption of AIoT technology is the need for increased trust in its reliability. Without confidence in AIoT, adopting the technology may lead to delays. Effective data handling relies heavily on accurate knowledge, which may be challenging for farmers who need to become tech-savvy and may need experts to understand and analyze the AIoT system. However, hiring experts and professionals with digital skills to implement and operate new systems and maintain new technology operations can be difficult for the industry. Also, privacy and security concerns can delay technology adoption (Qureshi, Sikandar and Dhawankar. 2022). The convergence of AI and IoT can generate novel security vulnerabilities, such as data breaches and cyberattacks. The increasing collection and transmission of substantial volumes of data by IoT devices have raised considerable privacy concerns, necessitating enterprises adhering to pertinent rules and regulations about data retention. The technology infrastructure holds significant importance across various industries as it is a critical factor in facilitating the effective integration of novel technological advancements (Ayaz et al. 2019). A company may be perceived as using outdated AIoT technology without proper infrastructure.

12.5 FUTURE TRENDS OF AIoT

The proliferation of AIoT devices has led to increased security challenges and threats. While AI has immense transformative potential in various sectors, it is currently being predominantly utilized for security purposes. Although AIoT is expected to be a significant area, the risks involved cannot be overlooked. In complex scenarios involving multiple variables, AIoT is still far from replacing human labor. However, it can save time and cost, optimize resource utilization, and provide intelligent solutions for traffic, homes, cities, stores, etc. By leveraging its capability to analyze and comprehend a given context, AI can facilitate the identification of anomalies, unusual activities, and early detection of attacks, thereby enhancing security measures.

Statista's (2016) research predicts that the global number of connected IoT devices will surpass 75 billion by 2025. The growing market is leading to an increase in the diversity and complexity of IoT networks. This heterogeneity challenges security professionals and researchers, as each manufacturer has their hardware and software, and numerous protocols are available for interconnecting objects. Consequently, AIoT networks are vulnerable to cyberattacks, and implementing a security solution requires considering various factors. However, no single security solution can safeguard all IoT devices from present and future threats (Javaid et al. 2022). Due to their limited resources, traditional security mechanisms and techniques like firewalls, intrusion detection systems, and anti-virus software are unsuitable for AIoT devices. As a result, wireless devices are more vulnerable to cyberattacks mainly because of their connection to computer networks and the Internet. The limited resources of AIoT systems have a direct impact on their IT security.

Although the security industry has started exploring the potential of AIoT, much remains to be done before it can reach its full potential. AI has progressed in advanced theory, but developing it into a complex decision-making system that can handle complex situations is still in its infancy. Despite this, many industry leaders believe that AI could revolutionize the industry. One of the key security concerns for connected devices is the lack of attention given to security during manufacturing. This has made it easier for hackers to exploit weaknesses in the design and configuration of these devices. Moreover, the complexity of AIoT data communication makes it difficult for humans to understand and predetermine normal data flow. Traditional security technologies can only protect against known attacks and vulnerabilities, leaving the system vulnerable to resourceful and innovative cyberattackers (Chen et al. 2021). To prevent exploiting AIoT devices, companies should adopt a zero-trust policy and respond promptly to any signs of compromise. AI technology plays a crucial role in identifying novel attacks and detecting blind spots by recognizing typical behavior in a digital environment. While hardware-related AIoT vulnerabilities are debated, local attacks can expose other vulnerabilities, creating a chain of compromises that can be exploited remotely.

It is important to note, however, that AI alone is not a complete security solution, especially if it is not well-designed. The effectiveness of an AI algorithm is highly dependent on its training, available datasets, and the quality of the algorithm itself. Poor data quality can result in weak AI, low detection rates, and poor security outcomes. To detect previously unknown cybersecurity threats, machine learning is utilized with both supervised and unsupervised algorithms. Supervised learning involves the analyst training the algorithm on the conclusions it should draw, while unsupervised learning is more efficient, with the algorithm generating information and making independent decisions about cyber threats without human guidance.

Using AI technology can help address the issue of limited security resources, freeing up security teams to focus on more critical tasks. This can also help mitigate the shortage of skilled workers in the security industry. Additionally, the use of blockchain technology is becoming more important in securing IoT devices, as it offers enhanced data storage security and guarantees data accessibility, allowing users to store their data on different devices and retrieve it as needed.

12.5.1 AIoT Implementation Advantage

The adoption of AI has the potential to provide numerous advantages. For instance, when combined with network and monitoring systems, AI can function as an extra surveillance mechanism. In the coming years, AI is expected to become a crucial necessity for businesses, promoting the creation of novel innovations and enhancing the performance of current products (Husin et al. 2021; Massaoudi et al. 2021). There are several advantages to using AI technology, including the following:

1. **Cost-effectiveness:** While AI technology may have high initial costs in some situations, it provides substantial cost benefits in the long run by avoiding expenses that would arise without it.

2. **Accuracy:** AI machines are generally more accurate than humans, regardless of the length of time they are utilized or the nature of the work.

3. **Predictive capability:** By continuously analyzing and immediately assessing diverse data sets, AI can independently generate predictions, which can be used to proactively service machines to prevent unnecessary downtime.

4. **Reliability:** AI offers reliable performance by eliminating the possibility of human errors once programmed correctly, leading to a consistent quality of outcome.

5. **Speed:** AI technology's ability to quickly identify patterns in repetitive processes allows it to diagnose problems or identify fraudulent activities much faster than human cognitive abilities, which are limited.

6. **Autonomy:** Once machines are programmed, they require minimal supervision for repetitive tasks. Moreover, AI technology can continuously learn and perform algorithms with high reliability and take corrective action when errors occur (Javaid, Mohd, et al. 2022).

12.6 CURRENT OPEN CHALLENGES AND FUTURE DIRECTIONS

The integration of AI and IoT into AIoT holds promise in delivering substantial convenience to individuals through its diverse range of applications in everyday activities. While the AIoT is currently in its nascent phase of evolution, it exhibits considerable potential for forthcoming progressions. Nevertheless, implementing AIoT in practical scenarios encounters various obstacles, including establishing a collaborative framework among end devices, edge servers, and the cloud. This section analyzes the current challenges and potential future directions for advancing AIoT.

12.6.1 Heterogeneity and Interoperability

The perception layer of the AIoT employs various devices, including Raspberry Pi and Field-Programmable Gate Array (FPGA) based products, along with smartphones, to effectively capture the intricacies of the physical environment (Qureshi, Qayyum, et al. 2021). The AIoT architecture's heterogeneity is evident in deploying various sensors and devices on separate servers to cater to the diverse requirements of different applications or services. This approach ensures a comprehensive perception of the environment, as each device is specifically chosen to meet the specific needs of its corresponding application or service. For instance, sensors designed for Advanced Driver (AD|) assistance systems are typically deployed on Roadside Units (RSUs), whereas sensors intended for smart homes are typically positioned on intelligent gateways.

To facilitate intelligent decision-making, networked devices within the architecture of the AIoT must engage in the interchange and consolidation of data across diverse networks such as Bluetooth, NB-IoT, ZigBee, Wi-Fi, HTTP/TCP, or UDP. Consequently, it is anticipated that AIoT systems would exhibit a significant level of heterogeneity about the diversity of devices, platforms, and frameworks. This emphasizes the criticality of ensuring interoperability and coordination among different devices and platforms. Exploring network software paradigms like Software Defined Network (SDN) (C. Wang et al. 2019; Huang et al. 2019) and utilizing SDN and Network Function Virtualization (NFV) can substantially improve efficiency and flexibility in managing systems. SDN solutions can streamline management processes by providing a cohesive framework for administering diverse devices and sensors. Moreover, SDN can virtualize physical devices and offer tailored services to tackle the issue of device heterogeneity. NFV employs virtualization technologies to transform network node functions into software modules. In recent times, there has been a notable endeavor to amalgamate SDN with NFV inside the realm of edge-cloud computing. The primary objective of this integration is to augment the Quality of Service (QoS) for applications driven by AIoT (Lv and Xiu. 2019; M. Wang et al. 2019).

In addition, for effective communication in the network layer, a uniform communication protocol is necessary for the diverse sensors and devices in the edge-cloud environment. The Open Flow protocol is a prevalent means of communication between an SDN controller and a switch, garnering significant interest from the academic community (Mondal, Misra and Maity. 2019). Implementing Deep Learning (DL) models on a Graphics Processing Unit (GPU) edge server can enhance their performance, but incorporating NFV into a GPU is still challenging. To effectively implement these paradigms, further research and development are required in domains like security, allocation of resources, deployment of runtime services, and computational offloading.

12.6.2 Resource Management

The progress of AIoT has led to the development of various applications, such as smart homes and Internet of Vehicles (IoV). These systems use multiple sensors and devices that are distributed across different locations to gather data. However, these sensors and devices have limited computational and storage capabilities, and are often battery-powered, making it difficult to perform low-latency computation tasks on them. To optimize the utilization of distributed resources across edge nodes and devices, it is recommended to break large AI models into smaller subtasks and assign them to various edge nodes and devices for collaborative training. The service environments of numerous intricate and heterogeneous AIoT applications, such as IoV, exhibit a significant degree of volatility, hence posing challenges in accurately forecasting results. Although AIoT has numerous applications in our daily lives and offers significant convenience to people, it is still a nascent technology with vast potential. To fully utilize the advantages of AIoT, numerous sensors, and devices are distributed throughout the network to gather data. Due to their typical reliance on battery power and limited processing and storage capacities, the execution of latency-sensitive tasks on the computing resources of these devices can present significant challenges. As a result, intricate AI models are frequently partitioned into smaller subtasks and distributed to diverse edge nodes and devices to facilitate collaborative training. The ability to orchestrate online edge resources and provision is essential to support substantial tasks in the continuously changing service environments of sophisticated AIoT applications. Comprehensive attention should be given to solutions that target the real-time optimization of coordination among heterogeneous end devices' computation, networking, and caching resources during the runtime (Sun et al. 2007). Two approaches are being taken by researchers to optimize the performance of AIoT systems. The initial approach focuses on reducing bandwidth costs in a wireless multicast channel by implementing integrated caching and computing strategies. The second methodology uses AI techniques, including deep reinforcement learning (DRL), to effectively handle resource allocation and scheduling (Tang, Zhou and Kato. 2020; Cheng et al. 2019).

12.6.3 Model Inference and Training

The process of optimizing various hyperparameters to enhance the compression and acceleration of AI inference methods typically necessitates the utilization of empirical experiments and expert knowledge. Consequently, it becomes crucial to fine-tune networks based on the insights gained from these trials. Hence, developing adaptive or automatic compression and acceleration techniques holds significant value, as seen by ongoing research endeavors in this domain. However, acceleration technologies, like pruning and quantization, may reduce performance, making it crucial to implement hardware acceleration to support the execution of AI models. The challenge of training AI models in parallel arises from constraints on processing, storage, and network resources. Federated Learning (FL) addresses the data-driven prerequisites and privacy protection obstacles encountered by AI models within a distributed computing framework, offering advantages such as minimal data transmission traffic, preservation of model quality, and data isolation. Nevertheless, it is essential to note that the bandwidth of edge nodes is constrained and exhibits heterogeneity, characterized by varying computational capabilities and unevenly distributed data. Consequently, these factors contribute to communication delays encountered during the distributed Stochastic Gradient Descent (SGD) process. Therefore, exploring diverse parallel communication mechanisms can improve efficiency further (Rothchild et al. 2020). Although existing quantization methods primarily apply to AI inference, fine-grained quantization-aware training can be utilized for AIoT applications (Chung, Chen and Chang. 2020).

12.6.4 Security and Privacy

AIoT also faces security and privacy concerns, such as privacy breaches and malicious attacks. Typically, AI models are deployed at the network's edge or on end devices to offer quick services. Unfortunately, edge servers and end devices frequently possess constrained computing and storage capabilities, rendering them susceptible to malevolent assaults, including DDoS operations, such as the infamous Mirai attack. The flooding-based DDoS attack continues to pose a significant concern within edge computing systems. Current security methods require significant computation and communication loads, which are impractical for resource-constrained end devices. Physical Unclonable Functions (PUFs) have emerged as an up-and-coming field of study in the realm of security authentication within edge computing environments. This is primarily due to their ability to provide robust protection against physical intrusion while exhibiting advantages such as low computational overhead, minimal resource utilization, straightforward implementation, and distinctive physical characteristics. Furthermore, it is imperative to investigate hardware-assisted protection techniques that are founded on the Reduced Instruction Set Computing (RISC-V) architecture. Preliminary efforts have already commenced in this particular trajectory (Long et al. 2019; De et al. 2020).

AIoT systems are highly susceptible to privacy concerns, with data and firmware attacks posing a severe threat to sensitive information, including user location and health records. End users and devices frequently generate this data and store it locally, making its protection critical. In addition, data transmission between edge infrastructures can lead to privacy breaches, and sufficient and diverse data are required for designing and training AI algorithms. One promising solution to address these issues is to use the FL method, which performs distributed data training while preserving privacy.

Various technologies can be employed in the edge computing environment to ensure privacy while creating AI models that share parameters. These technologies include differential privacy, homomorphic encryption, and secure multiparty computation. Blockchain technology is also significant in securing the AIoT and can be combined with FL and other methods to enhance privacy preservation further. However, blockchain technology developed for IoT networks may consume many network resources, such as communication bandwidth and computational resources, leading to performance issues. Researchers have proposed integrating blockchain with the AIoT in the upcoming 6G communication network, which can potentially improve AI, data storage, and analytics (Sekaran et al. 2020). Therefore, more exploration is needed to develop blockchain-based solutions that safeguard users and devices from malicious attacks in the AIoT.

12.6.5 Artificial Intelligence Ethics in AIoT

AI algorithms in the AIoT environment can make decisions rapidly without human supervision. Therefore, it is essential to develop algorithms that can autonomously learn without causing harm or violating human rights. To effectively navigate the ethical implications associated with AI technology, it is imperative to consider a range of design principles, including but not limited to justice, honesty, responsibility, safety, and sustainability. Justice is widely regarded as the foremost value within this context, encompassing the imperative to uphold fairness, prevent prejudice, and promote diversity across several facets, including data, algorithms, implementation strategies, and resultant consequences. Achieving AI justice involves avoiding prejudice and favoritism toward individuals. Honesty is an essential value that necessitates the presence of transparency, openness, and interpretability of data and technology to tackle ethical concerns related to AI effectively.

Accountability must be established throughout the entire design and implementation process, and AI developers, designers, and institutions must assume responsibility for the actions and consequences of AI. The paramount objective of AI ethics is to ensure safety, which encompasses the prioritization of accuracy, reliability, security, and robustness in AI systems. To enhance security, it is imperative for AI designers to explicitly state their commitment to preventing foreseen or inadvertent harm, including potential military confrontations and malevolent cyberattacks.

Sustainability is another important part of AI ethics, which stresses the need to protect the environment and improve the ecosystem while building and using AI systems. It is imperative to ensure that AI applications are meticulously created, implemented, and managed to achieve these objectives, focusing on optimizing energy efficiency and mitigating their ecological footprint.

12.7 CONCLUSION

AIoT is a new trend integrated with edge and cloud computing services. The rapid adoption of these network applications leads to new security, privacy, and trust challenges. These networks have suffered from new security and protection threats aimed at maintaining end nodes' or users' privacy and trust against disruptive attacks designed to incur financial losses. The existing services and security systems still suffer from many flaws and need to design more efficient and lightweight trust and privacy solutions. In this chapter, we discussed the privacy, trust, and security challenges and their possible solution. This chapter also discusses the new trend and usage of blockchain and AI in AIoT networks. For future AIoT networks, there is a need to design more smart systems by using cost-effective, lightweight, and energy-efficient solutions.

REFERENCES

Ahlgren, Bengt, Markus Hidell, and Edith C-H Ngai. "Internet of Things for Smart Cities: Interoperability and Open Data." *IEEE Internet Computing* 20.6 (2016): 52–56.

Alansari, Zainab, et al. *Internet of Things: Infrastructure, Architecture, Security and Privacy.* 2018 International Conference on Computing, Electronics & Communications Engineering (iCCECE). 2018. IEEE.

Alhalafi, N., and Prakash Veeraraghavan. *Privacy and Security Challenges and Solutions in IoT: A Review.* IOP Conference Series: Earth and Environmental Science. 2019. IOP Publishing.

Ayaz, Muhammad, et al. "Internet-of-Things (IoT)-Based Smart Agriculture: Toward Making the Fields Talk." *IEEE Access* 7 (2019): 129551–83.

Chen, Shu-Wen, et al. "AIoT Used for Covid-19 Pandemic Prevention and Control." *Contrast Media & Molecular Imaging* 2021 (2021).

Cheng, Nan, et al. "Space/Aerial-Assisted Computing Offloading for IoT Applications: A Learning-Based Approach." *IEEE Journal on Selected Areas in Communications* 37.5 (2019): 1117–29.

Chung, Ching-Che, Wei-Ting Chen, and Ya-Ching Chang. *Using Quantization-Aware Training Technique with Post-Training Fine-Tuning Quantization to Implement a Mobilenet Hardware Accelerator.* 2020 Indo–Taiwan 2nd International Conference on Computing, Analytics and Networks (Indo-Taiwan ICAN). 2020. IEEE.

De, Asmit, et al. "Hardware Assisted Buffer Protection Mechanisms for Embedded Risc-V." *IEEE Transactions on Computer-Aided Design of Integrated Circuits and Systems* 39.12 (2020): 4453–65.

Huang, Meitian, et al. "Reliability-Aware Virtualized Network Function Services Provisioning in Mobile Edge Computing." *IEEE Transactions on Mobile Computing* 19.11 (2019): 2699–713.

Husin, Ku Azmie Ku, et al. *Monitoring and Optimizing Solar Power Generation of Flat-Fixed and Auto-Tracking Solar Panels with IoT System.* IOP Conference Series: Materials Science and Engineering. 2021. IOP Publishing.

Javaid, Mohd, et al. "Enhancing Smart Farming through the Applications of Agriculture 4.0 Technologies." *International Journal of Intelligent Networks* 3 (2022): 150–64.

Kraijak, Surapon, and Panwit Tuwanut. *A Survey on Internet of Things Architecture, Protocols, Possible Applications, Security, Privacy, Real-World Implementation and Future Trends.* 2015 IEEE 16th International Conference on Communication Technology (ICCT). 2015. IEEE.

Long, Jing, et al. "PUF-Based Anonymous Authentication Scheme for Hardware Devices and IPS in Edge Computing Environment." *IEEE Access* 7 (2019): 124785–96.

Lv, Zhihan, and Wenqun Xiu. "Interaction of Edge-Cloud Computing Based on SDN and NFV for Next Generation IoT." *IEEE Internet of Things Journal* 7.7 (2019): 5706–12.

Massaoudi, Mohamed, et al. "Deep Learning in Smart Grid Technology: A Review of Recent Advancements and Future Prospects." *IEEE Access* 9 (2021): 54558–78.

Mondal, Ayan, Sudip Misra, and Ilora Maity. "AMOPE: Performance Analysis of OpenFlow Systems in Software-Defined Networks." *IEEE Systems Journal* 14.1 (2019): 124–31.

Musaddiq, Arslan, et al. "A Survey on Resource Management in IoT Operating Systems." *IEEE Access* 6 (2018): 8459–82.

Nozari, Hamed, Agnieszka Szmelter-Jarosz, and Javid Ghahremani-Nahr. "Analysis of the Challenges of Artificial Intelligence of Things (AIoT) for the Smart Supply Chain (Case Study: FMCG Industries)." *Sensors* 22.8 (2022): 2931.

Qureshi, K. N., and A. H. Abdullah, *Industrial Wireless Sensor Network Architecture Standards, Applications.* AsiaSense, the Sixth International Conference 2013, Melaka, Malaysia. 2013. AaiaSense.

Qureshi, Kashif Naseer, et al. "Data Analysis Based Dynamic Prediction Model for Public Security in Internet of Multimedia Things Networks." *Multimedia Tools and Applications* (2021).

Qureshi, Kashif Naseer, et al. "A Secure Data Parallel Processing Based Embedded System for Internet of Things Computer Vision Using Field Programmable Gate Array Devices." *International Journal of Circuit Theory and Applications* n/a.n/a (2021).

Qureshi, Kashif Naseer, Ajay Sikandar, and Piyush Dhawankar. "Next-Generation Connected Traffic Using UAVs/Drones." *Secure and Digitalized Future Mobility: Shaping the Ground and Air Vehicles Cooperation* (2022): 65.

Rothchild, Daniel, et al. *FetchSGD: Communication-Efficient Federated Learning with Sketching.* International Conference on Machine Learning. 2020. PMLR.

Statista. "Internet of Things – Number of Connected Devices Worldwide 2015–2025." Statista Research Department. 2016.

Sekaran, Ramesh, et al. "Survival Study on Blockchain Based 6G-Enabled Mobile Edge Computation for IoT Automation." *IEEE Access* 8 (2020): 143453–63.

Sun, Yaping, et al. "Bandwidth Gain from Mobile Edge Computing and Caching in Wireless Multicast Systems." *IEEE Transactions on Wireless Communications* 19.6 (2020): 3992–4007.

Tang, Fengxiao, Yibo Zhou, and Nei Kato. "Deep Reinforcement Learning for Dynamic Uplink/Downlink Resource Allocation in High Mobility 5G HetNet." *IEEE Journal on Selected Areas in Communications* 38.12 (2020): 2773–82.

Un Nisa, Khaleeq, et al. "Security Provision for Protecting Intelligent Sensors and Zero Touch Devices by Using Blockchain Method for the Smart Cities." *Microprocessors and Microsystems*, 90 (2022): 104503.

Wang, Cong, et al. "SDN-Based Handover Authentication Scheme for Mobile Edge Computing in Cyber-Physical Systems." *IEEE Internet of Things Journal* 6.5 (2019): 8692–701.

Wang, Meng, et al. *An Efficient Service Function Chain Placement Algorithm in a MEC-NFV Environment.* 2019 IEEE Global Communications Conference (GLOBECOM). 2019. IEEE.

Index